# MARY BERRY

## COOKS UP A FEAST

WITH **LUCY YOUNG**

# CONTENTS

# FOREWORD

We've worked together for 30 years and have written cookery books on a vast range of subjects. One of the many joys of publishing them is the feedback we get from you, our readers. We take your comments extremely seriously. And if there's one request that's kept on coming, it's for a book to serve numbers – a party book, with recipes for anything from a family get-together in the kitchen to a full-on feast. It's an area we feel well qualified to write on – in our personal lives as well as in our professional lives, there's nothing we like so much as cooking for family, friends, and neighbours – no matter the number.

At the same time, we're well aware of the worries that many of you have about cooking for more than six. "What can I make for so many people?" "How can I keep the food hot and will there be enough?" – these are the sorts of question we're asked, and we hope we have answered them in this book.

In *Mary Berry Cooks up a Feast* we give you all the advice you need to make cooking for a crowd easy and stress free. There are recipes for summer and winter, for formal occasions and informal occasions, inside the home and out. We give timings for Agas as well as conventional ovens, together with prepare-ahead and freezing information.

We kick off with the basics – how to plan your feast and how to guarantee there's enough for everyone to eat. We advise on ways to get the most from your kitchen and let you in on a few cheats and shortcuts to make life easier. We also give you ideas on setting the scene and on how to keep your cool on the day itself. Then it's on to the recipes.

Whether you are cooking for the family or entertaining for a larger number, the recipes in this book are perfect for a range of different styles. There are party bites for a drinks party, impressive mains for a sit-down dinner party, and bowl food for a more casual feast. The choice is yours – and we have included all the tips you'll need.

To take the effort out of estimating quantities, for the vast majority of recipes we give a list of ingredients to serve six and a list of ingredients to serve 12, with notes on any special equipment.

So here it is – the much-requested book to answer all your party needs and put your mind at rest when cooking for a crowd. We hope each and every one of you enjoys it and finds the inspiration and confidence you're looking for as you plan your special day.

Remember – no feast is worth stressing over. Whatever happens, fun will be had by everyone – including you!

Mary Berry          Lucy Young

# THE RIGHT EQUIPMENT

*If you haven't cooked for a crowd before, there's a chance your kitchen might not be geared up for it. Help is at hand – in various guises. Here are our tips for assembling the equipment you'll need for success.*

Once you've fine-tuned your menu, check you have all the pots, pans, and dishes you'll need. If you don't have absolutely everything, don't worry – there are often ways round it. In this book we've aimed to keep fancy equipment to a minimum and to use standard-sized pieces whenever possible. For cooking some dishes for larger numbers, you'll need to invest in a big 11 litre (20 pint) pan. Buy a long-handled spatula, too.

## CHOOSING DISHES

The majority of recipes for 12 in this book can be cooked in two standard dishes for six rather than in a single huge one. There's even an advantage to doing this – smaller dishes are a lot less heavy to handle. If you don't have a second dish, borrow one from a friend or buy a foil dish. The cooking times for two dishes should be the same as for one large dish, but keep an eye on the food towards the end of cooking – the important thing is that it's cooked right through to the middle.

Foil dishes are not as sturdy as porcelain cookware, so always sit them on a baking sheet, particularly when you're taking them in and out of the oven, and take care not to puncture them. Because they are made of metal, cooking times are slightly less. Again, check towards the end of cooking to see if the food is done.

## IMPROVISING

Take a look around your kitchen to see if there are any pieces of equipment you can improvise with. A roasting tin, for example, can stand in as an ovenproof dish, and we find no end of uses for our preserving pan. To check the capacity of a dish, fill it with water from a measuring jug. Slightly too big is better than too small – for obvious reasons.

## PERFECT TIMING

With so much going on in the kitchen when you're cooking for a crowd, it's worth putting your mind at rest by investing in a good digital kitchen timer. They are relatively inexpensive, extremely simple to use, and the best models can time up to four dishes at once.

## FRIDGE KNOW-HOW

If you are preparing food in advance, your fridge will be working hard in the run-up to your feast. The average domestic fridge isn't that big and when it's full to capacity, it has to work overtime to cope. As a result, the temperature inside can rise, even if the weather outside isn't that warm. A fridge that's full to capacity doesn't allow the cold air to circulate freely either, which can sometimes mean foods are inadequately chilled.

Check frequently that yours is working at the correct temperature – 4–5°C (39–41°F) – and adjust the controls to lower the temperature, if necessary. If your fridge doesn't have a temperature display, invest in a fridge thermometer – it's an inexpensive piece of equipment.

## STORING AND WRAPPING
Be mindful of not using single-use plastics. Beeswax sheets are a great product to use instead of cling film for storing and keeping food. Use recyclable materials whenever possible and reuse as much as you can.

## GLASSES
Provide all the right glasses for the drinks you have on offer – wine glasses (both red and white), beer glasses, and glasses for water or soft drinks – and make sure there are plenty of them. Some non-breakable glasses or plastic beakers are a good idea if there are going to be children present. You might want to supply an ice bucket and some recyclable paper straws, too. A corkscrew and a bottle opener are essential items, as is a container for corks and caps.
• Red wine can be swirled easily in a large-bowled glass to release aromas.

• White wine will keep cooler in a narrow glass with a stem to hold it by.
• Beer tastes better from a chalice glass, which also maintains the head.
• Soft drinks or water are best served in tall highball glasses.

*"Keep an eye on food cooked in one large dish towards the end of cooking – the important thing is that it's cooked right through to the middle."*

# SERVING THE RIGHT AMOUNT

*From experience, we know it's better to serve too much food than not enough. That said, you don't want so much left over that you do not know what to do with it. Here's how to get the quantities right.*

Almost every recipe in this book is designed to serve six or 12. These quantities depend to some extent, of course, on who your guests are. In general, though, we tend to err on the generous side. And to make doubly sure that there will be enough food, we always provide a plentiful supply of bread or potatoes, so that guests can tuck in and help themselves. How much food we serve also depends on the time of day.

## SUGGESTED SERVING QUANTITIES
### PARTY BITES
• 8–10 per person at an occasion such as a drinks party where you're serving no other food. Serve up to five different types – cold and/or hot – depending on the number of people you've invited.
• 3 per person at a meal with no first course. Serve two different types of canapé – cold and/or hot.
• 1–2 per person at a meal with a first course. Serve just one kind of party bite, either cold or hot.

### FIRST COURSES
• **Soup:** around 300ml (10fl oz) per serving, depending on the vessels used. Soup bowls usually hold 300ml; mugs a little less. For 12, you will need 3.5 litres (6 pints) soup; for 20–25, 6 litres (10½ pints) soup.
• **Rocket** (as a garnish): 200g (7oz) for 12; 400g (14oz) for 20–25.

### MAIN-COURSE SIDE DISHES
• **Baby new potatoes:** 1.5kg (3lb 3oz) for 12; 2.5kg (5½lb) for 20–25.
• **Jacket potatoes:** 1 medium potato per person.
• **Mashed potatoes:** 225g (8oz) (unpeeled weight of potatoes) per serving. So 2.7kg (6lb) for 12; 4.5kg (10lb) for 20–25.
• **Roast potatoes:** Three small potatoes per serving.
• **Green salad/mixed leaf salad:** 300g (11oz) for 12; 500g (1lb 2oz) for 20–25.
• **Tomato salad:** 1 small or ½ large tomato per serving.
• **Rice/bulghur wheat/couscous:** 600g (1lb 5oz) for 12; 1.25kg (2¾lb) for 20–25.
• **Noodles:** 1 nest per person.
• **Bread:** 1 large baguette cuts into 10–12 slices.
• **Green vegetables:** About 75g (2½oz) per serving. So 900g (2lb) for 12; 1.5kg (3lb 3oz) for 20–25.
• **Gravy:** 1.2 litres (2 pints) for 12; 1.4–1.7 litres (2½–3 pints) for 20. If your guests are helping themselves from the gravy boat, you might wish to make a little more, as they may serve themselves rather generously.

### FOR A BUFFET
• **Poached salmon:** 2.7–3kg (6–6½lb) salmon (head on, gutted) for 12; 6kg (13lb) salmon for 20–25.
• **Ham:** 2 slices per serving (if accompanied by

another meat or fish); 3 slices per serving (if served on its own).

- **Roast fillet of beef:** 140–175g (5–6oz) per serving when hot; 100g (3½oz) per serving when cold (cold beef is easier to carve thinly).

PUDDINGS

- **Pouring cream:** 600ml (1 pint) for 12; 1.2 litres (2 pints) for 20–25.
- **Crème fraîche/yogurt:** 400ml tub for 12; 2 x 400ml tubs for 20–25.
- **Custard:** 1.2 litres (2 pints) for 12; 2.4 litres (4 pints) for 20–25.
- **Ice cream:** 1 scoop per person served as an accompaniment; 2 scoops per person on its own.
- For a cheese board, serve 3–5 cheeses, about 750g (1lb 10oz) in total for 12; 1kg (2¼lb) for 20–25. Accompany with your favourite savoury biscuits, a good chutney, and some fresh figs or grapes.

TEA

- For a tea with cakes, serve one round of sandwiches (two slices of bread) per person.
- Most people will drink a couple of cups of tea. For 20 cups, you'll need about 15 teabags (although it depends of course on how strong you make it) and 600ml (1 pint) milk.

## COOKING FOR DIFFERENT NUMBERS

When cooking for 10 or 11 people, just cook for 12 (using the quantities in the book) and freeze any leftovers. When cooking for eight or nine people, use the quantities for six people and make one and a half portions where possible – this will work for some things, but not for all, as liquid quantities can be erratic. Recipes this will work for include Tiger prawn balti (page 210), Hot mustard spiced beef (page 150), Boneless winter lamb shanks (page 160), and 21st-century Coronation chicken (page 96). When this won't work, just cook for six and then add another element or dish – this helps with the 'feast' idea, too:

- **Serve soup** with a salad or salads from the book, or bread and oil on a platter.
- **Add extra veg** to bulk out sauces such as bolognese.
- **For casseroles and curries**, cook more rice; add breads.
- **For desserts** (such as cheesecakes) don't mess around with the quantities – just make two!

# CHEATS AND SHORTCUTS

*If you're cooking last minute, you might appreciate a helping hand. Luckily, cutting the odd corner won't affect the final quality of the dish — so long as you choose the right corners to cut. These cheats will take the pressure off.*

There are many ways you can cheat and make cooking for a party easier. A quick visit to your local supermarket or delicatessen will provide you with all the ready-prepared ingredients you need to rustle up a speedy dish like the Express Mediterranean platter (page 90), for instance — what could be more delicious and trouble-free to serve as your first course. Think simple and in season — if you don't have the time to make an elaborate pudding in the summer, simply serve fresh strawberries or raspberries with cream, or make our Magenta fruit compote with white chocolate sauce (page 298). Simplicity itself.

## SALADS AND VEGETABLES

Bags of prepared salads are an excellent timesaver. Buy the different varieties of leaves in separate packets, then you don't end up getting enormous amounts of shredded iceberg lettuce (not our favourite), and mix them together just before serving. A bottle of good-quality vinaigrette won't go amiss, either.

Due to over-use of plastics we are not so keen on ready-prepared vegetables, but they are available in bags should you need them. You could also team frozen vegetables with fresh vegetables — frozen peas go well with softened leeks or courgettes, for instance, and frozen baby broad beans can be mixed with any variety of fresh bean.

## EQUIPMENT

Certain pieces of equipment can save you time and effort as well. Cake-tin liners take the fiddle out of lining cake tins. They are also guaranteed to be a perfect fit. Recyclable foil containers, such as tart tins, casserole dishes, roasting tins, and platters are not only convenient, they don't need washing up either. You might appreciate that more than you think at the end of the day.

## PREPARING AHEAD

Okay, so preparing food in advance isn't exactly cheating, but it is a simple way of making life easier for yourself on the day. Throughout this book we give you advice on preparing ahead, but there are plenty of other little shortcuts you can take, too. When you're making the gravy for the Mini pork en croûtes (page 164), for instance, you can mix all the ingredients together, ready to add the juices from the meat at the last minute. We do this all the time.

We also keep fresh white breadcrumbs, grated Cheddar, grated Parmesan, and nuts in separate plastic containers in the freezer. They thaw in minutes, ready to cook with, and taste as fresh as they were the moment you put them in there.

## MAKING SERVING EASIER

Serving food to large numbers might seem daunting, but there are many ways of simplifying the task. When serving pies and lasagnes, we often lightly mark portion sizes on the surface with a knife so guests (or you) know where to cut. This works well with whole fish, too.

Cheesecakes, tarts, and quiches can be cut into slices or wedges, so you know they'll be enough to go round. Place them on a flat platter to serve, and reassemble them so they look whole. To make serving ice cream speedier, once it is frozen, scoop out the number of balls of ice cream you need and arrange on a tray. Cover with cling film and place in the freezer. Then all you need to do is arrange the balls in bowls when you are ready to serve, or pile them into a mound and let guests serve themselves.

*"Preparing food in advance isn't exactly cheating, but it is a simple way of making life easier for yourself on the day."*

# PLANNING THE OCCASION

*No matter the occasion, when you're having a party the first thing to do is to make a plan. Careful planning and meticulous organization are key to success. Here's our advice on the things to consider ahead of your feast.*

Take a look at your menu. What's sitting in the fridge waiting to be transferred to a dish or platter? What needs to be reheated or have the finishing touches put to it? And what has to be put together from scratch? Even if it's only the potatoes you're serving with your main course or a salad you have to dress, make sure they're on your list.

## CALCULATE THE WORKLOAD

With your proposed menu to hand, jot down what you can prepare ahead and what you can freeze in readiness for your big day. Will you be comfortable putting the finishing touches to dishes while your guests are there? Or would you rather it was just a simple matter of popping them in the oven? Dishes you can reheat and serve are ideal if you want to spend as much time as you can with your guests or if you think you might get flustered. Even better are cold dishes that will be sitting there ready for you to bring out and serve.

Remember to make a note if a dish can't be served straight away – roasted meats, for instance, need 15–20 minutes to rest before you carve them, and some tarts are tricky to cut when hot. Check, too, that you'll have enough room in your oven or on your hob and that you won't be trying to finish off too many dishes at once.

## CHOOSING WHAT TO SERVE

When choosing a first course, look at your menu as a whole. If you're serving fish as a main course, offer a meat or vegetarian dish as your starter, and vice versa. A simple first course is good before a more elaborate main course – you don't want to spoil people's appetites or fill them up before the meal has barely begun. But a rich or elaborate starter is fine before a simple main course.

A platter of tasty ingredients passed around the table makes a sociable starter. If you're serving 12, prepare two individual platters. If your guests are going to be standing up to eat, dot several platters around the room so they can help themselves.

A buffet usually consists of one or two main courses, with a selection of side dishes and a choice of puddings. Take care what dishes you serve together – most guests will want to sample everything, and poached salmon might not be the perfect partner for chicken tikka masala.

## HOT OR COLD?

A cold first course makes life easy when you're serving large numbers of people and is ideal in summer. Hot soup is perfect in winter, but bear in mind that if you're working singlehandedly it can be trickier than you think to serve soup to a crowd – it has to be piping hot, as have the bowls you pour it into. Again, look at your menu as a whole. You might feel more relaxed if you know one course is made, ready to take out of the fridge and serve.

Cold buffets are easier because almost everything can be prepared ahead. However, we always serve warm new potatoes or jacket potatoes, even at a cold buffet.

## WORK OUT THE SCHEDULE

Although you don't want to keep your guests hanging around, you don't want to hurry proceedings either. If you're not serving a starter, seat people before you bring out your main course. If you are serving a starter and your main course needs reheating, do it while you're eating the first course. Remember to allow 15–20 minutes for roast meats to rest before you carve them. Reheat your pudding, if necessary, while you're eating the main course.

## ASK FOR HELP IF YOU NEED IT

If you think you'll need help at some point during the party, make sure you line up volunteers in plenty of time. You might need someone to take people's coats and bags, for instance, or someone to go round with a plate of canapés or a bottle of wine. If you have any last-minute cooking to do, you might well appreciate a helping hand in the kitchen, too, even if it's only asking someone to toss the salad. But beware of enlisting too much help – people could end up getting in your way.

## TABLE TALK

Since you're pulling out the stops with the food, it makes sense to go to a little extra effort with the table decorations. Use your most impressive china, arrange fresh flowers in a vase, and light the candles before your guests come to the table to sit down. Easy-to-use LED fairy lights also give a lovely mood.

## IT'S ALL IN THE DETAILS

One of the lovely things about entertaining is sitting down after your guests have gone and looking back at the day, thinking of all the little things that went well. It could be how succulent the lamb was, how pretty the flowers looked on the table, and how happy people looked as they stood around and chatted. That's why we think that setting the scene is so important – joyful memories for you and joyful memories for them.

# PREPARING A FEAST

*The best way to stop last-minute panics is to prepare as much as you can, and do so well ahead of time. Follow these tips and you'll be able to relax and enjoy the company of your guests, knowing everything is in hand.*

Before you start any of the cooking, clear a space next to your cooker and lay out all the equipment you'll need – knives, utensils, oven gloves, a kitchen timer. Try to think of everything. Make space on a counter and pile the serving platters on it. Don't forget dishes for sauces and a basket for bread. Sort out all the plates, bowls, cutlery, napkins, and serving utensils you'll require and place them on your dining table or buffet table. If you're serving food hot, have the plates or bowls ready to pop in the oven to heat through.

## DEFROSTING FOOD

If you've frozen food ahead of time, it's important to defrost (thaw) it completely before cooking. We always advise defrosting in the fridge because it's the safest method of doing it. Overnight should be fine for small dishes, but a large deep dish can take up to two days. If time is against you, however, you can defrost non-meat and non-fish dishes at room temperature for a maximum of six hours. Once thawed, transfer to the fridge until needed. Never defrost in a warm oven or warm cupboard – the risk of attracting bacteria is high.

Transfer food into polythene bags or plastic containers to keep it in the fridge or freezer – they make better use of the limited space available.

## WHEN TO BRING OUT THE PARTY BITES

• Don't bring out your canapés until most of your guests have arrived. You don't want them all to have been gobbled up by the time everyone gets there.

• Start with your most stunning party bite – just like the curtain going up at the theatre, this is your signal that the action is about to commence.

• To begin with, serve one kind of canapé per plate or platter, so you can keep track of which guests have had what.

• Once the party bites have started to disappear, pass around mixed plates or platters instead of half-empty ones – these can look rather sad and uninviting.

• Allow 45 minutes to an hour for guests to enjoy their canapés before you serve your first course or main course. Don't rush things – you want to keep the atmosphere relaxed.

• At a drinks party you expect to last for 2–3 hours, serve the party bites for a couple of hours and then wind down.

• As a sign that it's knocking-off time and the curtain's about to come back down, we serve something sweet – brownies or cupcakes presented in paper truffle cases.

## BUFFETS

- Prepare all the dishes to serve the number of people you have coming. If you make them any smaller, there's the risk that some will run out. People will go back for second helpings, and any leftovers can be kept in the fridge for a few days or frozen.
- Make portions attractive and small. With guests tucking into more than one dish, you don't want to overwhelm them. We score suggested serving portions on the top of large dishes such as pies and lasagnes.
- If you're serving a whole ham, carve a few slices to get people going.
- If you're offering a first course at a formal meal, serve it at the tables where guests will sit.

## DRINKS

At a buffet, set the drink and glasses out on a separate table. Site it well away from the door – the first thing guests generally do at a party is pour themselves a drink and you don't want them blocking the entrance to the room.

## TEA

- Bake scones on the day. If you do have to prepare them in advance, freeze them and then gently reheat in a low oven once defrosted.

At a buffet, serve them with bowls of jam and cream (there's no need for butter) for guests to help themselves. Otherwise top them before you serve them.
- Although you can ice cakes ahead, the icing will be at its shiniest if you do it on the day itself. Provide forks with iced cakes as they can be messy to eat with your hands.
- Depending on the filling you're using, most sandwiches can be prepared up to a day ahead. Kept correctly, they will taste as fresh as the moment you made them. Other sandwiches, such as cucumber and tomato, are best made no more than 10 hours ahead. For more on this, turn to page 314.
- Offer fresh herb teas, mint from the garden, or infused herbal.

# ON THE DAY

*It's the day of your feast and the countdown's on. If you've prepared ahead and kept well organized, the pressure shouldn't be too intense. It's now time to make the final preparations. Here's what to keep in mind right before – and during – the party.*

No matter how much you are able to prepare in advance, there will still be plenty to do on the day itself. Before your guests arrive, lay the table, set out the drinks, arrange flowers in vases, and light candles.

## LAY THE TABLE
If you're having a buffet, arrange a stack of plates or bowls at one end of the table, with the cutlery and napkins at the other end. The flow of traffic can go from right to left or from left to right, depending on the layout of your room.

For a large sit-down meal, it's a good idea to have a seating plan. For special occasions, you might want to have name cards. If it's a family affair and you have young children, get them to decorate the cards for you. If you're having flowers in the centre of the table, arrange them in low vases so that people can still see each other and chat.

Think about the lighting, perhaps using lamps or candles to create a warm, relaxing atmosphere. Music can help to set the scene, too.

## WARM THE PLATES AND PLATTERS
Plates must be piping hot for food you're serving hot. Platters may need heating, too. The easiest way to do this is in a low oven or in the warming oven of the Aga. If your oven's already in use, you could either run them through a quick wash in the dishwasher (there's no need for any detergent) or stack them over a pan of simmering water. Swap them around every so often so they all get hot. Hot plates and hostess trolleys may not be high fashion any more, but they will certainly come in handy if you have one.

## TASTE THE FOOD
In the same way that you taste food as you're making it, it's important to taste it again before you serve it. Adjust the seasoning, if need be – that way, you can present it with confidence.

## SERVING PARTY BITES
If you've kept the canapés in the fridge, take them out about an hour before you want to serve them so they have a chance to come up to room temperature. The flavours will improve as a result. When serving hot canapés, work out timings carefully in advance – you don't want to keep people waiting. Nor do you want everything in the oven at once. Allow a little time for them to cool down before you take them out to serve.

## SERVING COLD FOOD
If you've prepared food ahead and kept it in the fridge ready to serve cold, transfer it to platters just before serving. If you want to cover the platters with

cling film, make sure it's only lightly secured under the rim – when too tightly wrapped, it can be time-consuming to remove and there's always the risk of damaging the arrangement as you do so.

## PORTION CONTROL

Whether you're serving individual plates of food or letting guests help themselves, it's important to keep an eye on the size of the portions. If you're serving guests, make sure the portions are a sensible size – you don't want to overwhelm people by putting too much on their plate to begin with. They can always have more. If you're serving food on platters for guests to help themselves, don't provide outsized utensils – they may seem practical, but guests will make full use of them and the food will be gone in no time.

## KEEPING FOOD HOT

It is essential to keep hot food hot. Use the top of your hob to keep pans on a gentle simmer or pop things into a low oven, but only after they have come to the boil on the hob.

## REHEATING FOOD

If you're going to reheat food, it needs to be done thoroughly. There can be serious health risks if you don't. We've indicated in the recipes when you can prepare a dish ahead and reheat it. If it doesn't say you can do this, don't do it – you'll spoil the dish.

If you've kept food you've prepared ahead in the fridge, allow time for it to come to room temperature before you reheat it. This can take much longer than you think – up to a few hours for a big dish. It depends to some extent on the temperature in your kitchen.

Whenever possible, reheat food in a wide shallow pan or dish – it will heat up more quickly than in a small deep one. On the hob, use a large-based pan that covers the whole of the hot plate. When reheating a casserole, bring it up to the boil, then cover with a lid and leave it to simmer gently, stirring occasionally.

Before you preheat the oven, arrange the shelves so that the dishes will all fit in. Preheat it well ahead of time and, halfway through cooking, switch the dishes around in case your oven has hotter parts to it.

Remember that the more dishes you're reheating in the oven at the same time, the longer they'll take. Check towards the end of cooking to see if they're done – they must be piping hot in the middle.

## GENTLY DOES IT

Don't rush to clear people's plates as soon as they've finished. Keep the atmosphere leisurely and relaxed. You might even encourage guests to swap places around the table before you serve the next course.

# PARTY BITES

*These tiny dishes will get your feast off with a flourish.*
*We like to offer a selection of meat, fish, and vegetarian*
*canapés to guarantee all tastes are catered for. At a drinks*
*party, offer no more than five different types, but lots of*
*them – people are much more likely to remember them.*

# SMOKED SALMON ON RYE WITH CUCUMBER PICKLE

### MAKES 60

4 tbsp light mayonnaise

2 tsp grainy mustard

1 tsp lemon juice

1 tbsp freshly chopped dill, plus extra to garnish

4 rectangular slices of rye bread, pumpernickel, or pumpkin seed bread

200g (7oz) smoked salmon slices

4 cucumber dill pickles, drained and very finely chopped

*These are always a hit. As a twist on the traditional recipe, we use rye bread, pumpernickel, or pumpkin-seed bread. You'll find the cucumbers in jars near the gherkins and olives at the supermarket.*

1. Mix the mayonnaise, mustard, lemon juice, and dill in a small bowl.

2. Lay the bread on a chopping board and spread evenly with the mixture.

3. Cover the mayonnaise with smoked salmon, then cut each piece of bread into 15 squares. Top each one with chopped pickle, arrange on a serving plate, then garnish with dill and serve.

### PREPARE AHEAD

*The bites can be made up to 6 hours ahead. Not suitable for freezing.*

# MINI CHICKEN SATAYS

MAKES 24

**Special equipment**
24 skewers (we prefer
wooden over metal)

4 large skinless boneless
chicken breasts

4 tsp white wine vinegar
or rice vinegar

4 tsp caster sugar

2 tbsp sunflower oil or
sesame oil

a little olive oil, to fry

**For the satay sauce**

1½ tbsp olive oil

1 large onion, finely
chopped

1 large red chilli, deseeded
and finely chopped

3 garlic cloves, crushed

1 tbsp medium curry
powder

6 heaped tbsp crunchy
peanut butter

350ml (12fl oz) water

1 heaped tsp caster sugar

juice of ½ large lime

salt and freshly ground
black pepper

a sprig of coriander,
to garnish

*These warm canapés always go down a storm and are
a cinch to make. If you'd like to serve them as a starter,
you'll need three to four per person. Soak wooden
skewers in water for about 8 hours before use so that
they don't burn during cooking. Serve with a little
ramekin of satay sauce.*

1.  Slice each chicken breast into six thin strips, then place them
in a mixing bowl. Add the vinegar, sugar, and sunflower oil and toss
together well. Leave to marinate in the fridge for about an hour.

2.  To make the sauce, heat the oil in a frying pan over a high
heat, add the onion, chilli, and garlic and fry for 1 minute.
Cover with a lid, lower the heat, and cook for 5 minutes or until
the onion is starting to soften.

3.  Stir in the curry powder and fry for 1 minute. Add the peanut
butter, water, sugar, and lime juice and stir over a high heat
until the sauce is quite thick and shiny, then season with salt
and freshly ground black pepper. Spoon into a serving bowl
and leave to cool completely.

4.  Thread each strip of chicken onto a skewer – they should be
fairly flat so that they will fry evenly, with room at one end so
they can be held comfortably.

5.  Heat a little olive oil in a large frying pan and fry the chicken
skewers for 1–2 minutes on each side or until golden all over
and cooked through. You may need to do this in batches.
Garnish the sauce with the coriander sprig and serve with the
warm chicken skewers.

## IN THE AGA
At step 2, start on the boiling plate, then cover with a lid and
transfer to the simmering oven for 10 minutes.

## PREPARE AHEAD
*The sauce can be made up to 3 days ahead.
The skewers can be threaded up to 2 days
ahead. Not suitable for freezing.*

# DUCK AND HOISIN SPRING ROLLS

MAKES 18

1 boneless duck breast,
skin removed

a little olive oil

salt and freshly ground
black pepper

6 sheets filo pastry

50g (1¾oz) butter, melted

3 tbsp hoisin sauce,
plus a little extra for
dipping

¼ cucumber, sliced in
half lengthways, seeds
removed, then cut
into 6cm (2½in) long
matchsticks

3 spring onions, cut
into 6cm (2½in) long
matchsticks

*These are our take on the crispy duck pancakes you get in Chinese restaurants. And very good they are, too. We use filo pastry because it is much easier to roll than shop-bought pancakes.*

1. Preheat the oven to 200°C (180°C fan/400°F/Gas 6). Meanwhile, rub both sides of the duck breasts with a little olive oil, season with salt and freshly ground black pepper, then fry over a high heat for 2 minutes on each side or until golden brown on the outside and still pink on the inside. Allow to cool slightly, then cut into very thin slices.

2. Lay a sheet of filo on the work surface and cut it into three 10 x 12cm (4 x 5in) strips (the dimensions of the filo will depend on the make, but cut strips that are roughly this size). Brush the edges of each strip with melted butter.

3. Spoon a little hoisin sauce near the bottom of each strip (leaving a gap around the edges), then sit a couple of slices of duck on top, followed by a few of the cucumber and spring onion matchsticks.

4. Fold the sides of each strip in, then, starting at the bottom, roll them up into neatly shaped spring rolls. Make 15 more in the same way.

5. Brush the spring rolls with a little more melted butter, arrange on a baking sheet, and bake, turning them halfway through cooking, for 10 minutes or until golden. Serve warm with extra hoisin sauce to dip into.

### IN THE AGA
Bake on the second set of runners in the roasting oven for 7–10 minutes.

### PREPARE AHEAD
*The spring rolls can be made up to the end of step 4 up to 8 hours ahead. Not suitable for freezing.*

# BEEF REMOULADE ROLLS

**MAKES 24**

2 large fat fillet steaks (weighing about 175g/6oz each)

1 tbsp olive oil

salt and freshly ground black pepper

1 small celeriac

4 tbsp good-quality mayonnaise

1 tbsp Dijon mustard

large handful of rocket

*Matchsticks of celeriac coated in mustardy mayonnaise, remoulade is a classic recipe – if you are short on time, cheat by buying 225g (8oz) ready-made remoulade from the deli counter of the supermarket. Here, the mixture is teamed with rocket and wrapped in wafer-thin slices of rare fillet steak.*

1. Rub the steaks with the oil and season with salt and freshly ground black pepper. Heat any remaining oil in a non-stick frying pan, add the steaks, and fry for 3 minutes on each side or until still rare (this will depend on the thickness). Set aside to cool completely.

2. Peel the celeriac with a sharp knife, chop into pieces, then cut into very thin matchsticks with the matchstick attachment of a food processor. Immerse in boiling salted water for 3 minutes or until soft. Drain and dry on kitchen paper.

3. Put the mayonnaise and mustard into a bowl, season with salt and freshly ground black pepper, and mix well. Stir in the celeriac.

4. Slice each cold steak into 12 thin slices (you may get more depending on the size of the steak). Spoon a little remoulade on one end of each slice, put a few rocket leaves on top, then roll them up and arrange on a platter. Serve with cocktail sticks, if you wish.

**PREPARE AHEAD**

*The remoulade can be made up to 3 days ahead. The rolls can be made up to 8 hours ahead. Not suitable for freezing.*

# PORK MEATBALLS WITH ORIENTAL DIPPING SAUCE

## MAKES ABOUT 50

450g (1lb) lean minced pork

1 red chilli, halved, deseeded, and finely diced

1 tsp freshly grated root ginger

½ onion, coarsely grated

50g (1¾oz) cream crackers, finely crushed

1 tsp five-spice powder

1 egg yolk

small bunch of coriander, roughly chopped

zest and juice of ½ lime

salt and freshly ground black pepper

a little sunflower oil, to fry

**For the dipping sauce**

juice of ½ lime

2 tbsp light muscovado sugar

100ml (3½fl oz) plum sauce

1 tbsp soy sauce

4 tbsp cold water

*Asian food always goes down well at a party. The consistency of the sauce is thin, as is traditional.*

1. Put the first nine ingredients into a bowl and mix together with your hands. Season well with salt and freshly ground black pepper, then shape into about 50 small meatballs.

2. Heat a little oil in a large frying pan, add the meatballs, and fry slowly for 10–15 minutes or until lightly golden and cooked through. You might need to do this in batches. Keep the meatballs warm while you make the dipping sauce.

3. Put all the ingredients for the sauce into a small saucepan and heat until the sugar dissolves. Pour into a bowl and serve with the meatballs.

**PREPARE AHEAD AND FREEZE**

*The meatballs can be made and fried up to 2 days ahead. The sauce can be made up to 3 days ahead. Freeze the uncooked meatballs for up to 2 months.*

# SAUSAGE AND APPLE FILO ROLLS

**MAKES 80**

*450g (1lb) pork sausagemeat*

*1 small Bramley apple, peeled, cored, and coarsely grated*

*1 tbsp grainy mustard*

*1 tbsp freshly chopped sage*

*salt and freshly ground black pepper*

*10 sheets filo pastry (each about 18 x 25cm/ 7 x 10in in size)*

*100g (3½oz) butter, melted*

*These are divine. They are also very tiny, but you could make them larger if you prefer. Just remember to bake them for a few minutes longer – and keep your eye on them. In spring we like to make a variation with asparagus – see below left.*

1. Put the sausagemeat, apple, mustard, and sage into a mixing bowl, season with salt and freshly ground black pepper, and mix well.

2. Divide the mixture into 10, then roll each one into a sausage about the diameter of a chipolata and as wide as a sheet of filo.

3. Brush one sheet of filo with melted butter. Arrange a sausage down one side and roll it up. Repeat with the remaining filo and sausages, then chill in the fridge for 30 minutes.

4. To serve, preheat the oven to 200°C (180°C fan/400°F/Gas 6). Slice each roll into eight diagonally and arrange on two baking sheets lined with baking parchment. Brush with melted butter.

5. Bake for 10–12 minutes or until golden and crisp. Serve hot or warm.

### IN THE AGA

Bake on the grid shelf on the floor of the roasting oven for about 8 minutes.

### ASPARAGUS, GOAT'S CHEESE, AND PARMA HAM FILO ROLLS

*Cook 18 trimmed asparagus spears in boiling salted water for 2–3 minutes or until just tender. Drain and refresh in cold water, then dry on kitchen paper. Lay pairs of slices of Parma ham next to each other lengthways on a board, and spread with soft goat's cheese (you will need 12 slices Parma ham and 6 tablespoons cheese in total). Arrange the asparagus spears along the long edges of the ham, then roll them up tightly. Then follow steps 4–5 as above, but using only 6 sheets of filo pastry, and cutting them into 48–60 pieces. Not suitable for freezing.*

### PREPARE AHEAD AND FREEZE

*The sausage and apple rolls can be made up to the end of step 4 up to 12 hours ahead. Alternatively, you can bake them and reheat to serve. Freeze the uncooked rolls for up to 2 months.*

# SAUSAGES AND MUSTARD MASH

MAKES 20

20 cocktail sausages

100g (3½oz) mashed potato

a little milk (optional)

a little butter (optional)

salt and freshly ground
black pepper

grainy mustard

a little freshly grated
Parmesan cheese

paprika, to dust

*We've been serving a version of this canapé for years and it is still one of our most popular. Our assistant, Lucinda, often cooks for parties and she says these are always the first to go.*

1. Grill the sausages, turning them halfway through, until cooked and evenly brown. Set aside to cool completely.

2. Heat the mashed potato in a pan (if it is a bit stiff, stir in a little milk and butter – the mixture should be smooth and fairly loose). Season with salt and freshly ground black pepper and add grainy mustard to taste. Transfer to a piping bag fitted with a plain narrow nozzle (don't worry if you don't have one – you can use a teaspoon).

3. Slice each sausage open lengthways. Squeezing the ends of each sausage together gently to create a recess, pipe or spoon the mashed potato into the opening.

4. Arrange on a baking tray, sprinkle with the Parmesan, and lightly dust with paprika.

5. To serve, preheat the oven to 200°C (180°C fan/400°F/Gas 6). Reheat the sausages for 10 minutes or until hot right the way through. Transfer to a platter and serve. Do warn your guests they may be hot!

### IN THE AGA
Reheat on the second set of runners in the roasting oven for about 8 minutes.

### PREPARE AHEAD AND FREEZE
*The sausages and mash can be prepared up to the end of step 3 up to 1 day ahead. Freeze at the end of step 3 for up to 1 month.*

# MINI SAUSAGES WITH MUSTARD AND BACON

**MAKES 18**

*6 long thin slices dry-cured unsmoked streaky bacon*

*1 tbsp grainy mustard*

*18 cocktail sausages*

*These little sausages make a great canapé for a festive gathering. They are also perfect for Christmas dinner to go with the turkey or a chicken.*

1.  Preheat the oven to 200°C (180°C fan/400°F/Gas 6).

2.  Lay the bacon in rows on a board. Spread a little grainy mustard on each rasher of bacon. Cut each piece into three.

3.  Wrap a piece of bacon (with the mustard on the inside) tightly around each sausage and put onto a baking tray ready for cooking. Cook in the preheated oven for about 25–30 minutes or until cooked and crisp.

## IN THE AGA
Roast on the grid shelf on the floor of the roasting oven for about 25 minutes, turning halfway through.

## PREPARE AHEAD AND FREEZE
*The sausages can be wrapped up to 1 day ahead. Cook up to 1 day ahead and reheat to serve. Freeze well raw and wrapped.*

# BACON AND WATER CHESTNUT BITES WITH MANGO CHUTNEY

MAKES ABOUT 21

*7 rashers thin unsmoked streaky bacon*

*4 tbsp mango chutney*

*220g can water chestnuts, drained and dried*

*Every can of water chestnuts we open seems to contain 21, but you may end up with one more or one less. It doesn't matter in the slightest for these, our version of the traditional devils on horseback.*

1. Preheat the oven to 220°C (200°C fan/425°F/Gas 7). Lay a rasher of bacon on a chopping board. Hold on to one end of the rasher and drag the blade of a large knife along the surface of the rasher to stretch it out. This will help to wrap it easily around the water chestnut. Cut across into three equal pieces. Repeat with the other rashers.

2. Lay all the rashers on the board. Spoon ½ teaspoon of the chutney on one end, sit a water chestnut on top, then roll the rashers up and arrange them on a baking sheet lined with parchment paper.

3. Spoon a little more chutney on top of each bite, then bake, turning them halfway through, for 15–20 minutes or until crisp and golden. Serve hot with a cocktail stick.

## IN THE AGA
Roast on the floor of the roasting oven for 15 minutes, turning them halfway through.

## PREPARE AHEAD
*The bites can be made up to the end of step 2 up to 1 day ahead. Not suitable for freezing.*

# CRISPY BACON AND QUAIL'S EGG TARTLETS

MAKES 24

2 large hen's eggs

12 quail's eggs

2 tbsp mayonnaise

dash of Tabasco

2 tbsp freshly snipped chives

salt and freshly ground black pepper

4 rashers streaky bacon

24 shop-bought pastry canapé cases

celery salt, for sprinkling

*These are utterly delicious – crispy bacon and egg mayonnaise tartlets, each topped with half a quail's egg. To make the eggs easier to peel, do it when they are just cool enough to handle. For speed, we use bought pastry cases, but you can make them yourself if you prefer.*

1. Put the hen's eggs in a saucepan. Cover with cold water, bring to the boil, and boil for 5 minutes. Add the quail's eggs and boil for a further 3 minutes. Drain and cover with cold water. Peel as soon as they are cool enough to handle.

2. Put the mayonnaise, Tabasco, and half the chives into a bowl with some salt and freshly ground black pepper and mix together. Quarter the large eggs, add to the mayonnaise, and mash well with a fork. Cut the quail's eggs in half and set aside.

3. Fry the bacon in a non-stick frying pan until crisp, then drain on kitchen paper and set aside.

4. Spoon the egg mayonnaise mixture into the pastry cases and sit half a quail's egg cut side up on top of each one. Snip the bacon into pieces and arrange a piece next to the quail's eggs.

5. Sprinkle with a pinch of celery salt, garnish with the remaining chives, and serve at once.

**PREPARE AHEAD**

*The tartlets can be prepared up to 3 hours ahead. Not suitable for freezing.*

# DIP PLATTER

*Dips are so easy to serve at a party. Here are two of our favourites. Vegetables such as peppers, carrots, and cucumbers are the classic dippers and always popular. If you're serving crisps, tortillas, or bread, choose plain varieties so they don't overpower the flavour of the dip.*

### SERVES 6–12 (DEPENDING ON WHAT YOU SERVE IT WITH)

*1 green chilli, halved, deseeded, and cut into three*

*3 small spring onions, finely chopped*

*3 garlic cloves, halved*

*small handful of flat-leaf parsley*

*small bunch of chives*

*200ml tub full-fat crème fraîche*

*1 tsp Dijon mustard*

*1 tbsp lemon juice*

*salt and freshly ground black pepper*

## GARLICKY HERB DIP

1. Put the chilli, spring onions, garlic, and parsley into a food processor and whiz until very finely chopped. Add the remaining ingredients, season with salt and freshly ground black pepper, and whiz again until smooth.

2. Spoon the dip into a bowl or ramekin and chill. To serve, place in the centre of a large plate, with your choice of dippers around the edge. The dip also goes well with potato wedges or dolloped on a jacket potato.

### SERVES 6–12 (DEPENDING ON WHAT YOU SERVE IT WITH)

*10 Peppadew peppers, drained, rinsed, and cut in half*

*1 red chilli, cut in half*

*2 tsp freshly grated root ginger*

*6 tbsp mayonnaise*

*2 tbsp mango chutney*

*100g (3½oz) full-fat cream cheese*

*a few drops of Tabasco*

*salt and freshly ground black pepper*

## SCORCHING CHILLI DIP

1. Put all the ingredients into a food processor and whiz until smooth. Season with salt and freshly ground black pepper.

2. Spoon the dip into a bowl or ramekin and place in the centre of a large plate. Arrange your choice of dippers around the edge.

### PREPARE AHEAD

*The dips can be made up to 4 days ahead. The flavours will get stronger the longer they keep. Not suitable for freezing.*

# GOLDEN DOUGH BALLS
# WITH CHEESE AND CHUTNEY

MAKES 32

16 ready-to-cook dough balls

25g (scant 1oz) butter

100g (3½oz) mature Cheddar cheese, grated

1 tbsp milk

salt and freshly ground black pepper

1 egg yolk

2 tbsp freshly snipped chives

3 tbsp mango chutney

*Dough balls are available in most supermarkets. They often come in a box with garlic butter, but you can also buy them in bags without the butter. They make an excellent base for hot canapés.*

1. Slice each dough ball in half horizontally, then cut a small piece off the rounded base so they'll sit flat on the baking sheet without toppling over.

2. Melt the butter in a saucepan, add the cheese, and stir to melt. Add the milk and stir until smooth. Leave to cool slightly, then season with salt and freshly ground black pepper and stir in the egg yolk and chives. Transfer to the fridge to firm up – when the mixture looks like soft butter, it will be easier to spread.

3. Preheat the oven to 200°C (180°C fan/400°F/Gas 6). Line a baking sheet with baking parchment or foil. Spread the cheese mixture over the flat side of each ball, spreading right to the edges. Spoon a small blob of the chutney on top.

4. Bake for 10–12 minutes or until golden brown and hot. Arrange on a platter and serve straightaway.

### IN THE AGA
Bake the dough balls on the top set of runners in the roasting oven for 10 minutes.

### RED PEPPER DOUGH BALLS
*As a variation on this scrummy recipe, cut small slices of chargrilled red peppers from a jar and arrange them in a cross on the top of each dough ball when they come out of the oven.*

### PREPARE AHEAD AND FREEZE
*The dough balls can be made up to the end of step 3 up to 12 hours ahead. Freeze without the chutney for up to 1 month.*

# SWEETCORN AND FETA FRITTERS

MAKES 40

4 rashers unsmoked back bacon

100g (3½oz) self-raising flour

2 eggs

100ml (3½fl oz) milk

salt and freshly ground black pepper

4 tbsp freshly snipped chives

150g can sweetcorn, drained

50g (1¾oz) feta cheese, finely crumbled

a little sunflower oil, to fry

200g (7oz) half-fat cream cheese

*These fritters are delicious and quick to make. Made a little larger, they are also great for brunch.*

1. Fry the bacon over a high heat until crisp. Set aside to cool, then snip into 40 pieces.

2. Put the flour into a mixing bowl, make a well in the centre, and add the eggs. Whisk by hand, gradually adding the milk, until you have a smooth batter. Season with salt and freshly ground black pepper, then stir in half the chives along with the sweetcorn and feta.

3. Heat the oil in a non-stick frying pan, add the batter to the pan half a teaspoon at a time, then fry for 2–3 minutes on each side or until golden and cooked through. You may need to do this in batches. Set aside to cool.

4. Put the cream cheese into a bowl, add the remaining chives, and season with salt and freshly ground black pepper.

5. Using a teaspoon, spoon the cream cheese mixture on top of the fritters, then top with a piece of crispy bacon. Arrange on a platter and serve.

## ON THE AGA

Fry the fritters on the simmering plate (grease it or cover it with baking parchment first) or in a non-stick frying pan.

## PREPARE AHEAD

*The fritters can be made up to 1 day ahead and assembled up to 6 hours ahead. Not suitable for freezing.*

# CROSTINI WITH SLOW-ROASTED TOMATOES AND HERBS

MAKES 30

1 very thin baguette

a little olive oil

15 small cherry tomatoes

salt and freshly ground black pepper

dash of caster sugar

2 tbsp full-fat cream cheese

2 heaped tsp freshly chopped mint

2 heaped tsp freshly chopped basil

*The time spent roasting the tomatoes is worth every moment – the depth of flavour they acquire is wonderful. Teamed with a herby cream cheese, they make a wonderful cold canapé.*

1. Preheat the oven to 140°C (120°C fan/275°F/Gas 1). Meanwhile, cut the bread into 30 thin slices and brush both sides with a little of the oil.

2. Slice the tomatoes in half and arrange cut side up on a baking sheet. Sprinkle with a little salt, some freshly ground black pepper, and a dash of sugar. Cook in the oven for 30 minutes or until just softened and beginning to shrivel.

3. Heat a little olive oil in a frying pan and fry the slices of bread over a high heat until golden brown on both sides. Set aside to cool.

4. Mix the cream cheese and herbs together in a bowl and season with salt and freshly ground black pepper. Spoon on to the cold crostini and top each one with a cold tomato half.

## IN THE AGA

Slide the tomatoes into the simmering oven and cook for 1 hour.

## PREPARE AHEAD AND FREEZE

*The crostini can be made up to 1 week ahead. Freeze without the topping for up to 4 months.*

# CROSTINI WITH PARMA HAM AND PEPPERED CREAM CHEESE

## MAKES 30

### For the onion marmalade

1 tbsp olive oil

1 red onion, thinly sliced

½ tsp balsamic vinegar

1 tsp brown sugar

salt and freshly ground black pepper

1 thin white baguette

a little olive oil

75g full-fat cream cheese

freshly ground black pepper

1 tbsp freshly snipped chives

6 slices Parma ham

*These are so popular whenever we serve them. If you are short on time, use onion marmalade from a jar.*

1.  Preheat the oven to 160°C (140°C fan/325°F/Gas 3). Meanwhile, make the onion marmalade. Heat the oil in a saucepan, add the onion, and fry over a high heat, stirring, for 5 minutes or until lightly coloured. Cover with a lid and cook slowly for 20 minutes or until soft. Add the vinegar and sugar and stir over a high heat for a few minutes until combined and glossy. Season with salt and freshly ground black pepper, then set aside to cool.

2.  Cut the bread into 30 slices. Brush each side with a little olive oil, then arrange on a baking sheet. Bake for 30–45 minutes or until crisp. Leave to cool.

3.  Spoon the cream cheese into a bowl, add the black pepper and the chives, and stir to combine.

4.  To serve, spread a little of the cream cheese mixture on top of each of the crostini. Snip each slice of Parma ham into 5 pieces and arrange on top of the cream cheese. Top with a little onion marmalade, arrange on a platter, and serve.

### IN THE AGA

Start the onion on the boiling plate, then cover with a lid and transfer to the simmering oven for 30 minutes. If there is any excess liquid left in the pan, return to the boiling plate for a couple of minutes. Bake the slices of bread on the floor of the roasting oven for 8 minutes on each side.

### PREPARE AHEAD AND FREEZE

*The marmalade and crostini can be made up to 1 week ahead. The topping can be added to the crostini up to 6 hours ahead. Freeze the crostini without the topping for up to 4 months.*

# HOME-MADE BLINIS WITH SALMON AND CRÈME FRAÎCHE

## MAKES 30

100g (3½oz) plain flour

½ tsp baking powder

2 eggs

4 tbsp milk

2 tbsp freshly snipped chives

1 tbsp sunflower oil

### For the topping

100g (3½oz) full-fat cream cheese

3 tbsp crème fraîche

2 tbsp freshly chopped dill, plus a few sprigs to garnish

1 tsp lemon juice

200g (7oz) smoked salmon

*We like our blinis quite thin, but the thickness is entirely up to you. If you make them too thick by mistake, simply slice them in half horizontally and you'll have twice the number.*

1. Put the flour, baking powder, eggs, milk, and chives into a bowl and mix to make a smooth batter. Heat the oil in a frying pan, add the batter half a teaspoon at a time, and fry for 1–2 minutes or until little bubbles form and the blinis start to curl at the edges. Turn over and lightly brown the other side, then transfer to a wire rack to cool. You may need to do this in batches.

2. To make the topping, mix the cream cheese, crème fraîche, chopped dill, and lemon juice in a small bowl, then spoon a little onto each blini.

3. Top the blinis with a small swirl of smoked salmon and a tiny sprig of dill. Arrange on a platter and serve.

### ON THE AGA
Fry the blinis directly on the simmering plate (grease it well beforehand) or in a frying pan on the simmering plate.

### PREPARE AHEAD AND FREEZE
*The blinis can be made up to the end of step 1 up to 2 days ahead. They can be assembled up to 6 hours ahead. Freeze at the end of step 1 for up to 3 months.*

# TOPPINGS FOR BLINIS AND CROSTINI

*Four delicious toppings for blinis or crostini. Each is enough to top 30. Prepare the blinis according to the method on page 48 and the crostini according to the method on page 47.*

6 heaped tbsp pesto

150g (5½oz) mozzarella, broken into pieces

8 cherry tomatoes, quartered

## MOZZARELLA, PESTO, AND CHERRY TOMATO

Spoon a little pesto onto each blini or crostini, top with a piece of mozzarella and then a quartered tomato. You should have two quarters left over.

8 tbsp cream cheese

10 slices Parma ham, each cut into three

6 Peppadew peppers, drained and each cut into five slices

## PARMA HAM, PEPPADEW PEPPER, AND CREAM CHEESE

Spread a little of the cream cheese onto each of the blinis or crostini, then arrange a swirl of Parma ham and a slice of pepper on top.

15 quail's eggs

30 asparagus tips

salt and freshly ground black pepper

170ml jar hollandaise sauce

## QUAIL'S EGG, HOLLANDAISE, AND ASPARAGUS

Put the quail's eggs into a pan, cover with cold water, and bring to the boil. Boil for 3 minutes, then plunge into cold water. When cool, peel and cut in half. Cook the asparagus tips in boiling salted water for 2–3 minutes or until tender. Drain and refresh in cold water. Spoon a blob of hollandaise onto each blini or crostini, sit half a quail's egg and an asparagus tip on top, then sprinkle with freshly ground black pepper. Serve cold or reheat in an oven preheated to 160°C (140°C fan/325°F/Gas 3) for 10 minutes or until warmed through.

170g can white crabmeat, drained

3 heaped tbsp cream cheese

3 tsp chilli dipping sauce

salt and freshly ground black pepper

## CRAB, CREAM CHEESE, AND CHILLI DIPPING SAUCE

Mix the ingredients together in a bowl, season with salt and freshly ground black pepper, then spoon onto the blinis or crostini.

CROSTINI, BLINIS, AND TARTLETS
Recipes on pages 49 and 53

# HUMMUS AND FETA TARTLETS

MAKES 48

**Special equipment** *12-hole mini muffin tin; 5cm (2in) round pastry cutter*

**For the tartlet cases**

*175g (6oz) plain flour, plus a little extra to dust*

*75g (2½oz) freshly grated Parmesan cheese*

*75g (2½oz) cold butter, cubed*

*2 tbsp pesto*

*2 tbsp cold water*

**For the filling**

*200g tub hummus*

*4 small carrots, grated*

*juice of ½ lemon*

*salt and freshly ground black pepper*

*200g (7oz) feta cheese, crumbled*

*200g (7oz) mixed pitted olives, sliced in half*

*The addition of Parmesan cheese and pesto makes the pastry for these tarlet cases out of this world!*

1.  Preheat the oven to 180°C (160°C fan/350°F/Gas 4). Meanwhile, put the flour, cheese, and butter into a food processor and whiz until the mixture resembles fine breadcrumbs. Add the pesto and water and whiz until the dough just comes together. Turn out on to a floured work surface and knead lightly into a ball. Roll out very thinly and then stamp out 48 rounds with a 5cm (2in) round cutter (don't worry if you don't get exactly 48). Use 12 of these to line the muffin tin.

2.  Bake for 12–15 minutes or until golden brown. Turn out onto a wire rack to cool and bake the remaining tartlet cases in the same way.

3.  When the tartlet cases are completely cold, spoon a little hummus into the base of each one. Mix the carrots and lemon juice together in a bowl and season with salt and freshly ground black pepper. Pile a little carrot on top of the hummus, then arrange some feta and half an olive on top. Serve cold.

### IN THE AGA

Bake the tartlets on the grid shelf on the floor of the roasting oven for 10 minutes.

---

**PREPARE AHEAD AND FREEZE**

*The tartlet cases can be made up to 10 days ahead and kept in the fridge. The tartlets can be filled up to 4 hours ahead. Freeze the empty tartlet cases for up to 2 months.*

# FILLINGS FOR TARTLETS

*Four excellent fillings for tartlets. Each recipe makes enough to fill 48 cases. Prepare the tartlets according to the recipe on page 52, but leave out the pesto.*

½ tbsp olive oil

225g (8oz) fillet steak

1 large cooked beetroot, coarsely grated

6 heaped tbsp creamed horseradish sauce

### RARE BEEF, BEETROOT, AND HORSERADISH

Heat the oil in a frying pan, add the steak, and fry for 3 minutes on each side or until cooked on the outside and rare on the inside. Leave to cool, then cut into 48 thin slices and arrange in the tartlet cases. Sprinkle with grated beetroot and a blob of horseradish sauce.

2 medium courgettes, cut in half lengthways and thinly sliced

2 red peppers, halved, deseeded, and cut into tiny dice

olive oil, to roast

salt and freshly ground black pepper

100g (3½oz) firm goat's cheese, cut into cubes

### GOAT'S CHEESE AND MEDITERRANEAN VEGETABLES

Preheat the oven to 200°C (180°C fan/400°F/Gas 6). Toss the courgettes and peppers with a little olive oil and season with salt and freshly ground black pepper. Roast in the oven for 15 minutes or until golden and tender. Spoon into the tartlet cases and top with the goat's cheese. Serve cold or reheat in an oven preheated to 160°C (140°C fan/325°F/Gas 3) for 10 minutes or until warmed through.

70g packet watercress

450g (1lb) dolcelatte cheese, cut into 48 small cubes

1 ripe pear, peeled, cored, and cut into 48 small cubes

### DOLCELATTE, WATERCRESS, AND PEAR

To serve cold, divide the watercress among the tartlets, then top with a cube of cheese and a cube of pear. To serve warm, top with the cheese and pear, then reheat in an oven preheated to 160°C (140°C fan/325°F/Gas 3) for 10 minutes or until the cheese has melted. Add the watercress before serving.

350g (12oz) cooked prawns

8 tbsp mayonnaise

1 tbsp tomato ketchup

2 tsp creamed horseradish sauce

1 tbsp lemon juice

salt and freshly ground black pepper

1 small mango, halved, stoned, and the flesh cut into 48 cubes

### PRAWN COCKTAIL WITH MANGO

Mix the prawns with the mayonnaise, ketchup, horseradish sauce, and lemon juice. Season with salt and freshly ground black pepper and spoon into the tartlet cases. Top each with a cube of mango.

# CHESTNUT, CRANBERRY, AND BRIE CHRISTMAS PARCELS

MAKES 24

1 tbsp olive oil

2 onions, chopped

125g chestnuts, finely chopped

salt and freshly ground black pepper

1 tbsp cranberry sauce

3 sheets filo pastry

100g butter, melted

100g firm brie, chopped into 24 small cubes

*A festive, crisp, delicious canapé for any special party. With the taste of Christmas in each bite, we call them parcels or moneybags. Use frozen or vacuum-packed chestnuts.*

1. Preheat the oven to 200°C (180°C fan/400°F/Gas 6).

2. To make the filling, heat the oil in a frying pan. Add the onions and fry over a high heat for a few minutes. Cover, lower the heat, and cook for about 10 minutes until soft. Add the chestnuts, then increase the heat and fry for 2 minutes until toasted. Spoon into a bowl and leave to cool. Season with salt and freshly ground black pepper and add the cranberry sauce.

3. Cut the pastry into 24 x 10cm squares. Brush each square with melted butter. Put a small tablespoon of the filling into the centre of the square. Place one cube of cheese on top. Crunch the end to seal in the middle so it looks like a moneybag. Repeat with the remaining squares.

4. Place the canapés on a baking sheet lined with non-stick paper. Bake for about 15 minutes until golden and crisp. Serve warm.

### IN THE AGA

Cook the parcels on the grid shelf on the floor of the roasting oven for about 10–12 minutes.

### PREPARE AHEAD AND FREEZE

*The parcels can be made and assembled up to 6 hours ahead. Freeze well uncooked for up to 1 month.*

# OUR BEST FIRST COURSES

*The first course is an opportunity to wow your guests.
If you are sitting down to eat, put the starter on the
table before guests come into the room. At a more
informal occasion, go round with the first course on
a platter – this is a very sociable way to entertain.*

# FENNEL AND SMOKED SALMON TARTLETS

*These are perfect as a first course, but you could equally serve them as a light lunch. Serve warm with dressed salad leaves. If you don't have time to make pastry, use shop bought – 225g (8oz) shortcrust pastry for eight tartlets and 350g (12oz) for 12 tartlets.*

**MAKES 8**

**Special equipment**
*2 x 4-hole Yorkshire pudding trays or 8 x 10cm (4in) tart tins*

**For the pastry**

*175g (6oz) plain flour, plus a little extra to dust*

*85g (3oz) butter*

*1 egg*

*1 tbsp water*

*a knob of butter*

*1 large fennel bulb, roughly chopped*

*1 small red chilli, deseeded and chopped*

*150g (5½oz) smoked salmon, chopped*

*large handful of freshly chopped parsley*

*200ml (7fl oz) pouring double cream*

*2 eggs*

*salt and freshly ground black pepper*

*50g (1¾oz) mature Cheddar cheese, grated*

**MAKES 12**

**Special equipment**
*3 x 4-hole Yorkshire pudding trays or 12 x 10cm (4in) tart tins*

**For the pastry**

*350g (12oz) plain flour, plus a little extra to dust*

*175g (6oz) butter*

*1 egg*

*1–2 tbsp water*

*a knob of butter*

*2 medium fennel bulbs, roughly chopped*

*1 large red chilli, deseeded and chopped*

*200g (7oz) smoked salmon, chopped*

*large handful of freshly chopped parsley*

*300ml (10fl oz) pouring double cream*

*3 eggs*

*salt and freshly ground black pepper*

*75g (2½oz) mature Cheddar cheese, grated*

1. To make the pastry, put the flour and butter into a food processor and whiz until the mixture resembles breadcrumbs. Add the egg and water and whiz until it forms a ball. Roll the pastry out thinly on a lightly floured work surface, then cut circles with a 12cm (5in) cutter or the bottom of a saucer. Place in the trays or tins and chill for 20 minutes.

2. Heat the knob of butter in a frying pan, add the fennel and chilli, and fry for 1 minute. Cover with a lid and cook over a low heat for 15 minutes or until soft. Set aside to cool.

3. Preheat the oven to 200°C (180°C fan/400°F/Gas 6) and put a baking sheet in to get hot (two sheets for 12). Meanwhile, divide the cooled fennel mixture among the pastry cases, then sprinkle over the smoked salmon and parsley. Whisk the cream and eggs together in a measuring jug, season with salt and freshly ground black pepper, and stir in half the cheese. Pour into the cases, then sprinkle over the remaining cheese.

4. Bake for 20 minutes (25 minutes for 12) or until golden brown and the pastry is crisp.

## IN THE AGA

Bake on the floor of the roasting oven for 15–20 minutes. If you're making 12 tartlets, bake a batch of eight and then a batch of four.

## PREPARE AHEAD AND FREEZE

*You can make the tartlets up to 2 days ahead. Freeze for up to 2 months.*

# DOUBLE SALMON AND EGG TERRINE

*This is ideal for any occasion – buffet, picnic, even a smart dinner party. Serve it with toast or on individual plates with dressed rocket leaves.*

## SERVES 6

**Special equipment** *450g (1lb) loaf tin lined with cling film*

*100g (3½oz) fresh salmon fillet, skinned*

*a knob of butter, plus 25g (scant 1oz), at room temperature*

*salt and freshly ground black pepper*

*100g (3½oz) smoked salmon trimmings*

*100g (3½oz) full-fat cream cheese*

*3 tbsp light mayonnaise*

*1 tbsp freshly chopped chives*

*2 tbsp lemon juice*

*4 large hard-boiled eggs, chopped fairly finely*

*cress, to garnish*

## SERVES 12

**Special equipment** *900g (2lb) loaf tin lined with cling film*

*225g (8oz) fresh salmon fillet, skinned*

*a large knob of butter, plus 50g (1¾oz), at room temperature*

*salt and freshly ground black pepper*

*170g packet smoked salmon trimmings*

*200g (7oz) full-fat cream cheese*

*6 tbsp light mayonnaise*

*2 tbsp freshly chopped chives*

*juice of ½ lemon*

*8 large hard-boiled eggs, chopped fairly finely*

*cress, to garnish*

1. Preheat the oven to 180°C (160°C fan/350°F/Gas 4). Place the salmon on some foil, spoon the knob of butter on top, and season with salt and freshly ground black pepper. Scrunch the sides of the foil together at the top to make a parcel, place on a baking sheet, and bake for 12–15 minutes (15–20 minutes for 12) or until just cooked. Set aside to cool in the foil.

2. Pick out the nicest pieces of smoked salmon (around half) and put the rest into a food processor with the cream cheese, the remaining butter, mayonnaise, chives, and lemon juice. Break up the cold salmon in the foil and add to the processor with the juices. Season with salt and freshly ground black pepper, then whiz until smooth. Spoon into a mixing bowl.

3. Add the eggs and stir until combined. Scatter the remaining smoked salmon trimmings (chopped, if necessary) on top of the cling film in the base of the loaf tin.

4. Spoon the mousse mixture on top and level the surface. Cover with cling film and chill in the fridge for at least 6 hours to firm up.

5. To serve, pop the terrine in the freezer for about 30 minutes to make slicing easier, then turn it out of the tin and cut into slices. Scatter with cress and serve.

### IN THE AGA
Cook the salmon parcel in the simmering oven for about 15 minutes or until just cooked.

### PREPARE AHEAD
*The terrine can be made up to the end of step 4 up to 2 days ahead. Not suitable for freezing.*

# PRAWN AND CRAYFISH COCKTAIL

*You can prepare this attractive starter ahead and have it ready and waiting in the fridge. Serve with lightly buttered brown bread.*

## SERVES 6

8 tbsp mayonnaise

juice of ½ lemon

2 tbsp tomato ketchup

2 tsp creamed horseradish sauce

3 tbsp capers, drained, rinsed, dried, and roughly chopped

salt and freshly ground black pepper

300g (11oz) small cooked shelled North Atlantic prawns

175g tub cooked crayfish tails, drained

4 Baby Gem lettuces

2 tbsp freshly chopped parsley

## SERVES 12

240ml (8fl oz) mayonnaise

juice of 1 lemon

4 tbsp tomato ketchup

1 heaped tbsp creamed horseradish sauce

6 tbsp capers, drained, rinsed, dried, and roughly chopped

salt and freshly ground black pepper

600g (1lb 5oz) small cooked shelled North Atlantic prawns

2 x 175g tubs cooked crayfish tails, drained

8 Baby Gem lettuces

4 tbsp freshly chopped parsley

1. Mix the first five ingredients together in a bowl and season with salt and freshly ground black pepper.

2. Dry the prawns and crayfish tails on kitchen paper and stir into the sauce.

3. Peel the lettuce leaves from the heart and arrange 18 leaves (36 for 12) on a platter or on individual plates, allowing three leaves per person. Spoon the prawn mixture into the leaves and sprinkle with a little of the parsley.

## PREPARE AHEAD

The sauce can be made up to 4 days ahead. The dish can be assembled up to 6 hours ahead. Not suitable for freezing.

# QUICK SALMON AND
# PRAWN DILL SALAD

*A first course with wow factor, yet it is surprisingly easy to make. These are perfect for a crowd because they are individual servings, so you'll always know you have the right number. For very special occasions, arrange a fresh king prawn in the shell on the top of each portion. Serve cold with warm brown rolls or some good brown bread.*

**SERVES 6**

200g (7oz) shelled cooked North Atlantic prawns

200g (7oz) sliced smoked salmon

small bunch of fresh dill

170ml tub full-fat soured cream

finely grated zest of 1 lemon

juice of ½ lemon

pinch of ground cayenne pepper

freshly ground black pepper

lamb's lettuce, a little vinaigrette, and 6 lemon wedges, to serve

**SERVES 12**

400g (14oz) shelled cooked North Atlantic prawns

400g (14oz) sliced smoked salmon

large bunch of fresh dill

2 x 170ml tubs full-fat soured cream

finely grated zest of 2 lemons

juice of 1 lemon

big pinch of ground cayenne pepper

freshly ground black pepper

lamb's lettuce, a little vinaigrette, and 12 lemon wedges, to serve

1. Lay the prawns on kitchen paper and squeeze out any excess liquid.

2. Cut one long strip, about 1 x 5cm (½ x 2in), per serving from the salmon slices and put to one side. Cut the remaining smoked salmon into small pieces about 1cm (½in) in size.

3. Set aside a sprig of dill per serving, then finely chop the rest of the bunch and tip into a mixing bowl. Add the soured cream, lemon zest, lemon juice, cayenne pepper, and some freshly ground black pepper and stir to combine.

4. Add the prawns and chopped salmon pieces.

5. Arrange the lamb's lettuce on individual plates, drizzle with vinaigrette, then pile the prawn mixture in the centre.

6. Arrange the reserved salmon strips on top of the prawns. Garnish with a sprig of dill and a wedge of lemon.

**PREPARE AHEAD**

*The prawn and salmon mixture can be made up to the end of step 4 up to 8 hours ahead – the flavours will actually improve. The plates can be arranged up to 3 hours ahead. Not suitable for freezing.*

# CRAB, AVOCADO, AND SMOKED SALMON TIANS

## SERVES 6

**Special equipment** *6 x 7cm (2¾in) metal cooking rings arranged on a baking sheet lined with cling film*

300g (11oz) fresh crab meat

100g (3½oz) full-fat cream cheese

bunch of dill, finely chopped

juice of 1 lemon

dash of Tabasco

½ tsp Dijon mustard

salt and freshly ground black pepper

3 small ripe avocados, halved, stoned, and peeled

6 handfuls of salad leaves such as watercress, rocket, or lamb's lettuce, to garnish

6 slices smoked salmon

## SERVES 12

**Special equipment** *12 x 7cm (2¾in) metal cooking rings arranged on a baking sheet lined with cling film*

600g (1lb 5oz) fresh crab meat

200g (7oz) full-fat cream cheese

large bunch of dill, finely chopped

juice of 2 lemons

generous dash of Tabasco

1 tsp Dijon mustard

salt and freshly ground black pepper

6 small ripe avocados, halved, stoned, and peeled

12 handfuls of salad leaves such as watercress, rocket, or lamb's lettuce, to garnish

12 slices smoked salmon

*A delicious and impressive starter, which looks stunning at a dinner party, wedding, or other celebration. If you don't have metal cooking rings to shape the tians, don't worry – you can use ramekins lined with cling film. Serve with dressed salad leaves, lemon wedges, and buttered brown bread.*

1. Mix the crab meat, cream cheese, dill, half the lemon juice, the Tabasco, and mustard in a bowl and season with salt and freshly ground black pepper.

2. Mash one avocado with a fork until smooth (two avocados for 12) and cut the remaining avocados into small pieces. Mix the mashed and chopped avocados together, stir in the remaining lemon juice, and season with salt and freshly ground black pepper.

3. Spoon the avocado mixture into the base of each cooking ring and press down with the back of a spoon.

4. Divide the crab mixture among the rings and spread to the edges to cover the avocado entirely. Cover with cling film and chill in the fridge for a few hours.

5. When ready to serve, arrange a handful of salad leaves on each plate, place a ring on top, then carefully remove the cling film and ring. Top each tian with a swirl of smoked salmon.

## PREPARE AHEAD

*The tians can be made up to 6 hours ahead.
Not suitable for freezing.*

# SMOKED MACKEREL
# AND WATERCRESS PÂTÉ

*A quick-to-prepare starter served with smoked trout. You'll find it in the chiller cabinets at the supermarket. Serve with warm rolls or toast.*

## SERVES 6

**Special equipment** *19cm (7½in) square cake tin, lined with cling film*

100g (3½oz) butter, at room temperature

175g (6oz) full-fat cream cheese

1 tbsp creamed horseradish

juice of ½ lemon

300g (11oz) smoked mackerel, skin removed

a few drops of Tabasco

25g (scant 1oz) fresh watercress, plus a little extra to garnish

freshly ground black pepper

6 small slices smoked trout

6 lemon wedges, to garnish

## SERVES 12

**Special equipment** *23 x 30cm (9 x 12in) traybake tin or roasting tin, lined with cling film*

225g (8oz) butter, at room temperature

350g (12oz) full-fat cream cheese

2 tbsp creamed horseradish

juice of 1 lemon

600g (1lb 5oz) smoked mackerel, skin removed

a few drops of Tabasco

50g (1¾oz) fresh watercress, plus a little extra to garnish

freshly ground black pepper

12 small slices smoked trout

12 lemon wedges, to garnish

1. Put the butter, cream cheese, horseradish, and lemon juice into a food processor and whiz until completely smooth.

2. Remove any tiny bones from the mackerel, then break the flesh into pieces and add to the processor. Add the Tabasco and watercress, season with freshly ground black pepper, and whiz again until just blended.

3. Spoon into the tin and level the top. Cover with cling film and chill overnight.

4. To serve, pop the pâté in the freezer for about 30 minutes to make slicing easier, then turn it out and cut into squares, triangles, slices, or rounds. Arrange a piece on each plate, top with a slice of smoked trout in a swirl, then garnish with watercress and a lemon wedge, and serve with toast or brown bread.

## PREPARE AHEAD

*The pâté can be made up to the end of step 3 up to 2 days ahead. Not suitable for freezing.*

# RUSTIC MUSHROOM LIVER PÂTÉ

*This is so easy to make in a food processor. What's more, it requires no oven-baking. Serve with toast and slices of gherkin, if liked.*

## SERVES 6

**Special equipment** *450g (1lb) loaf tin, lined with cling film*

15g (½oz) dried porcini mushrooms

2 tbsp olive oil

1 onion, roughly chopped

50g (1¾oz) smoked streaky bacon, snipped into small pieces and rind removed

1 garlic clove, crushed

50g (1¾oz) chestnut mushrooms, thinly sliced

1 tsp each freshly chopped parsley and thyme leaves

200g (7oz) fresh chicken livers

25g (scant 1oz) fresh white breadcrumbs

50g (1¾oz) butter, at room temperature

100g (3½oz) full-fat cream cheese

2 tsp Worcestershire sauce

salt and freshly ground black pepper

a little freshly chopped parsley, to garnish

## SERVES 12

**Special equipment** *900g (2lb) loaf tin, lined with cling film*

25g (scant 1oz) dried porcini mushrooms

4 tbsp olive oil

1 large onion, roughly chopped

100g (3½oz) smoked streaky bacon, snipped into small pieces and rind removed

2 garlic cloves, crushed

100g (3½oz) chestnut mushrooms, thinly sliced

2 tsp each freshly chopped parsley and thyme leaves

400g (14oz) fresh chicken livers

50g (1¾oz) fresh white breadcrumbs

100g (3½oz) butter, at room temperature

200g (7oz) full-fat cream cheese

1 tbsp Worcestershire sauce

salt and freshly ground black pepper

a little freshly chopped parsley, to garnish

1. Put the porcini into a bowl and pour over just enough boiling water to cover. Set aside to soften for about 30 minutes, then drain and dry well with kitchen paper.

2. Heat half the oil in a frying pan, add the onion, bacon, and porcini, and fry for 1 minute. Cover with a lid and cook over a low heat for 10 minutes or until the bacon is cooked. Add the garlic, mushrooms, parsley, and thyme and fry for 5 minutes or until the mushrooms are just cooked. Transfer to a mixing bowl.

3. Heat the remaining oil in the unwashed pan and fry the chicken livers for 1–2 minutes on each side or until brown on the outside and still pink in the centre. Add to the bowl with the porcini mixture and leave to cool.

4. Spoon half the cold chicken liver mixture into a food processor, add the breadcrumbs, butter, cream cheese, and Worcestershire sauce, and whiz until smooth. Season with salt and freshly ground black pepper and whiz again until smooth and combined. Tip into a bowl.

5. Chop the remaining cold chicken liver mixture coarsely, then add to the bowl with the smooth pâté and stir to combine. Spoon into the prepared tin and level the top. Cover with cling film and chill for a minimum of 6 hours or overnight.

6. To serve, turn the tin upside down onto a serving plate and remove the cling film. Press some chopped parsley on top, cut the pâté in fairly thick slices, and serve.

### IN THE AGA
At step 2, cover with a lid and transfer to the simmering oven for 20 minutes to soften.

### PREPARE AHEAD
*The pâté can be made up to 3 days ahead. Not suitable for freezing.*

# CELEBRATORY FISH PLATTER

*Mary made this as part of a New Year's Eve pot luck supper party. The tray was quick to prepare and easy to bundle into the car with a plate of brown bread and butter.*

SERVES 6

## SERVES 6

**For the gravadlax**

500g (1lb 2oz) piece salmon fillet, from the thick end, skin on

2 tbsp dried dill

2 tbsp coarse sea salt

2 tbsp caster sugar

salt and freshly ground black pepper

6 tbsp mayonnaise

1 tsp Dijon mustard

2 tsp freshly chopped dill

**For the prawn cocktail**

300g (11oz) small cooked shelled North Atlantic prawns

6 tbsp light mayonnaise

juice of ½ lemon

2 tbsp tomato ketchup

2 tbsp creamed horseradish sauce

**To serve**

75g (2½ oz) lamb's lettuce or rocket

6 large Little Gem lettuce leaves

6 large cooked king prawns, shells removed but heads on

lemon wedges

## SERVES 12

**For the gravadlax**

1kg (2¼lb) piece salmon fillet, from the thick end, skin on

4 tbsp dried dill

4 tbsp coarse sea salt

4 tbsp caster sugar

salt and freshly ground black pepper

12 tbsp mayonnaise

1 tbsp Dijon mustard

1 tbsp freshly chopped dill

**For the prawn cocktail**

600g (1lb 5oz) small cooked shelled North Atlantic prawns

12 tbsp light mayonnaise

juice of 1 small lemon

4 tbsp tomato ketchup

4 tbsp creamed horseradish sauce

**To serve**

175g (6 oz) lamb's lettuce or rocket

12 large Little Gem lettuce leaves

12 large cooked king prawns, shells removed but heads on

lemon wedges

1. To make the gravadlax, place the salmon skin side down on a large piece of foil, then pull out any bones with tweezers or a small knife. Sprinkle over the dill, salt, sugar, and some freshly ground black pepper, making sure all the salmon is covered. Wrap in the foil and place on a tray or baking sheet. Place another baking sheet on top and put some heavy weights or tinned food on it to weigh the fish down. Transfer to the fridge for 12 hours or overnight.

2. Take the salmon from the fridge and pour away any juices. Place in the freezer for 30 minutes to make slicing easier. Then, using a sharp knife, cut into thin slices. Keep the knife angled at about 45 degrees so the slices are wide. Discard the skin.

3. To make the prawn cocktail, dry the prawns thoroughly with kitchen paper. Mix the mayonnaise, lemon juice, ketchup, and horseradish in a bowl, add the prawns, and season with salt and freshly ground black pepper.

4. To serve, scatter the lamb's lettuce or rocket over the base of a platter. Spoon the prawn cocktail into the Little Gem lettuce leaves, then arrange on one area of the platter. Arrange the gravadlax and the king prawns alongside, then add the lemon wedges. Mix the mayonnaise for the gravadlax with the mustard and dill, season with salt and freshly ground black pepper, and serve in a bowl.

## PREPARE AHEAD AND FREEZE

*The gravadlax can be made up to 2 days ahead. Freeze for up to 1 month. The cocktail sauce can be made up to 12 hours ahead. Not suitable for freezing. The platter can be assembled up to 4 hours ahead.*

# FILLET OF BEEF WITH BEETROOT AND HORSERADISH DRESSING

*When you're serving numbers at a smart dinner party, it's always a good feeling to know the first course is made and waiting in the fridge. This recipe is perfect for that. When you carve the fillet, you want the slices to be long and thin rather than round – middle-cut fillets give you the correct shape. Serve with brown bread rolls.*

## SERVES 6

300g (11oz) middle-cut fillet steak, trimmed

1 tbsp olive oil, plus a little extra to serve

salt and freshly ground black pepper

4 medium-sized cooked beetroot, thinly sliced

50g (1¾oz) rocket

50g (1¾oz) piece Parmesan cheese

**For the horseradish dressing**

2 tbsp creamed horseradish sauce

3 tbsp light mayonnaise

2 tbsp lemon juice

## SERVES 12

2 x 300g (11oz) middle-cut fillet steaks, trimmed

2 tbsp olive oil, plus a little extra to serve

salt and freshly ground black pepper

8 medium-sized cooked beetroot, thinly sliced

100g (3½oz) rocket

100g (3½oz) piece Parmesan cheese

**For the horseradish dressing**

4 tbsp creamed horseradish sauce

6 tbsp light mayonnaise

4 tbsp lemon juice

1. Rub the steak with the oil and season with salt and freshly ground black pepper.

2. Heat a frying pan until very hot, then fry the fillet for 2½ minutes on each side (fry each fillet separately for 12). This will give you a rare steak. If you prefer medium, cook for another minute on each side. Remove from the pan and leave to cool.

3. To make the dressing, put the ingredients into a small bowl and whisk with a hand whisk until smooth and combined. Season with salt and freshly ground black pepper.

4. When the steak is cold, carve it into very thin slices – you're aiming to get 30 slices per fillet. Arrange five thin slices in a star shape on each plate. Arrange five slices of beetroot in the middle of the plate in a spiral shape, then drizzle with the horseradish dressing.

5. Gather together a little bundle of rocket leaves for each plate and place on top of the beetroot. Using a potato peeler, shave little shavings of Parmesan over the top.

6. Drizzle with a little olive oil and serve straightaway.

## PREPARE AHEAD

*The plates can be prepared up to the end of step 5 up to 6 hours ahead. Drizzle with oil just before serving. Not suitable for freezing.*

# ROASTED FIGS WITH PARMA HAM AND GOAT'S CHEESE

*Mary was given this recipe by a friend in Portugal who makes full use of fruits in season. We use vacuum-packed dry-cured ham, as it comes in convenient even-sized slices. Swap the figs for tomatoes, if you like – see below left.*

## SERVES 6

2 x 100g rolls firm goat's cheese, such as Capricorn

6 fresh figs

12 slices Parma ham

rocket or salad leaves, to serve

balsamic vinegar, to serve

olive oil, to serve

## SERVES 12

4 x 100g rolls firm goat's cheese, such as Capricorn

12 fresh figs

24 slices Parma ham

rocket or salad leaves, to serve

balsamic vinegar, to serve

olive oil, to serve

1. Pop the goat's cheese in the freezer for about an hour or until firm.

2. Preheat the oven to 220°C (200°C fan/425°F/Gas 7). Cut off the pointed stem at the top of each fig, then stand the figs upright on a board. Cut a cross in the top of each one, but don't cut right down to the base.

3. Trim the ends off the cheese and discard, then cut each roll into three slices. Cut each slice in half to give semi-circles. Cut half the semi-circles in half again to give quarters.

4. Lie each slice of ham out flat and trim off any excess fat.

5. Put a semi-circle of cheese into each fig where you've made the cross. Use the quarters to fit in either side, so the complete cross is filled with goat's cheese.

6. Wrap each fig in a piece of ham, then wrap it in another piece, working in the other direction. Squeeze the ham together at the top.

7. Roast for 8 minutes (10 minutes for 12) or until the cheese has melted and the ham is crisp.

8. Arrange the figs on serving plates with some rocket or salad leaves, drizzle with a little balsamic vinegar and olive oil, and serve at once.

### IN THE AGA

Bake on the second set of runners in the roasting oven for 6–8 minutes.

## ROASTED TOMATOES WITH PESTO

*When figs are not in season, we use skinned, medium-sized, slightly under-ripe tomatoes prepared in the same way. Spoon a teaspoon of pesto over the cheese and tomato before wrapping it in the Parma ham.*

## PREPARE AHEAD

*You can prepare the figs up to the end of step 6 up to 12 hours ahead. Not suitable for freezing.*

# ASPARAGUS WITH PARMESAN AND MUSTARD SAUCE

*This is such an easy first course for when asparagus is plentiful and at its best in the months of May and June. We like to cook the asparagus on a baking sheet and serve them in individual portions, but you can bake them in a large ovenproof dish and take it to the table if you prefer.*

## SERVES 6

750g (1lb 10oz) asparagus spears, woody ends removed

salt and freshly ground black pepper

50g (1¾oz) Parmesan cheese, freshly grated

**For the mustard sauce**

4 tsp Dijon mustard

2 tsp white wine vinegar

4 tbsp sunflower oil

2 tbsp mayonnaise

juice of ½ lemon

1 tsp caster sugar

## SERVES 12

1.5kg (3lb 3oz) asparagus spears, woody ends removed

salt and freshly ground black pepper

100g (3½oz) Parmesan cheese, freshly grated

**For the mustard sauce**

2 heaped tbsp Dijon mustard

1½ tbsp white wine vinegar

8 tbsp sunflower oil

4 tbsp mayonnaise

juice of 1 lemon

2 tsp caster sugar

1. Preheat the oven to 220°C (200°C fan/425°F/Gas 7). Meanwhile, put the asparagus spears into a shallow pan of boiling salted water and bring back up to the boil. Boil for 3 minutes, then drain, refresh in cold water, and dry on kitchen paper.

2. Arrange six bundles of asparagus on a large baking sheet lined with baking parchment (12 bundles on two baking sheets for 12), season with salt and freshly ground black pepper, and sprinkle with the cheese.

3. Bake for 8 minutes (12 minutes for 12) or until the cheese has melted and browned and the asparagus is piping hot.

4. Meanwhile, make the sauce: put all the ingredients into a bowl and whisk with a hand whisk until well combined, then season with salt and freshly ground black pepper.

5. Carefully transfer the bundles onto hot plates and serve with the mustard sauce.

### IN THE AGA

Bake on the top set of runners in the roasting oven for 7–8 minutes (8–10 minutes for 12).

### PREPARE AHEAD

*The asparagus can be prepared up to the end of step 2 up to 1 day ahead. The sauce can be made up to 4 days ahead. Not suitable for freezing.*

# ROQUEFORT AND PARSLEY MOUSSELINE CREAMS

*These make a delicious creamy starter. Serve them in ramekins with crusty bread alongside.*

**SERVES 6**

**Special equipment** *6 x size 1 (150ml/5fl oz) ramekins, greased*

*45g (1½oz) butter*

*45g (1½oz) plain flour*

*300ml (10fl oz) hot milk*

*3 large eggs, separated*

*100g (3½oz) Roquefort, coarsely grated*

*1 tbsp freshly chopped parsley*

*salt and freshly ground black pepper*

*dash of Tabasco*

**SERVES 12**

**Special equipment** *12 x size 1 (150ml/5fl oz) ramekins, greased*

*75g (2½oz) butter*

*75g (2½oz) plain flour*

*600ml (1 pint) hot milk*

*6 large eggs, separated*

*225g (8oz) Roquefort, coarsely grated*

*2 tbsp freshly chopped parsley*

*salt and freshly ground black pepper*

*dash of Tabasco*

1. Preheat the oven to 190°C (170°C fan/375°F/Gas 5). Meanwhile, melt the butter in a large saucepan, add the flour and then the milk, and whisk until the mixture thickens to a smooth white sauce. Remove from the heat and allow to cool slightly.

2. Meanwhile, whisk the egg whites in a bowl with an electric hand whisk until stiff.

3. Stir the cheese and parsley into the warm sauce and season with salt and freshly ground black pepper (not too much salt, as the cheese is salty). Add the egg yolks and Tabasco and stir to combine.

4. Mix a spoonful of the egg whites into the sauce until smooth, then fold in the rest so the mixture is light and combined. Spoon evenly into the ramekins and sit on a baking sheet.

5. Bake for 15–20 minutes (20–25 minutes for 12) or until risen and golden.

6. Serve hot in the ramekins with a dressed salad alongside.

### IN THE AGA
Bake on the second set of runners in the roasting oven for 15 minutes (15–20 minutes for 12).

### PREPARE AHEAD
*The creams can be made up to the end of step 4 up to 6 hours ahead. Not suitable for freezing.*

# SWEET POTATO SOUP
# WITH CUMIN AND GINGER

**SERVES 6**

1 tbsp olive oil

900g (2lb) sweet potatoes, peeled and cut into 1cm (½in) cubes

450g (1lb) carrots, cut into 1cm (½in) cubes

2cm (¾in) piece fresh root ginger, peeled and finely grated

1 tsp ground cumin

1.4 litres (2½ pints) vegetable stock

salt and freshly ground black pepper

double cream, to garnish

chopped chives, to garnish

**SERVES 12**

2 tbsp olive oil

1.8kg (4lb) sweet potatoes, peeled and cut into 1cm (½in) cubes

900g (2lb) carrots, cut into 1cm (½in) cubes

5cm (2in) piece fresh root ginger, peeled and finely grated

2 tsp ground cumin

3 litres (5¼ pints) vegetable stock

salt and freshly ground black pepper

double cream, to garnish

chopped chives, to garnish

*Vibrant in colour and quick to make, this soup is ideal for any winter party. Serve with croûtons or crispy bread, if liked.*

1. Heat the oil in a deep saucepan, add the sweet potatoes, carrots, ginger, and cumin and fry over a high heat, stirring, for 10 minutes or until starting to brown.

2. Add the stock, bring to the boil, then season with salt and freshly ground black pepper. Cover with a lid and simmer over a low heat for 20–30 minutes (35–40 minutes for 12) or until the sweet potatoes and carrots are tender.

3. Carefully scoop out half the vegetables into a bowl using a slotted spoon. Whiz the remainder in a food processor or blender until smooth, then return to the pan.

4. Add the reserved vegetables, bring to the boil again, and check the seasoning.

5. To serve, garnish with a swirl of double cream and some chopped chives.

**IN THE AGA**

At step 2, cover with a lid and transfer to the simmering oven for 30 minutes (40 minutes for 12) or until tender.

**PREPARE AHEAD AND FREEZE**

*The soup can be made up to 3 days ahead. Freeze for up to 3 months.*

# HONEY-GLAZED PARSNIP SOUP

*Our lovely friend Jane gave us the idea for this recipe. It's creamy and luxurious – ideal before a light meal. Garnish with croûtons and cracked black pepper, and a drizzle of cream if you like.*

### SERVES 6

1 tbsp olive oil

900g (2lb) parsnips, roughly chopped

2 large onions, roughly chopped

4 celery sticks, sliced

1 leek, roughly chopped

1½ tbsp runny honey

1.4 litres (2½ pints) vegetable stock

salt and freshly ground black pepper

150ml (5fl oz) double cream

### SERVES 12

2 tbsp olive oil

1.5kg (3lb 3oz) parsnips, roughly chopped

4 large onions, roughly chopped

8 celery sticks, sliced

2 leeks, roughly chopped

3 tbsp runny honey

2.8 litres (5 pints) vegetable stock

salt and freshly ground black pepper

300ml (10fl oz) double cream

1. Heat the oil in a deep saucepan, add the vegetables, and fry over a high heat for a few minutes. Stir in the honey and fry for 4–5 minutes or until the vegetables are becoming golden brown and caramelized.

2. Add the stock and season with salt and freshly ground black pepper. Cover with a lid, lower the heat, and simmer for 20–30 minutes (35–40 minutes for 12) or until the parsnips are completely tender.

3. Transfer to a food processor or blender and whiz until completely smooth.

4. Return to the pan to reheat, stir in the cream, and check the seasoning. Serve piping hot.

### IN THE AGA

At step 2, cover with a lid and transfer to the simmering oven for 30 minutes (45 minutes for 12) or until the parsnips are tender.

### PREPARE AHEAD AND FREEZE

*The soup can be made up to the end of step 3 up to 2 days ahead. Freeze at the end of step 3 for up to 1 month.*

# FRENCH ONION SOUP WITH MUSTARD GRUYÈRE CROÛTONS

*The onions are caramelized in sugar in this traditional recipe. We toast the croûtons to make a perfect winter starter or lunch dish.*

## SERVES 6

25g (scant 1oz) butter

4 large onions (about 675g/1½lb), thinly sliced

2 tsp soft light brown sugar

1.7 litres (3 pints) chicken stock

1 tbsp cornflour

salt and freshly ground black pepper

1½ tbsp balsamic vinegar

### For the croûtons

1 small thin soft bread stick

25g (scant 1oz) butter, at room temperature

2 tbsp Dijon mustard

50g (1¾oz) Gruyère, finely grated

## SERVES 12

50g (1¾oz) butter

8 large onions (about 1.35kg/3lb), thinly sliced

2 tbsp soft light brown sugar

3.6 litres (6¼ pints) chicken stock

2 tbsp cornflour

salt and freshly ground black pepper

4 tbsp balsamic vinegar

### For the croûtons

1 large thin soft bread stick

50g (1¾oz) butter, at room temperature

4 tbsp Dijon mustard

100g (3½oz) Gruyère, finely grated

1. Melt the butter in a deep saucepan, add the onions, and fry for 5 minutes, stirring. Lower the heat, cover with a lid, and cook for 20 minutes or until completely soft.

2. Remove the lid, stir in the sugar, and continue to fry the onions over a high heat for 10 minutes or until lightly browned. Add the stock, bring to the boil, cover with a lid again, and simmer for 5–10 minutes.

3. Mix the cornflour in a cup with a little cold water to make a thin paste, then stir into the soup. Season with salt and freshly ground black pepper, add the vinegar, and stir well. Bring to the boil, stirring continuously, until slightly thickened.

4. To make the croûtons, preheat the grill. Slice the bread into 18 thin slices (36 for 12), butter both sides, then toast on one side until golden. Turn the croûtons over, spread a little mustard on the untoasted side and top with the cheese. Slide back under the grill for 3–5 minutes or until the cheese is golden and melted.

5. Serve the soup in hot bowls with three croûtons per person.

### IN THE AGA

At step 1, cover with a lid and soften the onion in the simmering oven for 15 minutes or until tender. Continue on the boiling plate.

### PREPARE AHEAD AND FREEZE

*The soup can be made up to 3 days ahead. The croûtons can be assembled up to 6 hours ahead and popped under the grill before serving. Freeze the soup without the croûtons for up to 3 months.*

# PUY LENTIL AND PEARL BARLEY SOUP

**SERVES 6**

1 tbsp olive oil

1 large onion, finely chopped

2 carrots, finely diced

2 garlic cloves, crushed

100g (3½oz) dried Puy lentils

100g (3½oz) pearl barley

680g jar passata

1.5 litres (2¾ pints) chicken stock or vegetable stock

salt and freshly ground black pepper

2 tsp sugar

1 tbsp balsamic vinegar

**SERVES 12**

2 tbsp olive oil

2 onions, finely chopped

2 large carrots, finely diced

4 garlic cloves, crushed

225g (8oz) dried Puy lentils

225g (8oz) pearl barley

2 x 680g jars passata

3 litres (5½ pints) chicken stock or vegetable stock

salt and freshly ground black pepper

1 tbsp sugar

2 tbsp balsamic vinegar

*This is a hearty, healthy soup full of flavour and goodness. Serve it piping hot with some crusty bread.*

1. Heat the oil in a deep frying pan, add the onion and carrots, and fry over a high heat, stirring, for 10 minutes or until lightly brown.

2. Add the garlic, lentils, and barley and fry for 1 minute. Blend in the passata and stock and season with salt and freshly ground black pepper.

3. Bring to the boil, cover with a lid, and simmer for 40–45 minutes (50–55 minutes for 12) or until the lentils and barley are tender.

4. Add the sugar and vinegar, check the seasoning, and serve.

**IN THE AGA**

At step 3, cover with a lid and transfer to the simmering oven for 45–55 minutes.

**PREPARE AHEAD**

*The soup can be made up to 3 days ahead. Not suitable for freezing.*

# EXPRESS MEDITERRANEAN PLATTER

*A very sociable first course that's also a bit of a cheat. For a variation on this platter, try the quick, flavoursome tapenade recipe given below. If you are serving 12, arrange the food on two platters or a large wooden board.*

## SERVES 6

8 Peppadew peppers, drained and sliced

1 tbsp freshly chopped parsley

200g tub hummus

salt and freshly ground black pepper

6 stuffed vine leaves

200g (7oz) feta cheese, cut into bite-sized cubes

200g (7oz) marinated chargrilled artichokes in oil, drained and oil reserved

200g (7oz) Kalamata olives in oil, drained and oil reserved

6 pitta breads

## SERVES 12

16 Peppadew peppers, drained and sliced

2 tbsp freshly chopped parsley

2 x 200g tubs hummus

salt and freshly ground black pepper

12 stuffed vine leaves

400g (14oz) feta cheese, cut into bite-sized cubes

400g (14oz) marinated chargrilled artichokes in oil, drained and oil reserved

400g (14oz) Kalamata olives in oil, drained and oil reserved

12 pitta breads

1. Take a large flat platter or round tart plate and put a small bowl in the centre. Mix the Peppadew pepper slices and parsley with the hummus, season with salt and freshly ground black pepper, and spoon into the bowl.

2. Arrange the vine leaves, feta, artichokes, and olives in piles around the platter.

3. Toast the pitta and slice into fingers, then arrange in a pile alongside the artichokes.

4. Drizzle the feta with some of the oil from the olives or artichokes and serve chilled or at room temperature.

## TAPENADE AND TOMATO PLATTER

*Swap the olives for baby tomatoes on the vine, if you like. To make a green olive, basil, and tomato tapenade, mix a sliced clove of garlic, 2 tbsp sundried tomato paste, 3 tbsp drained capers, 70g pitted green olives, 2 tbsp olive oil, and a small bunch of basil, chopped, in a processor. Season with freshly ground black pepper and spoon into a bowl. Serve as a dip or to go with bread and cheeses.*

## PREPARE AHEAD

*The hummus can be mixed with the parsley and peppers up to 4 days ahead. The platter can be assembled up to 8 hours ahead.*

# ANTIPASTI

*You can use any variety of sliced meats you like for this appetizing selection of roasted vegetables with an aubergine and mint dip. Serve with chunky bread, flat bread, or toasted pitta bread.*

## SERVES 6

**For the aubergine and mint dip**

2 large aubergines

2 tbsp olive oil

3 fat garlic cloves (unpeeled)

100ml (3½fl oz) full-fat Greek yogurt

juice of ½ lemon

3 tbsp freshly chopped mint, plus a sprig to garnish

salt and freshly ground black pepper

**For the roasted vegetables**

4 courgettes, thickly sliced

1 yellow pepper, halved, deseeded, and sliced into large chunks

1 red pepper, halved, deseeded, and sliced into large chunks

2 tbsp olive oil

2 tbsp balsamic vinegar

**Sliced meats**

6 slices Parma ham

6 slices salami

6 slices chorizo

## SERVES 12

**For the aubergine and mint dip**

4 large aubergines

4 tbsp olive oil

6 fat garlic cloves (unpeeled)

200ml (7fl oz) full-fat Greek yogurt

juice of 1 lemon

6 tbsp freshly chopped mint, plus 2 sprigs to garnish

salt and freshly ground black pepper

**For the roasted vegetables**

8 courgettes, thickly sliced

2 yellow peppers, halved, deseeded, and sliced into large chunks

2 red peppers, halved, deseeded, and sliced into large chunks

4 tbsp olive oil

4 tbsp balsamic vinegar

**Sliced meats**

12 slices Parma ham

12 slices salami

12 slices chorizo

1. Preheat the oven to 220°C (200°C fan/425°F/Gas 7).

2. To make the aubergine and mint dip, slice the aubergines in half lengthways, arrange cut side up in a roasting tin, and drizzle with the oil. Add the garlic to the tin and roast for 30–35 minutes or until the aubergine flesh is soft.

3. Scoop the flesh out of the aubergines and place in a food processor. Discard the skins. Squeeze the garlic from their skins and add to the aubergines, then whiz together until smooth. Add the yogurt, lemon juice, and mint, season with salt and freshly ground black pepper, and whiz again until combined. Spoon into a serving bowl (two bowls for 12) and set aside to cool.

4. Meanwhile, make the roasted vegetables. Arrange the courgettes, yellow pepper, and red pepper in a roasting tin, drizzle over the oil, and roast in the preheated oven for 30–40 minutes or until just cooked. Drizzle over the vinegar, season with salt and freshly ground black pepper, and set aside to cool.

5. To assemble the dish, arrange the cold meats in piles on a platter (two platters for 12), garnish the dip with mint and place at one end, then arrange the roasted vegetables alongside the meats. Serve with bread of your choice.

### IN THE AGA

Roast the aubergines, courgettes, and peppers on the floor of the roasting oven for 25–30 minutes or until tender.

### PREPARE AHEAD

*The dip can be made up to 3 days ahead. The vegetables can be roasted up to 1 day ahead. The platter can be assembled up to 8 hours ahead. Not suitable for freezing.*

# MAIN COURSES
# POULTRY AND GAME

*These recipes are low on effort, but high on impact –
perfect for when you're cooking for a crowd. Chicken
is always popular, and the duck and game dishes
at the end of this chapter are even more special.*

# 21ST-CENTURY CORONATION CHICKEN

*No buffet would be complete without coronation chicken. It's also delicious made with cooked turkey – ideal for a Boxing Day bowl party. Serve with baby new potatoes and dressed salad.*

## SERVES 6

2 tbsp apricot jam

1 tbsp curry powder

300ml (10fl oz) mayonnaise

150ml (5fl oz) half-fat crème fraîche

1 tbsp tomato purée

finely grated zest and juice of 1 lemon

450g (1lb) cooked chicken, cut into bite-sized pieces

2 spring onions, finely chopped

salt and freshly ground black pepper

175g (6oz) black and green seedless grapes, cut in half lengthways

rocket, to garnish

## SERVES 12

4 tbsp apricot jam

2 tbsp curry powder

600ml (1 pint) mayonnaise

300ml (10fl oz) half-fat crème fraîche

2 tbsp tomato purée

finely grated zest and juice of 2 lemons

900g (2lb) cooked chicken, cut into bite-sized pieces

4 spring onions, finely chopped

salt and freshly ground black pepper

300g (11oz) black and green seedless grapes, cut in half lengthways

rocket, to garnish

1. Put the jam and curry powder in a small saucepan and heat gently, stirring until the jam has melted. Set aside to cool a little.

2. Meanwhile, put the mayonnaise, crème fraîche, and tomato purée in a mixing bowl with the lemon zest and lemon juice and mix together until combined.

3. Stir in the jam mixture, then add the chicken and spring onions. Season with salt and freshly ground black pepper, add half the grapes, and stir until combined.

4. Spoon onto a serving platter and garnish with the remaining grapes and the rocket.

### PREPARE AHEAD

*The dish can be made up to 1 day ahead.*
*The sauce can be made up to 3 days ahead.*
*Not suitable for freezing.*

# HERB CHICKEN WITH GARLIC SAUCE

**SERVES 6**

150g full-fat cream cheese

75g (2½oz) mature Cheddar cheese, grated

2 tsp chopped fresh basil

2 tsp chopped chives

1 small garlic clove, crushed

6 skinless boneless chicken breasts

salt and freshly ground black pepper

1 tbsp runny honey

a pinch of paprika

200ml (7fl oz) dry white wine

2 large garlic cloves, sliced in half

300ml (10fl oz) double cream

2 tbsp sun-dried tomato paste

200g (7oz) French beans, trimmed and sliced into three

300g (11oz) frozen broad beans

300g (11oz) frozen petits pois

a knob of butter

2 tbsp freshly chopped basil

**SERVES 12**

300g full-fat cream cheese

175g (6oz) mature Cheddar cheese, grated

2 tbsp chopped fresh basil

2 tbsp chopped chives

2 garlic cloves, crushed

12 skinless boneless chicken breasts

salt and freshly ground black pepper

2 tbsp runny honey

a pinch of paprika

400ml (14fl oz) dry white wine

4 large garlic cloves, sliced in half

600ml (1 pint) double cream

4 tbsp sun-dried tomato paste

400g (14oz) French beans, trimmed and sliced into three

600g (1lb 5oz) frozen broad beans

600g (1lb 5oz) frozen petits pois

a large knob of butter

4 tbsp freshly chopped basil

*This is such a simple yet classy dish, easy to cook for a crowd on formal occasions. Serve with new potatoes and green vegetables.*

1. Preheat the oven to 220°C (200°C fan/425°F/Gas 7). Mash the cream cheese, Cheddar, herbs, and crushed garlic together with a fork in a small bowl. Make three diagonal slashes in the top of each chicken breast, cutting about half the way through. Season with salt and freshly ground black pepper, then spoon the cheese into the gaps. Arrange in a flat ovenproof dish.

2. Drizzle with the honey and sprinkle with paprika. Roast in the oven for 20–25 minutes or until cooked, then remove from the oven and leave to rest for 5 minutes.

3. Meanwhile, put the wine and sliced garlic into a saucepan and boil until reduced by half. Add the cream and boil until reduced by one-third or until the sauce has thickened to a pouring consistency. Remove the garlic and season with salt and freshly ground black pepper, then stir in the tomato paste.

4. Bring a pan of salted water to the boil. Add the French beans, broad beans, and petits pois and boil for 4 minutes or until just cooked. Drain and toss with the butter.

5. Reheat the sauce and add the basil. Spoon the vegetables onto plates. Slice a chicken breast into thick pieces and arrange on top of each one. Serve with a little of the sauce.

### IN THE AGA

Roast the chicken on the second set of runners in the roasting oven for 18–20 minutes (25–30 minutes for 12).

### PREPARE AHEAD

*The chicken breasts can be prepared up to the end of step 1 up to 1 day ahead. The sauce can be made up to 3 days ahead. Add the basil just before serving. Not suitable for freezing.*

# PAN-FRIED CHICKEN WITH MUSHROOMS AND TARRAGON

*This is one of Lucy's fail-safe recipes that can be rustled up quickly while everyone is enjoying a glass of wine. Serve with plain rice, or mashed potato.*

### SERVES 6

1 tbsp olive oil

5 small skinless boneless chicken breasts, cut into thin strips

salt and freshly ground black pepper

1 large onion, finely chopped

2 medium courgettes, cut into thick matchsticks

350g (12oz) button mushrooms, quartered

2 large garlic cloves

200ml (7fl oz) dry white wine

200ml (7fl oz) double cream

juice of ½ lemon

1 heaped tbsp freshly chopped tarragon

### SERVES 12

This dish is not suitable for more than six because the sauce would not reduce to a thick consistency and would be wet from the large quantity of vegetables.

1. Heat the oil in a deep frying pan, add half the chicken strips, season with salt and freshly ground black pepper, and brown over a high heat until golden all over. Remove with a slotted spoon and set aside on a plate. Cook the rest of the chicken strips in the same way.

2. Add the onion and fry over a high heat for a few minutes or until golden. Cover with a lid, lower the heat, and cook for 15 minutes or until tender. Turn up the heat, add the courgettes, mushrooms, and garlic, and fry for 3 minutes or until the vegetables start to soften. Remove from the pan and set aside with the chicken.

3. Add the wine to the pan and boil over a high heat until it has reduced in volume to about 4 tablespoons. Stir in the cream and boil again for a few minutes until the sauce thickens. Stir in the lemon juice and season with salt and freshly ground black pepper. Return the chicken and vegetables to the pan for a couple of minutes to heat through.

4. Add the tarragon and serve immediately.

# TRADITIONAL CHICKEN, LEEK, AND MUSHROOM PIE

## SERVES 6

**Special equipment** *2.4 litre (4 pint) ovenproof pie dish*

*75g (2½oz) butter*

*3 large leeks, sliced*

*75g (2½oz) plain flour, plus a little extra to dust*

*300ml (10fl oz) apple juice*

*450ml (15fl oz) chicken stock*

*250g (9oz) portabella mushrooms, sliced*

*1 tbsp Dijon mustard*

*1 tbsp freshly chopped thyme leaves*

*3 tbsp full-fat crème fraîche*

*750g (1lb 10oz) cooked chicken, sliced*

*salt and freshly ground black pepper*

*500g packet all-butter puff pastry*

*1 egg, beaten with a little milk*

## SERVES 12

**Special equipment** *2 x 2.4 litre (4 pint) ovenproof pie dishes or 1 x 4 litre (7 pint) dish*

*175g (6oz) butter*

*6 leeks, sliced*

*175g (6oz) plain flour, plus a little extra to dust*

*600ml (1 pint) apple juice*

*900ml (1½ pints) chicken stock*

*450g (1lb) portabella mushrooms, sliced*

*2 tbsp Dijon mustard*

*2 tbsp freshly chopped thyme leaves*

*6 tbsp full-fat crème fraîche*

*1.5kg (3lb 3oz) cooked chicken, sliced*

*salt and freshly ground black pepper*

*2 x 500g packets all-butter puff pastry*

*2 eggs, beaten with a little milk*

*This is an old-fashioned pie, perfect for a winter Sunday lunch. If you're cooking for 12, we think it is easier to make two pies rather than one really large one, but it's up to you.*

1. Preheat the oven to 200°C (180°C fan/400°F/Gas 6). Meanwhile, melt the butter in a large frying pan, add the leeks, and fry over a high heat for 2 minutes. Cover with a lid, lower the heat, and cook for 10 minutes or until tender.

2. Turn up the heat, stir in the flour, then blend in the apple juice and stock. Bring to the boil, stirring all the time, then add the mushrooms, mustard, thyme, and crème fraîche. Add the chicken, season with salt and freshly ground black pepper, and simmer for 5 minutes. Spoon into the pie dish and set aside to cool.

3. Meanwhile, make the pastry top. On a worktop lightly dusted with flour, roll out the pastry until it is a little bigger than the dish. Cut strips of pastry to the size of the lip of the dish, then wet the lip with water and attach the strips on top. Wet the top of the strips with water, then lay the pastry lid on them and press to seal the edges. Crimp the edges with your fingers.

4. Brush the pastry with the egg and bake in the oven for 35 minutes (1 hour for a large pie for 12 – cover it with foil if it begins to get too brown) or until the pastry is crisp and golden and the filling is piping hot.

### IN THE AGA
Bake on the lowest set of runners in the roasting oven for 30 minutes (50 minutes for 12).

### PREPARE AHEAD AND FREEZE
*The pie can be made up to the end of step 3 up to 1 day ahead. Freeze at the end of step 3 for up to 2 months.*

# STICKY CHICKEN DRUMSTICKS

## SERVES 6

6 tbsp tomato ketchup

2 tbsp Worcestershire sauce

2 tbsp grainy mustard

2 tbsp runny honey

salt and freshly ground black pepper

6 chicken drumsticks (skin on)

## SERVES 12

175ml (6fl oz) tomato ketchup

4 tbsp Worcestershire sauce

4 tbsp grainy mustard

4 tbsp runny honey

salt and freshly ground black pepper

12 chicken drumsticks (skin on)

*Drumsticks are always a favourite at a barbecue – with adults and children alike. Marinating aside, they are also quick to make. Serve hot or cold with salad and jacket potatoes.*

1.  Put the first four ingredients into a bowl, mix together well, then season with salt and freshly ground black pepper.

2.  Add the chicken and marinate for a minimum of 2 hours or overnight.

3.  Preheat the oven to 220°C (200°C fan/425°F/Gas 7). Season the drumsticks with salt and freshly ground black pepper and cook for 30–40 minutes (45 minutes for 12) or until golden brown and sticky. Turn halfway through. Alternatively, cook on the barbecue.

### IN THE AGA

Cook on the second set of runners in the roasting oven for 20 minutes (30 minutes for 12), turning them over halfway through.

### PREPARE AHEAD AND FREEZE

*The drumsticks can be marinated overnight. Freeze in the marinade for up to 2 months.*

# SPICY MARINATED CHICKEN WITH SUMMER SALSA

## SERVES 6

2 red chillies, halved, deseeded, and finely diced

4 garlic cloves, crushed

6 tbsp freshly chopped parsley

zest and juice of 1 large lemon

4 tbsp olive oil

2 tbsp runny honey

4 tsp paprika

6 skinless boneless chicken breasts

### For the salsa

2 large tomatoes, cut in half, deseeded, and diced

6 spring onions, finely sliced

½ cucumber, peeled, halved, deseeded, and diced

small bunch of coriander, roughly chopped

finely grated zest and juice of 1 lime

2 tsp balsamic vinegar

2 tbsp olive oil

1 tsp caster sugar

salt and freshly ground black pepper

## SERVES 12

4 red chillies, halved, deseeded, and finely diced

8 garlic cloves, crushed

bunch of parsley, chopped

zest and juice of 2 lemons

8 tbsp olive oil

4 tbsp runny honey

2 heaped tbsp paprika

12 skinless boneless chicken breasts

### For the salsa

4 large tomatoes, cut in half, deseeded, and diced

12 spring onions, finely sliced

1 cucumber, peeled, halved, deseeded, and diced

large bunch of coriander, roughly chopped

finely grated zest and juice of 2 limes

1 tbsp balsamic vinegar

4 tbsp olive oil

2 tsp caster sugar

salt and freshly ground black pepper

*Fresh and healthy, this dish is great for garden parties. Marinate it overnight for maximum flavour. Serve with salad and new potatoes.*

1. Mix the first seven ingredients together in a large bowl. Add the chicken breasts and turn to coat. Leave to marinate in the fridge for 1–2 hours or overnight.

2. Preheat the oven to 220°C (200°C fan/425°F/Gas 7). Heat a griddle pan until hot, add the chicken, and brown for 20–30 seconds on each side or until griddle marks are left. You may need to do this in batches. Arrange on a baking sheet lined with baking parchment.

3. Roast for 25 minutes (35 minutes for 12) or until golden and cooked through. Remove from the oven and allow to rest for 5 minutes.

4. Meanwhile, make the salsa: mix all the ingredients in a large bowl and season with salt and freshly ground black pepper.

5. Carve the chicken into thick slices and serve with the salsa.

### IN THE AGA

Roast the chicken in the middle of the roasting oven for 25 minutes (35 minutes for 12).

### PREPARE AHEAD

*The chicken can be prepared up to the end of step 2 up to 1 day ahead. The salsa ingredients can be prepared up to 1 day ahead and mixed together 1 hour ahead. Not suitable for freezing.*

# SUN-BLUSHED TOMATO AND HERB CHICKEN

*A quick recipe that you can either prepare ahead or at the last minute. Partly dried (rather than completely dried) tomatoes are sold under different names in different shops, but sun-blushed and sun-ripened tomatoes are the same thing. Serve with new potatoes and green vegetables or salad.*

**SERVES 6**

1 tbsp freshly chopped parsley

3 tbsp freshly snipped chives

1 tbsp freshly chopped basil

200g tub full-fat cream cheese

1 egg yolk

2 tsp lemon juice

50g (1¾oz) sun-blushed or sun-ripened tomatoes, snipped into small pieces

salt and freshly ground black pepper

6 boneless chicken breasts, skin on

a little runny honey

**For the sauce**

150ml (5fl oz) dry white wine

300ml (10fl oz) double cream

1 tbsp freshly chopped parsley

**SERVES 12**

2 tbsp freshly chopped parsley

6 tbsp freshly snipped chives

2 tbsp freshly chopped basil

2 x 200g tubs full-fat cream cheese

2 egg yolks

1 tbsp lemon juice

100g (3½oz) sun-blushed or sun-ripened tomatoes, snipped into small pieces

salt and freshly ground black pepper

12 boneless chicken breasts, skin on

a little runny honey

**For the sauce**

300ml (10fl oz) dry white wine

600ml (1 pint) double cream

2 tbsp freshly chopped parsley

1. Preheat the oven to 200°C (180°C fan/400°F/Gas 6). Put the first seven ingredients into a bowl, season with salt and freshly ground black pepper, and stir until combined.

2. Loosen the skin from the chicken breasts, but keep it attached at one side. Spoon the filling underneath and replace the skin.

3. Arrange the chicken breasts in a roasting tin, season with salt and freshly ground black pepper, then drizzle with a little honey.

4. Roast for 25–30 minutes (35–40 minutes for 12) or until golden and cooked through.

5. Meanwhile, make the sauce: put the wine into a pan (use a wide-based pan for 12, to make the reduction quicker) and boil over a high heat until it has reduced to about 3 tablespoons (6 tablespoons for 12). Add the cream and boil for a couple of minutes to thicken. Season with salt and freshly ground black pepper.

6. Allow the chicken breasts to rest for a few minutes after roasting, then add any juices from the tin to the sauce. Carve each breast into three or serve whole. Add the parsley to the hot sauce and serve with the chicken.

**IN THE AGA**

Roast on the second set of runners in the roasting oven for 25 minutes (35 minutes for 12).

**PREPARE AHEAD**

The chicken can be prepared up to the end of step 2 up to 1 day ahead. The sauce can be made up to 2 days ahead. Not suitable for freezing.

# CHICKEN WITH PESTO, TALEGGIO, AND ROASTED TOMATOES

*This is truly scrumptious. It's also quick to make. Home-made pesto is best, but you can use good-quality pesto from a jar if you're short of time. Serve with potatoes and salad.*

**SERVES 6**

6 skinless boneless chicken breasts

salt and freshly ground black pepper

175g (6oz) Taleggio cheese (straight from the fridge), cut into small cubes

3 tbsp pesto

2 tbsp freshly chopped basil

3 tbsp full-fat cream cheese

50g (1¾oz) fresh breadcrumbs

a pinch of paprika

400g (14oz) cherry tomatoes on the vine

2 tbsp olive oil

1 tbsp balsamic vinegar

**SERVES 12**

12 skinless boneless chicken breasts

salt and freshly ground black pepper

300g (11oz) Taleggio cheese (straight from the fridge), cut into cubes

5 tbsp pesto

4 tbsp freshly chopped basil

5 tbsp full-fat cream cheese

75g (2½oz) fresh breadcrumbs

a pinch of paprika

900g (2lb) cherry tomatoes on the vine

3 tbsp olive oil

2 tbsp balsamic vinegar

1. Preheat the oven to 220°C (200°C fan/425°F/Gas 7). Arrange the chicken breasts in a single layer in an ovenproof dish or roasting tin and season with salt and freshly ground black pepper.

2. Mix the Taleggio, pesto, basil, and cream cheese in a bowl and season with salt and freshly ground black pepper. Spoon onto the chicken breasts, spreading the mixture out to cover them completely. Sprinkle with the breadcrumbs and dust with a little paprika.

3. Bake for 20 minutes, then arrange the tomatoes around the chicken, pour the oil and vinegar over them, and return to the oven for a further 10 minutes (30 minutes for 12) or until the chicken is just cooked through. Be careful not to overcook it.

4. To serve, arrange a chicken breast on each plate with a few tomatoes, then spoon over some of the juices from the dish.

**IN THE AGA**
Roast on the second set of runners in the roasting oven for 15 minutes, add the tomatoes, and cook for 10 minutes more (30 minutes for 12).

**PREPARE AHEAD AND FREEZE**
*The chicken can be prepared up to the end of step 2 up to 12 hours ahead. Freeze at the end of step 2 for up to 2 months.*

# CHICKEN AND BACON
# CAESAR SALAD

## SERVES 6

200g packet smoked bacon lardons

4 thick slices white bread, crusts removed

3 tbsp olive oil

3 boneless skinless chicken breasts

2 romaine lettuces, cut into 5cm (2in) slices

50g (1¾oz) coarsely grated Parmesan cheese

salt and freshly ground black pepper

### For the dressing

¼ garlic clove, crushed

2 tbsp white wine vinegar

½ tsp Dijon mustard

2 tbsp olive oil

6 tbsp mayonnaise

3 tbsp water

25g (scant 1oz) finely grated Parmesan cheese

1 tsp caster sugar

## SERVES 12

400g packet smoked bacon lardons

8 thick slices white bread, crusts removed

6 tbsp olive oil

6 boneless skinless chicken breasts

4 romaine lettuces, cut into 5cm (2in) slices

100g (3½oz) coarsely grated Parmesan cheese

salt and freshly ground black pepper

### For the dressing

½ garlic clove, crushed

4 tbsp white wine vinegar

1 tsp Dijon mustard

4 tbsp olive oil

175ml (6fl oz) mayonnaise

4 tbsp water

50g (1¾oz) finely grated Parmesan cheese

2 tsp caster sugar

*A meal in itself. We serve it cold with crusty bread, but you can keep the bacon, croûtons, and chicken warm and add just before serving.*

1. Preheat the oven to 220°C (200°C fan/425°F/Gas 7). Meanwhile, scatter the lardons over the base of a roasting tin. Cut each slice of bread into 20 even-sized cubes and scatter next to the lardons. Drizzle over two-thirds of the oil and cook in the oven for 15–20 minutes (20 minutes for 12) or until golden and crisp. Shake the tin occasionally.

2. Lay the chicken breasts between two sheets of cling film and bash with a rolling pin until half as thick. Heat the remaining oil in a frying pan, add the chicken, and fry for 3 minutes on each side or until golden all over and cooked through. You may need to do this in batches. Allow to cool slightly, then cut into thin slices.

3. Put the lettuce and Parmesan into a large salad bowl and season with salt and freshly ground black pepper. Add the lardons and croûtons and toss together.

4. To make the dressing, put the garlic, vinegar, mustard, and oil into a bowl and whisk by hand until smooth. Add all the other ingredients and whisk again. Season with salt and freshly ground black pepper. Pour the dressing over the salad and toss to combine. Arrange the chicken on top and serve at once.

### IN THE AGA

Cook the lardons and croûtons on the floor of the roasting oven for 10–15 minutes or until golden and crisp.

### PREPARE AHEAD

*The lettuce and Parmesan can be placed in a bowl up to 6 hours ahead. The dressing can be made up to 3 days ahead. Not suitable for freezing.*

# MEDITERRANEAN LEMON AND HERB CHICKEN SALAD

*This is a wonderfully fresh, light salad, perfect for a picnic or for eating al fresco. You can replace the chicken with turkey if you prefer. Serve with salad leaves and your favourite bread.*

## SERVES 6

**For the dressing**

2 tbsp Dijon mustard

2 tbsp pesto

juice of 1 lemon

4 tbsp olive oil

1 tbsp caster sugar

salt and freshly ground black pepper

750g (1lb 10oz) cooked boneless skinless chicken, cut into thin strips

150g (5½oz) pitted green olives, halved

290g jar chargrilled red peppers, drained and thinly sliced

2 tbsp freshly chopped basil

2 tbsp freshly chopped flat-leaf parsley

200g (7oz) feta cheese, broken into small pieces

## SERVES 12

**For the dressing**

4 tbsp Dijon mustard

4 tbsp pesto

juice of 2 lemons

8 tbsp olive oil

2 tbsp caster sugar

salt and freshly ground black pepper

1.5kg (3lb 3oz) cooked boneless skinless chicken, cut into thin strips

300g (11oz) pitted green olives, halved

2 x 290g jars chargrilled red peppers, drained and thinly sliced

4 tbsp freshly chopped basil

4 tbsp freshly chopped flat-leaf parsley

400g (14oz) feta cheese, broken into small pieces

1. Put all the ingredients for the dressing into a large bowl and whisk by hand until well combined.

2. Add the chicken and toss well. Add the olives, half the peppers, the basil, parsley, and two-thirds of the feta. Season with salt and freshly ground black pepper and toss to combine.

3. Arrange on a platter and scatter the remaining peppers and feta attractively along the centre. Chill in the fridge before serving.

## PREPARE AHEAD

*The salad can be made up to 8 hours ahead. Not suitable for freezing.*

# SARDINIAN CHICKEN

**SERVES 6**

2 tbsp olive oil

75g (2½oz) pancetta, cut into strips

6 large chicken thighs (bone in), skinned

1 large onion, chopped

1 small red pepper, halved, deseeded, and diced

3 garlic cloves, crushed

225g (8oz) button mushrooms, quartered

120ml (4fl oz) red wine

1 level tbsp plain flour

400g can chopped tomatoes

5 tbsp tomato purée

salt and freshly ground black pepper

1 tsp freshly chopped thyme leaves

grated zest of 1 lemon

2 tbsp capers, drained and chopped

**SERVES 12**

4 tbsp olive oil

175g (6oz) pancetta, cut into strips

12 large chicken thighs (bone in), skinned

2 large onions, chopped

1 large red pepper, halved, deseeded and diced

6 garlic cloves, crushed

450g (1lb) button mushrooms, quartered

250ml (8fl oz) red wine

1 heaped tbsp plain flour

2 x 400g cans chopped tomatoes

150ml (5fl oz) tomato purée

salt and freshly ground black pepper

2 tsp freshly chopped thyme leaves

grated zest of 2 lemons

4 tbsp capers, drained and chopped

*Mary's sister-in-law, Margaret, made this for 90 people for a charity lunch and it was a triumph. You can use boned thighs if you prefer; they'll take about 30 minutes less to cook. Serve with new potatoes or mash and green vegetables.*

1. Preheat the oven to 180°C (160°C fan/350°F/Gas 4). Heat half the oil in a large deep frying pan or casserole, add the pancetta and chicken, and cook over a high heat for a few minutes or until the pancetta is crisp and the chicken golden all over. You may need to do this in batches. Remove with a slotted spoon and set aside.

2. Add the remaining oil to the pan, then add the onion, pepper, garlic, and mushrooms and fry for a few minutes or until starting to soften.

3. Put the wine into a jug and blend to a smooth paste with the flour.

4. Add the tomatoes and tomato purée to the pan, then blend in the wine mixture, season with salt and freshly ground black pepper, and bring to the boil. Return the chicken and pancetta to the pan, add the thyme, lemon zest, and capers, and bring to the boil.

5. Cover with a lid and transfer to the oven for 1 hour (1¼ hours for 12) or until the chicken is tender. Serve piping hot.

**IN THE AGA**
Cook in the simmering oven for 1–1¼ hours or until the chicken is tender.

**PREPARE AHEAD AND FREEZE**
*The casserole can be made up to 2 days ahead. Freeze for up to 2 months.*

# ITALIAN FARMHOUSE CHICKEN

*If time is short, you can use peppers from a jar for this. Serve with rice or mashed potatoes and a green vegetable.*

## SERVES 6

1 tbsp olive oil

1 large onion, coarsely chopped

2 garlic cloves, crushed

2 x 400g cans chopped tomatoes

2 tbsp tomato purée

1 tsp caster sugar

salt and freshly ground black pepper

3 red peppers, cut in half and deseeded

### For the stuffing

450g (1lb) pork sausagemeat

finely grated zest of ½ lemon

small bunch of basil leaves, torn

1 tbsp Dijon mustard

12 boneless skinless chicken thighs

## SERVES 12

2 tbsp olive oil

2 large onions, coarsely chopped

4 garlic cloves, crushed

4 x 400g cans chopped tomatoes

4 tbsp tomato purée

2 tsp caster sugar

salt and freshly ground black pepper

6 red peppers, cut in half and deseeded

### For the stuffing

900g (2lb) pork sausagemeat

finely grated zest of 1 lemon

large bunch of basil leaves, torn

2 tbsp Dijon mustard

24 boneless skinless chicken thighs

1. Preheat the oven to 200°C (180°C fan/400°F/Gas 6). Heat the oil in a frying pan, add the onion and garlic, and fry over a high heat for a few minutes or until starting to soften. Stir in the tomatoes, tomato purée, sugar, and 100ml (3½fl oz) water (200ml (7fl oz) for 12), season with salt and freshly ground black pepper, and bring to the boil. Cover with a lid and simmer for 15 minutes or until the onion is tender.

2. Meanwhile, arrange the peppers cut side down on a baking sheet and bake for 20 minutes or until the skin has started to blacken. Transfer to a polythene bag, seal the top, and set aside (this makes it easier to remove the skin). Once cool, peel and cut each half in two.

3. To make the stuffing, put the sausagemeat into a mixing bowl, add the lemon zest, basil, and mustard, season with salt and freshly ground black pepper, and mix well. Divide the mixture into 12 (24 for 12) and shape into little sausages.

4. Place the chicken thighs skinned side down on a board between sheets of cling film, opened up flat, and bash with a rolling pin to make them a little thinner. Make sure each thigh is the same thickness. Season with salt and freshly ground black pepper.

5. Place a slice of pepper on each thigh, add one of the sausages, and roll the thigh up. Repeat with the other thighs. Arrange join side down in a single layer in a large shallow ovenproof dish and pour over the tomato sauce.

6. Bake for 40–45 minutes (45–50 minutes for 12) or until bubbling and the chicken is cooked.

### IN THE AGA

Roast the peppers at the top of the roasting oven for 12 minutes. Bake the thighs on the grid shelf on the floor of the roasting oven for 40–45 minutes (45–55 minutes for 12).

### PREPARE AHEAD AND FREEZE

*The chicken thighs can be prepared up to the end of step 5 up to 12 hours ahead. Freeze the uncooked stuffed rolled chicken thighs for up to 2 months.*

# CHICKEN TIKKA MASALA

*Bright and full of flavour, this is one of the country's favourite curries. It is ideal for making in one large batch. Make sure you measure the spices accurately to get the right balance of flavours, and stir often. Serve with naan breads and Pilaf rice (pages 246–247).*

## SERVES 6

12 skinless boneless chicken thighs, each cut into 6 pieces

1 tbsp medium curry powder

1 tsp paprika

1 tbsp olive oil

3 onions, roughly chopped

2 garlic cloves, crushed

6cm (2½in) piece fresh root ginger, peeled and finely grated

2 tbsp garam masala

½ tsp turmeric

200ml (7fl oz) water

500ml carton passata

2 tbsp tomato purée

1 tbsp sugar

salt and freshly ground black pepper

juice of ½ lime

200ml (7fl oz) double cream

1 heaped tbsp freshly chopped coriander, to garnish

## SERVES 12

24 skinless boneless chicken thighs, each cut into 6 pieces

2 tbsp medium curry powder

2 tsp paprika

2 tbsp olive oil

5 onions, roughly chopped

4 garlic cloves, crushed

7.5cm (3in) piece fresh root ginger, peeled and finely grated

4 tbsp garam masala

1 tsp turmeric

400ml (14fl oz) water

2 x 500ml cartons passata

4 tbsp tomato purée

2 tbsp sugar

salt and freshly ground black pepper

juice of 1 lime

300ml (10fl oz) double cream

2 tbsp freshly chopped coriander, to garnish

1. Put the chicken pieces into a bowl, sprinkle over the curry powder and paprika, cover, and chill for 15 minutes.

2. Heat the oil in a deep frying pan or casserole, add the chicken, and quickly brown all over. Remove with a slotted spoon and set aside. You may need to do this in batches.

3. Add the onions, garlic, and ginger and fry for 2 minutes or until starting to soften. Add the garam masala and turmeric and fry for 1 minute. Blend in the water, passata, tomato purée, and sugar, return the chicken to the pan, and season with salt and freshly ground black pepper.

4. Bring to the boil, cover with a lid, and simmer, stirring occasionally, for 30–40 minutes (1 hour for 12) or until the chicken is tender.

5. Add the lime juice, check the seasoning, bring to the boil again, then add the cream. Serve garnished with the coriander.

### IN THE AGA
At step 4, bring to the boil on the boiling plate, cover with a lid, and transfer to the simmering oven for 40–45 minutes or until the chicken is tender.

### PREPARE AHEAD AND FREEZE
*The curry can be made up to the end of step 4 up to 2 days ahead. Freeze without the lime juice and cream for up to 2 months.*

# MINI CHICKEN BURGERS

*These chicken burgers are so easy to make and are perfect for a barbecue. Make them larger if you prefer, but cook them for a little longer.*

## SERVES 6

**Special equipment** *6cm (2½in) round cutter*

*2 slices white bread*

*500g (1lb 2oz) skinless boneless chicken breasts or thighs, roughly chopped*

*zest and juice of ½ small lemon*

*50g (1¾oz) freshly grated Parmesan cheese*

*small bunch of chives, snipped*

*1 egg yolk*

*salt and freshly ground black pepper*

*a little olive oil, to fry*

**To serve**

*6 sesame burger buns*

*grainy mustard*

*lettuce leaves*

*mayonnaise*

*2 tomatoes, sliced*

## SERVES 12

**Special equipment** *6cm (2½in) round cutter*

*4 slices white bread*

*1kg (2¼lb) skinless boneless chicken breasts or thighs, roughly chopped*

*zest and juice of 1 small lemon*

*100g (3½oz) freshly grated Parmesan cheese*

*large bunch of chives, snipped*

*1 large egg*

*salt and freshly ground black pepper*

*a little olive oil, to fry*

**To serve**

*12 sesame burger buns*

*grainy mustard*

*lettuce leaves*

*mayonnaise*

*4 tomatoes, sliced*

1. Put the bread into a food processor and whiz to fine breadcrumbs. Transfer to a large mixing bowl. Put the chicken into the processor and whiz until coarsely minced. You may need to do this in batches. Add to the bowl with the breadcrumbs.

2. Add the lemon zest, lemon juice, cheese, chives, and egg yolk (whole egg for 12) and mix together with your hands. Season with salt and freshly ground black pepper, then shape the mixture into 12 small burgers (24 for 12) and chill in the fridge for 30 minutes.

3. Heat a little oil in a frying pan and fry the burgers for 3–3½ minutes on each side or until lightly golden and cooked through. You may need to do this in batches. Alternatively, cook on a barbecue.

4. Slice the buns in half horizontally. Stamp out 12 rounds (24 for 12), using a 6cm (2½in) round cutter. Use the top and bottom of the buns. Spread each with a little mustard, then add a lettuce leaf. Place a burger on top, add a blob of mayonnaise, and garnish with a slice of tomato. Arrange the burgers on a platter and serve.

**PREPARE AHEAD AND FREEZE**

*The burgers can be prepared up to the end of step 2 up to 1 day ahead. Freeze for up to 3 months.*

# DUCK BREASTS WITH A PIQUANT LIME AND GINGER SAUCE

*This is an easy way to cook duck breasts, as you brown them well ahead. You then cook them at the last minute, without the worry about whether they will be golden or not. Serve with green beans.*

### SERVES 6

6 duck breasts, skinned

salt and freshly ground black pepper

1 tbsp olive oil

2 tsp freshly grated root ginger

300ml (10fl oz) full-fat crème fraîche

juice of 1 lime

small knob of butter, at room temperature

3 tbsp lime marmalade

chives, to garnish

### SERVES 12

12 duck breasts, skinned

salt and freshly ground black pepper

2 tbsp olive oil

4 tsp freshly grated root ginger

600ml (1 pint) full-fat crème fraîche

juice of 2 limes

large knob of butter, at room temperature

6 tbsp lime marmalade

chives, to garnish

1. Season the duck breasts with salt and freshly ground black pepper, then heat the oil in a frying pan and brown each one on its skinned side for a minute or so or until golden. Set aside. Add the ginger to the pan and heat over a low heat for 1 minute. Whisk in the crème fraîche and lime juice until smooth and combined. Set aside until needed.

2. Mix the butter and marmalade together in a bowl, then spread over the browned side of the cold duck breasts. Arrange in a roasting tin, browned side up.

3. When ready to serve, preheat the oven to 220°C (200°C fan/ 425°F/Gas 7). Roast the duck for 12–15 minutes (15–20 minutes for 12) or until cooked but still pink. Set aside to rest.

4. Meanwhile, place the roasting tin on the hob, add the lime and ginger sauce, and heat until hot, scraping up any sticky bits from the bottom of the tin.

5. Carve each duck breast diagonally into three and serve on the hot sauce with a garnish of chives.

### IN THE AGA

Roast the duck on the top set of runners in the roasting oven for 12 minutes.

### PREPARE AHEAD

*You can prepare the duck up to the end of step 2 up to 1 day ahead. Not suitable for freezing.*

# PHEASANT BREASTS WITH MUSHROOMS AND MADEIRA

*A warming dish that's perfect for sharing with friends when game is in season. Serve with mash and red cabbage or green vegetables.*

### SERVES 6

2 onions, sliced

3 thyme sprigs

3 young pheasants

600ml (1 pint) hot game stock or chicken stock

50g (1¾oz) butter

250g (9oz) small chestnut mushrooms, quartered

45g (1½oz) plain flour

4 tbsp cold water

150ml (5fl oz) Madeira

1 tbsp balsamic vinegar

1 tbsp freshly chopped thyme leaves

1 tbsp full-fat crème fraîche

salt and freshly ground black pepper

### SERVES 12

4 onions, sliced

6 thyme sprigs

6 young pheasants

1.2 litres (2 pints) hot game stock or chicken stock

100g (3½oz) butter

500g (1lb 2oz) small chestnut mushrooms, quartered

85g (3oz) plain flour

8 tbsp cold water

300ml (10fl oz) Madeira

2 tbsp balsamic vinegar

2 tbsp freshly chopped thyme leaves

2 tbsp full-fat crème fraîche

salt and freshly ground black pepper

1. Preheat the oven to 200°C (180°C fan/400°F/Gas 6). Line a large roasting tin with foil and scatter the onions over the base.

2. Put a sprig of thyme in the cavity of each bird. Arrange them breast side down on top of the onions in the tin.

3. Pour over the hot stock, cover with foil, and roast for 1 hour and 10 minutes (1 hour and 20 minutes for 12) or until the breasts are tender. Remove the birds from the tin and allow to rest. Reserve the stock.

4. Melt the butter in a saucepan, add the mushrooms, and fry over a high heat for a few minutes or until soft. Strain the stock from the roasting tin into a measuring jug until you have 450ml/15fl oz (900ml/1½ pints for 12), and discard the onions.

5. Mix the flour to a runny paste with the cold water, then stir in with the mushrooms and fry for 1 minute. Gradually add the measured stock and Madeira, stirring until blended. Bring to the boil, add the vinegar, thyme, and crème fraîche, and season with salt and freshly ground black pepper.

6. Using a sharp knife, detach the pheasant breasts from the carcass and cut each into three diagonally. Arrange in a serving dish and pour over the hot sauce. If the thighs are tender, they can also be served. If tough, use to make game stock with the carcass.

### IN THE AGA
Roast the pheasants in the centre of the roasting oven for 45 minutes (55 minutes–1 hour for 12).

### PREPARE AHEAD
*The dish can be prepared up to 1 day ahead and reheated. Not suitable for freezing.*

# GAME CASSEROLE WITH THYME AND MUSTARD DUMPLINGS

## SERVES 6

900g (2lb) mixed game, sliced into large pieces

150ml (5fl oz) Port

2 tbsp sunflower oil

30g (1oz) butter

2 large leeks, sliced

4 celery sticks, sliced

1 apple, peeled, cored, and chopped into small cubes

1 tbsp brown sugar

45g (1½oz) plain flour

450ml (15fl oz) chicken stock or game stock

1 tbsp Worcestershire sauce

2 tsp Dijon mustard

1 tbsp balsamic vinegar

salt and freshly ground black pepper

### For the dumplings

175g (6oz) self-raising flour

85g (3oz) suet

2 tbsp grainy mustard

1 tsp freshly chopped thyme leaves, plus extra to garnish

## SERVES 12

1.8kg (4lb) mixed game, sliced into large pieces

300ml (10fl oz) Port

4 tbsp sunflower oil

50g (1¾oz) butter

4 large leeks, sliced

8 celery sticks, sliced

2 apples, peeled, cored, and chopped into small cubes

2 tbsp brown sugar

85g (3oz) plain flour

900ml (1½ pints) chicken stock or game stock

2 tbsp Worcestershire sauce

1 heaped tbsp Dijon mustard

2 tbsp balsamic vinegar

salt and freshly ground black pepper

### For the dumplings

350g (12oz) self-raising flour

175g (6oz) suet

4 tbsp grainy mustard

2 tsp freshly chopped thyme leaves, plus extra to garnish

*This is the perfect casserole for a winter buffet. Start it the day before so that the game has time to absorb the flavours of the Port. If you don't have quite enough game, make up the weight with stewing beef. Serve with creamy mashed potatoes.*

1. Put the game and Port into a bowl and leave to marinate for a few hours or overnight.

2. Preheat the oven to 160°C (140°C fan/325°F/Gas 3). Meanwhile, heat the oil in a large frying pan or casserole. Drain the meat from the marinade (reserving the marinade) and brown quickly over a high heat. Remove with a slotted spoon and set aside. You may need to do this in batches.

3. Melt the butter in the frying pan, add the leeks, celery, and apple, and fry for 2 minutes. Add the sugar and fry for 2 minutes more or until the leeks are starting to soften.

4. Add the flour, then blend in the reserved marinade and stock. Return the meat to the pan and add the Worcestershire sauce, mustard, vinegar, and some salt and freshly ground black pepper.

5. Bring to the boil, cover with a lid, then transfer to the oven for 1–1½ hours (1½–2 hours for 12) or until the meat is tender.

6. Remove from the oven and increase the temperature to 200°C (180°C fan/400°F/Gas 6).

7. To make the dumplings, mix all the ingredients together in a large mixing bowl. Add about 150ml (5fl oz) cold water (300ml/10fl oz for 12) to make a sticky but manageable dough. Lightly knead the dough in the bowl, then shape into 12 small balls (24 for 12).

8. Put the dumplings on top of the casserole and bake without a lid near the top of the oven for 20 minutes or until the dumplings have risen and are golden brown on top. Garnish with chopped thyme.

### IN THE AGA

Cook the casserole in the simmering oven for 1½–2 hours or until tender. Add the dumplings and cook near the top of the roasting oven for 20 minutes or until risen and golden brown.

### PREPARE AHEAD AND FREEZE

*The casserole can be made up to the end of step 5 up to 2 days ahead. The dumplings are best freshly made. Freeze without the dumplings for up to 2 months.*

# HIGHLAND GAME PIE

SERVES 10

**Special equipment** *1.7 litre (3 pint) ovenproof pie dish with a wide base, about 23 x 33cm (9 x 13in)*

2 tbsp olive oil

1.4kg (3lb 2oz) game meat, such as pheasant, guinea fowl, partridge, or venison, cut into 4cm (1½in) cubes

salt and freshly ground black pepper

3 large onions, chopped

60g (2oz) plain flour

300ml (10fl oz) red wine

1.2 litres (2 pints) chicken or game stock

2 tbsp Worcestershire sauce

a little gravy browning, optional

10 pickled walnuts from a jar, quartered

**For the suet pastry**

200g (7oz) self raising flour

100g (3½oz) shredded suet

½ tsp salt

about 150ml (5fl oz) water

1 egg, beaten

*Full of flavour and perfect for feeding a crowd for that special occasion. You can easily buy game casserole meat from supermarkets, which comes diced and is perfect for this recipe.*

1. Preheat the oven to 160°C (140°C fan/320°F/Gas 3).

2. Heat the oil in a large deep casserole dish or sauté pan. Season the game meat with salt and freshly ground black pepper. Fry in the hot oil until brown all over, stirring over a high heat. Remove with a slotted spoon and set aside.

3. Add the onions to the pan and fry for a few minutes. Sprinkle in the flour and cook for 30 seconds. Gradually add the red wine and stock, then bring to the boil while stirring until smooth. Add the Worcestershire sauce and gravy browning, if using, and check the seasoning. Boil for few minutes, then cover and transfer to the oven for about 2 hours or until the meat is tender.

4. Stir in the walnuts and tip the mixture into the pie dish. Leave to cool before adding the pastry. Increase the oven to 200°C (180°C fan/400°F/Gas 6).

5. To make the pastry, measure the flour, suet, and salt into a bowl, and mix with your hand. Gradually add the water and mix with a fork or knife to combine. Bring together on a board and knead for 1 minute into a ball (there is no need to knead it like other pastries).

6. Roll out the pastry to the size of the dish. Brush the rim of the dish with beaten egg. Lay the pastry on top, press the edge of the pastry against the side of the dish firmly, and brush with beaten egg. Using a sharp knife, make a hole in the centre of the pastry.

7. Bake in preheated oven for about 35 minutes or until golden brown and bubbling. Serve piping hot with vegetables.

## IN THE AGA

To cook the casserole, bring to the boil on the boiling plate, cover, and transfer to the simmering oven for about 2 hours. Cook the pie with the pastry lid in the centre of the roasting oven for 25–30 minutes.

## PREPARE AHEAD AND FREEZE

*The casserole can be made up to 2 days ahead. The assembled pie can be made up to 12 hours ahead. Freezes well uncooked with the pastry lid for up to 1 month. Defrost before cooking.*

# MAIN COURSES MEAT

*This chapter is full of classics, alongside some more unusual dishes. From hearty winter feasts to summer barbecues, these recipes will be enjoyed by your family and friends time and again.*

# FILLET STEAK WITH A CREAMY MUSHROOM SAUCE

*This is a joy because it can be prepared ahead and reheated just before serving. Serve with new potatoes and a green vegetable.*

## SERVES 6

225g (8oz) chestnut mushrooms, thinly sliced

2 tbsp brandy

300ml (10fl oz) double cream

salt and freshly ground black pepper

6 x 150g (5½oz) middle-cut fillet steaks

1 tbsp olive oil

225g (8oz) baby spinach

50g (1¾oz) fresh white breadcrumbs

a little paprika, to dust

## SERVES 12

450g (1lb) chestnut mushrooms, thinly sliced

4 tbsp brandy

600ml (1 pint) double cream

salt and freshly ground black pepper

12 x 150g (5½oz) middle-cut fillet steaks

2 tbsp olive oil

450g (1lb) baby spinach

75g (2½oz) fresh white breadcrumbs

a little paprika, to dust

1. Put the mushrooms and brandy into a wide-based pan and toss over a high heat for 2–3 minutes or until the liquid has reduced slightly. Scoop out the mushrooms with a slotted spoon, add the cream, and boil for 5 minutes or until it has reduced by half and reached a coating consistency. Return the mushrooms to the pan, season with salt and freshly ground black pepper, then set aside to cool completely.

2. Heat a large non-stick frying pan over a high heat. Brush each steak with a little oil and season with salt and freshly ground black pepper. Pan-fry each steak for 1–2 minutes on each side or until golden and sealed. Transfer to a baking sheet. You will need to do this in batches.

3. Add the spinach to the pan and cook for a few minutes or until just wilted. Place a mound on top of each steak. Spoon the cold mushroom sauce on top of the spinach (just enough to cover – you should have some sauce left over to reheat and serve with the steaks).

4. Preheat the oven to 220°C (200°C fan/425°F/Gas 7). Sprinkle the steaks with the breadcrumbs and a dusting of paprika and bake for 8 minutes (11 minutes for 12) or until piping hot but just rare in the middle. Add 2 minutes for medium and 4 minutes for medium to well done. Rest for a couple of minutes before serving. Reheat the remaining mushroom sauce in a pan.

5. Serve the steaks piping hot with the sauce alongside.

### IN THE AGA
Cook on the top set of runners in the roasting oven for 8 minutes (11 minutes for 12). Add 2 minutes for medium, 4 for medium to well done.

## PREPARE AHEAD

*The steaks can be prepared up to the end of step 3 up to 12 hours ahead. Not suitable for freezing.*

# TERIYAKI STEAK

## SERVES 6

100ml (3½fl oz) mirin

3 tbsp soy sauce

2 tbsp light brown sugar

1 garlic clove, crushed

6 x 150g (5½oz) sirloin steaks or rump steaks

2 tbsp olive oil

225g (8oz) mixed wild mushrooms, such as oyster, shiitake, and chestnut, sliced

## SERVES 12

We think this dish is not suitable for more than six people because you would have to cook it in two batches, which would mean some steaks would end up being overcooked.

*Apart from the marinating – which is vital for the flavour of the sauce to come through – this is a very quick dish. You'll find mirin in a bottle in the world food section of the supermarket. It is a traditional Japanese rice seasoning, similar to rice wine or sake, but with a low alcohol content. Buy steaks of the same thickness, so they cook at the same rate. Serve with noodles.*

1. Put the mirin, soy sauce, sugar, and garlic into a wide shallow dish and stir together.

2. Add the steaks and turn to coat. Leave to marinate for a minimum of 30 minutes and up to 8 hours.

3. Heat half the oil in a non-stick frying pan. Remove the steaks from the marinade (reserving the marinade) and fry for 2½ minutes on each side – they should be medium rare. Transfer to a hot plate to rest. You may need to do this in batches.

4. Heat the remaining oil in the pan, add the mushrooms, and fry over a high heat for a few minutes or until just cooked. Pour in the reserved marinade and bring to the boil.

5. Serve the steaks whole or in slices with the mushrooms and sauce spooned on top.

## PREPARE AHEAD

The marinade can be made up to 4 days ahead. The steaks can be marinated for up to 8 hours. Not suitable for freezing.

# THAI BEEF WITH LIME AND CHILLI

*The advantage of using centre-cut beef fillet is that it's the same diameter all along, which means it roasts evenly and won't overcook at one end. This is delicious with our Thai green rice on page 248.*

## SERVES 6

900g (2lb) centre-cut beef fillet

1 tbsp olive oil

1 large red chilli, deseeded and roughly chopped

2.5cm (1in) fresh root ginger, peeled and roughly chopped

1 fat garlic clove, roughly chopped

small bunch of mint, stalks removed

finely grated zest and juice of 1 lime

100g (3½oz) coconut cream

200ml tub full-fat crème fraîche

1 tbsp sweet chilli dipping sauce

1 tbsp sugar

½ tbsp fish sauce

3 heaped tbsp light mayonnaise

## SERVES 12

1.8kg (4lb) centre-cut beef fillet

2 tbsp olive oil

2 large red chillies, deseeded and roughly chopped

5cm (2in) fresh root ginger, peeled and roughly chopped

2 fat garlic cloves, roughly chopped

large bunch of mint, stalks removed

finely grated zest and juice of 2 limes

200g carton coconut cream

2 x 200ml tubs full-fat crème fraîche

2 tbsp sweet chilli dipping sauce

2 tbsp sugar

1 tbsp fish sauce

6 heaped tbsp light mayonnaise

1. Preheat the oven to 220°C (200°C fan/425°F/Gas 7). Rub the beef with the oil and brown quickly on all sides in a large pan.

2. Transfer to a roasting tin and roast for 20 minutes (30 minutes for 12) – it should be medium rare – then cover loosely with foil and leave to rest for 15–20 minutes.

3. Meanwhile, put the chilli, ginger, garlic, mint, lime zest, and lime juice into a food processor and whiz until finely chopped. Add the six remaining ingredients and whiz again.

4. Carve the beef, allowing 2–3 slices per person, and arrange on a platter with the Thai green rice, if serving. Place the sauce alongside in a bowl.

### IN THE AGA

Roast the beef in the centre of the roasting oven for the same timings as above.

### PREPARE AHEAD

*The sauce can be made up to 3 days ahead.*
*The beef can be browned up to 12 hours ahead.*
*Not suitable for freezing.*

# SIRLOIN STEAK AND VEGETABLE STIR-FRY

*Light and fresh, this stir-fry is the perfect dish to rustle up as a speedy supper for up to six people. Serve with noodles or rice.*

## SERVES 6

350g (12oz) thin sirloin steak or fillet steak, sliced into very thin strips

1 tbsp runny honey

salt and freshly ground black pepper

2 tbsp olive oil

2 carrots, sliced into matchsticks

6 spring onions, sliced

150g (5½oz) baby corn, cut into thick slices

150g (5½oz) sugarsnap peas, sliced in half lengthways

250g (9oz) pak choi, white and green separated and cut into thick slices

### For the sauce

3 tbsp mirin

2 tbsp soy sauce

2 tbsp hoisin sauce

2 tbsp water

2 tsp cornflour

## SERVES 12

*We think this dish is not suitable for more than six people because the vegetables would release too much water and make the stir-fry soggy.*

1. Toss the steak in the honey and season well with salt and freshly ground black pepper.

2. Heat the oil in a large frying pan or wok over a high heat, add the steak, and stir-fry for 1–2 minutes or until brown and just cooked. Transfer to a plate with a slotted spoon.

3. Add the carrots, spring onions, and corn and stir-fry over a high heat for 3 minutes. Add the sugarsnap peas and the white part of the pak choi and stir-fry for 3 minutes.

4. To make the sauce, put the mirin, soy sauce, and hoisin sauce in a small bowl. Mix the water and cornflour to a smooth paste in another bowl, then add to the sauce. Pour the sauce into the frying pan with the steak and the green leaves of the pak choi and fry for 1–2 minutes or until the green leaves have just wilted.

5. Season with salt and freshly ground black pepper and serve at once.

## PREPARE AHEAD

*You can prepare all the ingredients up to 4 hours ahead. The sauce can be made up to 1 day ahead. Not suitable for freezing.*

# CLASSIC BEEF LASAGNE

*Although there are many trendy new lasagnes out there, we are often asked for a classic lasagne. This is a recipe we've perfected over the years. Leave it to stand for six hours before cooking.*

## SERVES 6

**Special equipment** *2.4 litre (4 pint) shallow wide-based ovenproof dish*

1 tbsp sunflower oil

900g (2lb) raw minced beef

2 onions, roughly chopped

4 celery sticks, diced

2 garlic cloves, crushed

2 level tbsp plain flour

2 x 400g cans chopped tomatoes

150ml (5fl oz) beef stock

3 tbsp tomato purée

1 tsp sugar

1 tbsp freshly chopped thyme leaves

**For the white sauce**

50g (1¾oz) butter

50g (1¾oz) plain flour

750ml (1¼ pints) hot milk

2 tsp Dijon mustard

50g (1¾oz) Parmesan cheese, freshly grated

salt and freshly ground black pepper

6–8 sheets lasagne

85g (3oz) mature Cheddar cheese, grated

## SERVES 12

**Special equipment** *2 x 2.4 litre (4 pint) shallow wide-based ovenproof dishes or 1 x 4 litre (7 pint) dish*

1 tbsp sunflower oil

1.8kg (4lb) raw minced beef

4 onions, roughly chopped

8 celery sticks, diced

4 garlic cloves, crushed

4 level tbsp plain flour

4 x 400g cans chopped tomatoes

300ml (10fl oz) beef stock

6 tbsp tomato purée

2 tsp sugar

2 tbsp freshly chopped thyme leaves

**For the white sauce**

100g (3½oz) butter

100g (3½oz) plain flour

1.5 litres (2¾ pints) hot milk

1 heaped tbsp Dijon mustard

100g (3½oz) Parmesan cheese, freshly grated

salt and freshly ground black pepper

12–16 sheets lasagne

175g (6oz) mature Cheddar cheese, grated

1. Preheat the oven to 160°C (140°C fan/325°F/Gas 3). Heat the oil in a large frying pan until hot, then add the mince and cook until brown all over. Stir in the onions, celery, and garlic.

2. Add the flour and stir to coat the vegetables and beef, then blend in the tomatoes, stock, tomato purée, sugar, and thyme. Bring to the boil, cover with a lid, then transfer to the oven for 1–1½ hours or until the beef is tender.

3. Meanwhile, make the white sauce. Melt the butter in a saucepan, add the flour, and cook over the heat for 1 minute, stirring. Slowly add the hot milk, whisking until the sauce is thick and smooth. Add the mustard and Parmesan and season well with salt and freshly ground black pepper.

4. Remove the meat sauce from the oven and put one-third into the base of the ovenproof dish (two dishes for 12). Spoon one-third of the white sauce on top and arrange a layer of lasagne on top of that. Season with salt and freshly ground black pepper.

5. Spoon half the remaining meat sauce on top, then half the remaining white sauce. Put another layer of lasagne on top and season with salt and freshly ground black pepper. Add the rest of the meat sauce followed by the rest of the white sauce.

6. Sprinkle over the Cheddar, then transfer to the fridge for a minimum of 6 hours before cooking so the pasta has time to soften.

7. To serve, preheat the oven to 200°C (180°C fan/400°F/Gas 6), then cook the lasagne in the middle of the oven for 45 minutes (1 hour for 12) or until golden brown on top, bubbling around the edges, and the pasta is soft.

## IN THE AGA

Cook the meat sauce in the simmering oven for 1–1½ hours or until the beef is tender. Cook the assembled lasagne in the middle of the roasting oven for 40–45 minutes (1 hour for 12), using the cold sheet if it is getting too brown.

## PREPARE AHEAD AND FREEZE

*The lasagne can be made up to the end of step 6 up to 2 days ahead. Freeze the lasagne at the end of step 6 for up to 2 months.*

# CLASSIC SPAGHETTI BOLOGNESE

*This is a traditional bolognese sauce, with chicken livers for a lovely depth of flavour. It's well worth making double the quantity, so you can freeze a batch for another day.*

## SERVES 6

2 tbsp sunflower oil

200g (7oz) fresh chicken livers, trimmed of any sinew and cut into small pieces

900g (2lb) raw lean minced beef

2 onions, finely chopped

2 garlic cloves, crushed

100ml (3½fl oz) Port

2 x 400g cans chopped tomatoes

3 tbsp tomato purée

1 tsp caster sugar

salt and freshly ground black pepper

500g (1lb 2oz) spaghetti

Parmesan cheese, grated

## SERVES 12

4 tbsp sunflower oil

450g (1lb) fresh chicken livers, trimmed of any sinew and cut into small pieces

1.8kg (4lb) raw lean minced beef

4 onions, finely chopped

4 garlic cloves, crushed

200ml (7fl oz) Port

4 x 400g cans chopped tomatoes

6 tbsp tomato purée

2 tsp caster sugar

salt and freshly ground black pepper

1kg (2¼lb) spaghetti

Parmesan cheese, grated

1. Preheat the oven to 160°C (140°C fan/325°F/Gas 3). Heat the oil in a large non-stick frying pan over a high heat, add the chicken livers, and brown quickly all over. Remove with a slotted spoon and set aside.

2. Add the minced beef in batches and brown all over, adding a little more oil if the pan's getting dry. Return the chicken livers to the pan along with all the beef.

3. Add the onions and garlic and fry for 2 minutes. Stir in the Port, tomatoes, tomato purée, and sugar and bring to the boil. Season with salt and freshly ground black pepper, cover with a lid, and transfer to the oven for 1–1¼ hours or until tender.

4. To serve, cook the spaghetti in boiling salted water according to the packet instructions. Drain well, transfer to a serving bowl, and top with the bolognese sauce. Scatter with the grated Parmesan to serve.

### IN THE AGA

Cook in the simmering oven for 1–1½ hours or until tender.

### PREPARE AHEAD AND FREEZE

*The sauce can be made up to 2 days ahead. Freeze for up to 3 months.*

# COLD FILLET OF BEEF
# WITH MUSTARD SAUCE

**SERVES 6**

*1.25kg (2¾lb) middle-cut fillet of beef*

*salt and freshly ground black pepper*

*1 tbsp olive oil*

*a small knob of butter*

**For the mustard sauce**

*200ml tub full-fat crème fraîche*

*2 tbsp Dijon mustard*

*1 tsp white wine vinegar*

*1 tsp black mustard seeds*

*1 tsp caster sugar*

**SERVES 12**

*1.8kg (4lb) whole middle-cut fillet of beef*

*salt and freshly ground black pepper*

*2 tbsp olive oil*

*a knob of butter*

**For the mustard sauce**

*500ml tub full-fat crème fraîche*

*4 tbsp Dijon mustard*

*2 tsp white wine vinegar*

*2 tsp black mustard seeds*

*2 tsp caster sugar*

*To avoid the meat turning grey once carved and exposed to the air, carve the cold beef up to 3 hours ahead, then reassemble into its original shape and wrap tightly in cling film. Chill until needed and arrange on the plate just before serving. Serve with new potatoes and the salad on page 226.*

1. Preheat the oven to 220°C (200°C fan/425°F/Gas 7). Meanwhile, season the beef with salt and freshly ground black pepper, then rub the oil over the meat.

2. Heat a wide-based frying pan over a high heat until very hot and brown the beef quickly on all sides.

3. Transfer to a small roasting tin, spread with the butter, and roast for 18–20 minutes (25 minutes for 12) or until medium rare. Set aside until cold.

4. To make the sauce, put all the ingredients into a bowl, season with salt and freshly ground black pepper, and stir to combine.

5. Thinly carve the beef and serve cold with the sauce.

**IN THE AGA**
Roast on the second set of runners in the roasting oven for 18 minutes (25 minutes for 12).

**PREPARE AHEAD**

*The fillet can be roasted up to 2 days ahead.*
*The sauce can be made up to 3 days ahead.*
*Not suitable for freezing.*

# GOOD OLD-FASHIONED BEEF STEW WITH RED WINE AND THYME

*This traditional stew has lots of flavour and is a favourite of Lucy's family, especially at holiday times when everyone is gathered together. Serve with creamy mashed potatoes and green vegetables.*

## SERVES 6

2 tbsp sunflower oil

900g (2lb) stewing beef, cut into bite-sized pieces

12 small shallots, peeled

2 medium carrots, diced

4 level tbsp plain flour

300ml (10fl oz) red wine

450ml (15fl oz) beef stock

1 tbsp redcurrant jelly

1 tbsp Worcestershire sauce

5 thyme sprigs

salt and freshly ground black pepper

250g (9oz) button mushrooms

## SERVES 12

2 tbsp sunflower oil

1.8kg (4lb) stewing beef, cut into bite-sized pieces

24 small shallots, peeled

4 medium carrots, diced

100g (3½oz) plain flour

600ml (1 pint) red wine

900ml (1½ pints) beef stock

2 tbsp redcurrant jelly

2 tbsp Worcestershire sauce

small bunch of thyme sprigs

salt and freshly ground black pepper

500g (1lb 2oz) button mushrooms

1. Preheat the oven to 160°C (140°C fan/325°F/Gas 3). Meanwhile, heat the oil in a large frying pan or casserole and quickly brown the beef all over. Remove with a slotted spoon and set aside. You may need to do this in batches.

2. Add the shallots and carrots to the pan and brown over a high heat. Add the flour and stir to coat the vegetables, then blend in the wine and stock. Add the redcurrant jelly, Worcestershire sauce, thyme, and some salt and freshly ground black pepper. Add the mushrooms and return the beef to the pan.

3. Bring to the boil, cover with a lid, and cook in the oven for 2–2½ hours (2½–3 hours for 12) or until the beef is tender. Serve piping hot.

### IN THE AGA
Cook in the simmering oven for 2–2½ hours or until tender.

### PREPARE AHEAD AND FREEZE
The stew can be made up to 1 day ahead. Freeze for up to 2 months.

# HOT MUSTARD SPICED BEEF

*A wonderful untemperamental casserole – warming and spicy. Serve with Cheese-topped dauphinois potatoes (page 253) and peas.*

| SERVES 6 | SERVES 12 |
|---|---|
| 1 tbsp sunflower oil | 2 tbsp sunflower oil |
| 900g (2lb) chuck steak, cut into 2cm (¾in) cubes | 1.8kg (4lb) chuck steak, cut into 2cm (¾in) cubes |
| 2 large onions, chopped | 4 large onions, chopped |
| 100g (3½oz) button mushrooms, cut into quarters | 225g (8oz) button mushrooms, cut into quarters |
| 1 tbsp Dijon mustard | 2 tbsp Dijon mustard |
| 2 tsp medium curry powder | 4 tsp medium curry powder |
| 1 tbsp muscovado sugar | 2 tbsp muscovado sugar |
| 2 tbsp Worcestershire sauce | 4 tbsp Worcestershire sauce |
| 25g (scant 1oz) plain flour | 50g (1¾oz) plain flour |
| 600ml (1 pint) beef stock or 2 beef stock cubes dissolved in 600ml (1 pint) water | 1.2 litres (2 pints) beef stock or 4 beef stock cubes dissolved in 1.2 litres (2 pints) water |
| salt and freshly ground black pepper | salt and freshly ground black pepper |
| 450g (1lb) Chantenay or baby carrots | 900g (2lb) Chantenay or baby carrots |
| freshly chopped parsley, to garnish (optional) | freshly chopped parsley, to garnish (optional) |

1. Preheat the oven to 160°C (140°C fan/325°F/Gas 3). Meanwhile, heat the oil in a large non-stick frying pan or casserole, add the cubes of meat, and fry quickly until golden brown all over. Remove with a slotted spoon and drain on kitchen paper. You may need to do this in batches.

2. Add the onions and mushrooms to the pan and fry over a high heat, stirring occasionally, for 3 minutes or until starting to soften.

3. Put the mustard, curry powder, sugar, Worcestershire sauce, and flour into a bowl and add 75ml (2½fl oz) of the stock (150ml/5fl oz for 12). Whisk by hand until smooth.

4. Add the remaining stock to the pan and bring to the boil. Spoon about half the hot stock into the mustard mixture and whisk by hand to give a smooth paste. Pour the mixture back into the pan, whisking over a high heat until thickened.

5. Season with salt and freshly ground black pepper, then return the meat to the pan. Bring to the boil, cover with a lid, and transfer to the oven for 2–2½ hours (2½–3 hours for 12) or until the meat is tender.

6. While the meat is cooking, cook the carrots – sliced in half lengthways if they are a little on the large size – in boiling salted water for a few minutes or until just tender. Drain and refresh in cold water.

7. To serve, bring the casserole to the boil on the hob. Add the carrots, check the seasoning, and boil for a few minutes or until the carrots are hot. Sprinkle with parsley, if using, and serve.

IN THE AGA

Cook in the simmering oven for 2–2½ hours.

PREPARE AHEAD AND FREEZE

*The dish can be made up to the end of step 5 up to 2 days ahead. Freeze without the carrots for up to 2 months.*

# AROMATIC BEEF CURRY WITH GINGER AND TOMATOES

## SERVES 6

1 heaped tsp each ground cumin, ground coriander, and garam masala

½ tsp turmeric

10 cardamom pods, crushed, pods discarded, and seeds finely crushed

2 tbsp olive oil

900g (2lb) stewing beef, chopped into 2.5cm (1in) pieces

1 large onion, roughly chopped

1 red chilli, halved, deseeded, and chopped

4 garlic cloves, crushed

2cm (¾in) piece fresh root ginger, peeled and grated

400g can chopped tomatoes

300ml (10fl oz) beef stock

1 cinnamon stick

4 tbsp tomato purée

3 tbsp mango chutney

salt and freshly ground pepper

200g (7oz) okra or green beans, sliced into 2cm (¾in) pieces

## SERVES 12

2 heaped tsp each ground cumin, ground coriander, and garam masala

1 tsp turmeric

20 cardamom pods, crushed, pods discarded, and seeds finely crushed

4 tbsp olive oil

1.8kg (4lb) stewing beef, chopped into 2.5cm (1in) pieces

2 large onions, roughly chopped

2 red chillies, halved, deseeded, and chopped

8 garlic cloves, crushed

5cm (2in) piece fresh root ginger, peeled and grated

2 x 400g cans chopped tomatoes

600ml (1 pint) beef stock

2 cinnamon sticks

8 tbsp tomato purée

6 tbsp mango chutney

salt and freshly ground pepper

450g (1lb) okra or green beans, sliced into 2cm (¾in) pieces

*A warming curry with lots of spice. Serve with poppadoms, naan breads, and Pilaf rice (pages 246–247).*

1. Preheat the oven to 160°C (140°C fan/325°F/Gas 3). Heat a large frying pan or casserole over a high heat, add all the spices, and fry, stirring constantly, for 1 minute or until just toasted, then spoon into a small bowl.

2. Add the oil to the pan and quickly brown the beef until golden all over. Remove with a slotted spoon and set aside. You may need to do this in batches. Add the onion to the pan with the toasted spices, the chilli, garlic, and ginger and fry for 3–4 minutes.

3. Add the chopped tomatoes, stock, cinnamon, tomato purée, and chutney. Return the beef to the pan, season with salt and freshly ground pepper, cover with a lid, and transfer to the oven for about 2–2¼ hours (2½ hours for 12) or until the beef is tender.

4. Cook the okra or green beans in boiling salted water for 3 minutes, drain, and stir into the pan. Fish out the cinnamon and discard. Serve straightaway.

### IN THE AGA

Cook in the simmering oven for about 2–2¼ hours or until tender.

### PREPARE AHEAD AND FREEZE

*The curry can be made up to 2 days ahead. Freeze without the okra or green beans for up to 2 months.*

# CHILLI CON CARNE

**SERVES 6**

1 tbsp olive oil

900g (2lb) raw minced beef

2 medium onions, coarsely chopped

2 garlic cloves, crushed

2 red chillies, halved, deseeded, and finely chopped

2 tbsp paprika

2 tsp cumin powder

½–1 tsp hot chilli powder (depending on taste)

200ml (7fl oz) red wine

2 x 400g cans chopped tomatoes

2 tbsp tomato purée

salt and freshly ground black pepper

2 x 400g cans kidney beans in water, drained and rinsed

1–2 tbsp mango chutney (depending on taste)

**SERVES 12**

2 tbsp olive oil

1.8kg (4lb) raw minced beef

3 large onions, coarsely chopped

4 garlic cloves, crushed

4 red chillies, halved, deseeded, and finely chopped

4 tbsp paprika

1 heaped tbsp cumin powder

1–2 tsp hot chilli powder (depending on taste)

400ml (14fl oz) red wine

4 x 400g cans chopped tomatoes

4 tbsp tomato purée

salt and freshly ground black pepper

4 x 400g cans kidney beans in water, drained and rinsed

2–3 tbsp mango chutney (depending on taste)

*The hotness of chilli con carne is a personal choice. Taste it at the end and, if you like yours hot, add more chilli powder, then bring to the boil to cook it through. The chutney adds a touch of sweetness. Serve with long-grain rice, grated Cheddar or Red Leceister cheese, and a dollop of soured cream.*

1.  Preheat the oven to 180°C (160°C fan/350°F/Gas 4). Meanwhile, heat the oil in a deep, non-stick frying pan or casserole, add the mince, and fry over a high heat for 5 minutes or until brown all over. You may need to do this in batches.

2.  Add the onions, garlic, and chillies and fry with the mince for a few minutes.

3.  Sprinkle in the paprika, cumin, and chilli powder and fry for a few minutes more. Blend in the wine, tomatoes, and tomato purée and stir as you bring to the boil. Season with salt and freshly ground black pepper, cover with a lid, and transfer to the oven for about an hour.

4.  Add the kidney beans and chutney, return to the oven, and continue to cook for a further 30 minutes (1 hour for 12) or until the meat is completely tender. Serve straightaway.

**IN THE AGA**

Cook in the simmering oven for 1½ hours. Add the beans and chutney after 1 hour.

**PREPARE AHEAD AND FREEZE**

*The chilli can be made up to 2 days ahead. Freeze for up to 2 months.*

# MARINATED MARMALADE AND WHISKY LAMB FILLET

*Lamb loin fillet is lean, tender, and very quick to cook. It's also quite expensive, so this recipe is for extra special occasions. Serve with creamy mashed potatoes and a green vegetable.*

**SERVES 6**

3 large lamb loin fillets, trimmed

3 heaped tbsp thin-cut Seville orange marmalade

finely grated zest of ½ lemon

1 garlic clove, crushed

2 tbsp whisky

2 tbsp olive oil

salt and freshly ground black pepper

**For the sauce**

300ml (10fl oz) chicken stock

1½ tbsp soy sauce

2 tsp balsamic vinegar

2 level tsp cornflour

1 tbsp cold water

**SERVES 12**

6 large lamb loin fillets, trimmed

6 heaped tbsp thin-cut Seville orange marmalade

finely grated zest of 1 lemon

2 garlic cloves, crushed

4 tbsp whisky

4 tbsp olive oil

salt and freshly ground black pepper

**For the sauce**

600ml (1 pint) chicken stock

3 tbsp soy sauce

4 tsp balsamic vinegar

4 level tsp cornflour

2 tbsp cold water

1. Arrange the lamb fillets in a flat dish. Put the marmalade, lemon zest, garlic, and whisky into a small bowl and mix together. Pour over the lamb, cover, and leave to marinate in the fridge for about an hour or up to 6 hours.

2. Preheat the oven to 220°C (200°C fan/425°F/Gas 7). Heat the oil in large frying pan. Scrape the marinade off the fillets and reserve for the sauce. Season the lamb with salt and freshly ground black pepper, then fry quickly until brown on all sides. You may need to do this in batches. Arrange on a baking sheet.

3. Roast for 8 minutes (12 minutes for 12) or until cooked but still pink in the middle. Set aside to rest.

4. Meanwhile, make the sauce. Rinse the frying pan, add the reserved marinade along with the stock, soy sauce, and balsamic vinegar, and bring to the boil. Put the cornflour into a cup, add the cold water, and mix until smooth. Add a little of the hot sauce and mix again, then stir into the frying pan and bring to the boil to thicken it slightly.

5. Carve the lamb into slices, strain the sauce, and serve alongside.

### IN THE AGA
Roast the lamb fillets on the second set of runners in the roasting oven for 8 minutes (10 minutes for 12).

---

**PREPARE AHEAD AND FREEZE**

*The lamb can be marinated for up to 6 hours.
The sauce can be made up to 3 days ahead.
Freeze the sauce for up to 3 months.*

# SLOW-ROAST LEG OF LAMB

*Slow-roasted lamb is ideal for a crowd – it looks after itself in the oven, it's tender, and easy to carve. No wonder it's Mary's family lunch most Sundays. Serve with mint sauce and redcurrant jelly.*

## SERVES 6

1.5kg (3lb 3oz) half-boned leg of lamb

8 garlic cloves, thinly sliced

bunch of fresh thyme

2 red onions, roughly chopped

1 tbsp olive oil

salt and freshly ground black pepper

750ml (1¼ pints) water mixed with 1 beef stock cube

1 heaped tbsp plain flour

3 tbsp water

1 heaped tbsp redcurrant jelly

a little gravy browning (optional)

## SERVES 12

2 x 1.5kg (3lb 3oz) half-boned legs of lamb

16 garlic cloves, thinly sliced

large bunch of fresh thyme

4 red onions, roughly chopped

2 tbsp olive oil

salt and freshly ground black pepper

1.5 litres (2¾ pints) water mixed with 2 beef stock cubes

2 heaped tbsp plain flour

6 tbsp water

2 heaped tbsp redcurrant jelly

a little gravy browning (optional)

1. Preheat the oven to 220°C (200°C fan/425°F/Gas 7). Lay the lamb on a board and use a small sharp knife to make holes in the flesh. Push the garlic and thyme into the holes.

2. Arrange the onions in the base of a large roasting tin. Sit a grill rack over the onions and place the lamb on top. Drizzle over the oil and season with salt and freshly ground black pepper.

3. Roast for 30–40 minutes or until brown. Remove the tin from the oven and reduce the oven temperature to 160°C (140°C fan/325°F/Gas 3).

4. Pour the stock around the lamb, cover the tin with foil, and return to the oven for 5 hours (5½ hours for 12) or until the meat is tender and just falling off the bone.

5. Transfer the lamb to a board, cover with foil, and leave to rest while you make the gravy.

6. Put the flour into a cup and mix to a smooth runny paste with the water. Heat the roasting tin on the hob, whisk in the flour mixture and the redcurrant jelly, and bring to the boil, stirring all the time until smooth. Check the seasoning and add a little gravy browning if you'd like the gravy to be a rich brown colour. Strain through a sieve for a smooth gravy.

7. Carve the lamb and serve with the hot gravy.

### IN THE AGA

At step 3, roast on the second set of runners in the roasting oven for 30 minutes (40 minutes for 12). At step 4, transfer to the simmering oven for 5–6 hours.

### PREPARE AHEAD

*The lamb can be prepared up to the end of step 2 up to 1 day ahead. Not suitable for freezing.*

# BONELESS WINTER LAMB SHANKS

*A whole lamb shank can look too filling. Our recipe gives guests the option of having half. It tastes even better when made the day before. Serve with mashed potato and cabbage.*

**Special equipment** *2.4 litre (4 pint) shallow ovenproof dish*

*2 tbsp olive oil*

*6 lamb shanks, trimmed of any excess fat*

*2 medium onions, thinly sliced*

*3 garlic cloves, crushed*

*50g (1¾oz) plain flour*

*600ml (1 pint) cold chicken stock*

*3 tbsp sun-dried tomato paste*

*150ml (5fl oz) red wine or Port*

*3 tbsp soy sauce*

*1 tbsp freshly chopped thyme leaves*

*salt and freshly ground black pepper*

*1½ tbsp balsamic vinegar*

**Special equipment** *2 x 2.4 litre (4 pint) shallow ovenproof dishes*

*4 tbsp olive oil*

*12 lamb shanks, trimmed of any excess fat*

*4 medium onions, thinly sliced*

*6 garlic cloves, crushed*

*100g (3½oz) plain flour*

*1.2 litres (2 pints) cold chicken stock*

*6 tbsp sun-dried tomato paste*

*300ml (10fl oz) red wine or Port*

*6 tbsp soy sauce*

*2 tbsp freshly chopped thyme leaves*

*salt and freshly ground black pepper*

*3 tbsp balsamic vinegar*

1. Preheat the oven to 160°C (140°C fan/325°F/Gas 3). Heat half the oil in a large deep saucepan or casserole. Brown the shanks all over until golden. Remove and set aside. You may need to do this in batches.

2. Add the remaining oil to the pan, add the onions and garlic, and cook over a high heat for 5 minutes or until starting to soften. Put the flour into a jug and slowly whisk in the cold stock until smooth. Add to the pan with the tomato paste and red wine or Port and bring to the boil.

3. Return the lamb to the pan, add the soy sauce and thyme, and season with salt and freshly ground black pepper. Stir well, cover with a lid, and transfer to the oven for 3–4 hours (4 hours for 12) or until the meat is tender and starting to fall off the bone. Stir in the vinegar.

4. Remove the shanks from the sauce, wrap in foil, and set aside to cool. Pour the sauce into a 2.4 litre (4 pint) shallow ovenproof dish (two dishes for 12), cool, and cover with foil. When the sauce and shanks are completely cold, transfer to the fridge overnight, if time allows.

5. To serve, preheat the oven to 180°C (160°C fan/350°F/Gas 4). Using a spoon, remove the fat from the surface of the sauce and discard. Remove the meat from the bone in one piece, then cut each piece in half. Add to the sauce and cover with foil.

6. Reheat in the oven for 45–50 minutes (1 hour for 12) or until piping hot.

### IN THE AGA

At step 3, transfer to the simmering oven for 4–5 hours or until the meat is tender and falling off the bone. At step 6, slide on to the second set of runners in the roasting oven for 45 minutes (1 hour for 12). Stir from time to time.

### PREPARE AHEAD AND FREEZE

*This is best made the day before and reheated. Freeze for up to 6 weeks.*

# SHEPHERD'S PIE DAUPHINOIS

*This variation on the classic shepherd's pie has a layered topping of potato and cream instead of mash. Liquid gravy browning can be rather hard to track down these days, but it's well worth the hunt. Not only does it make a sauce or gravy an appetizing rich brown, it saves you time, too, as you don't have to brown the onions for so long. Serve with a green vegetable.*

## SERVES 6

**Special equipment** *2.4 litre (4 pint) shallow wide-based ovenproof dish*

*900g (2lb) raw minced lamb*

*2 onions, chopped*

*2 large carrots, finely diced*

*45g (1½oz) plain flour*

*300ml (10fl oz) red wine*

*300ml (10fl oz) beef stock*

*1 tbsp Worcestershire sauce*

*1 tbsp tomato purée*

*dash of gravy browning (optional)*

*salt and freshly ground black pepper*

### For the topping

*900g (2lb) old King Edward potatoes or other floury potatoes, cut into 3mm (⅛in) slices*

*150ml (5fl oz) double cream*

*75g (2½oz) mature Cheddar cheese, grated*

## SERVES 12

**Special equipment** *2 x 2.4 litre (4 pint) shallow wide-based ovenproof dishes*

*1.8kg (4lb) raw minced lamb*

*4 onions, chopped*

*4 large carrots, finely diced*

*75g (2½oz) plain flour*

*600ml (1 pint) red wine*

*600ml (1 pint) beef stock*

*2 tbsp Worcestershire sauce*

*2 tbsp tomato purée*

*dash of gravy browning (optional)*

*salt and freshly ground black pepper*

### For the topping

*1.8kg (4lb) old King Edward potatoes or other floury potatoes, cut into 3mm (⅛in) slices*

*300ml (10fl oz) double cream*

*175g (6oz) mature Cheddar cheese, grated*

1. Preheat the oven to 160°C (140°C fan/325°F/Gas 3). Meanwhile, put the minced lamb, onions, and carrots into a deep frying pan or casserole and fry over a high heat, stirring frequently, for 5 minutes or until the meat is brown. Drain away any fat.

2. Stir in the flour and, over a high heat, add the wine, stock, Worcestershire sauce, and tomato purée (add the gravy browning, too, if you want the sauce to be a rich dark colour). Stir until blended, then bring to the boil. Season with salt and freshly ground black pepper, cover with a lid, and transfer to the oven for 1–1½ hours or until the mince is tender.

3. Check the seasoning, then tip the meat into the ovenproof dish(es) and set aside to cool. Increase the oven temperature to 220°C (200°C fan/425°F/Gas 7).

4. Put the potatoes in a pan of boiling salted water for 4–5 minutes to blanch them. Drain, refresh in cold water, and dry well with kitchen paper.

5. Arrange a layer of potato on top of the cold mince, then pour over half the cream and season with salt and freshly ground black pepper. Arrange the remaining potatoes on top, pour over the remaining cream, and sprinkle over the cheese.

6. Bake for 30 minutes (45–50 minutes for 12) or until golden and bubbling.

### IN THE AGA

At step 2, transfer to the simmering oven for 2 hours or until the mince is tender. At step 6, bake on the second set of runners in the roasting oven for 30 minutes (45–50 minutes for 12).

## PREPARE AHEAD AND FREEZE

*The pie can be prepared up to the end of step 5 up to 1 day ahead. Freeze for up to 2 months.*

# MINI PORK EN CROÛTES

*As a team, we like to go to the pub occasionally, to chat and have a moment off from cooking. One evening we had a recipe similar to this – delicious and beautifully presented. Serve with spinach.*

**SERVES 6**

75g (2½oz) mature Cheddar cheese, grated

50g (1¾oz) fresh white breadcrumbs

2 tbsp freshly chopped parsley

1 tsp freshly chopped thyme

1 egg

salt and freshly ground black pepper

dash of Tabasco

2 x 350g (12oz) pork fillets, trimmed

8 slices Parma ham

a little plain flour, to dust

375g packet ready-rolled puff pastry

1 egg, beaten with a little milk

**For the apple gravy**

a knob of butter

1 large onion, finely chopped

50g (1¾oz) plain flour

400ml (14fl oz) chicken stock

400ml (14fl oz) unsweetened apple juice

salt and freshly ground pepper

2 tbsp Worcestershire sauce

a little gravy browning, optional

**SERVES 12**

150g (5oz) mature Cheddar cheese, grated

100g (3½oz) fresh white breadcrumbs

4 tbsp freshly chopped parsley

2 tsp freshly chopped thyme

2 eggs

salt and freshly ground black pepper

generous dash of Tabasco

4 x 350g (12oz) pork fillets, trimmed

16 slices Parma ham

a little plain flour, to dust

2 x 375g packets ready-rolled puff pastry

1 egg, beaten with a little milk

**For the apple gravy**

a large knob of butter

2 large onions, finely chopped

100g (3½oz) plain flour

750ml (1¼ pints) chicken stock

750ml (1¼ pints) unsweetened apple juice

salt and freshly ground pepper

4 tbsp Worcestershire sauce

a little gravy browning, optional

1.  Put the cheese, breadcrumbs, herbs, and egg into a small bowl. Season with salt and freshly ground black pepper, add the Tabasco, and mix well.

2.  Slice each pork fillet in half horizontally, then cover with cling film and bash with a rolling pin until they are slightly thinner. Spread the cheese mixture on top of the halved fillets, then put the fillet halves together again, with the cheese mixture in the middle.

3.  Arrange four slices of the ham side by side on a board. With the edges overlapping slightly, they should be about as wide as one of the pork fillets. Sit a fillet across the ham at one end and roll it up so the pork is encased in the ham. Do the same with the other fillet(s).

4.  On a lightly floured work surface, roll the pastry into a 33 x 40cm (13 x 16in) rectangle (two rectangles for 12). Slice in half widthways and brush with egg. Wrap each fillet in pastry and place join side down on a baking sheet. Brush with egg and chill for an hour.

5.  Preheat the oven to 220°C (200°C fan/425°F/Gas 7). Bake the parcels for 25–30 minutes (45 minutes for 12) or until golden and crisp. Allow to rest for 5–10 minutes before carving.

6.  Meanwhile, make the apple gravy. Heat the butter in a saucepan, add the onion, and fry for 2 minutes. Cover with a lid and cook over a low heat for 15 minutes or until soft. Sprinkle in the flour, blend in the stock and apple juice, and bring to the boil, stirring. Season and add the Worcestershire sauce and a little gravy browning, if you'd like the gravy to be a rich brown. Push through a sieve and discard the onion.

7.  Slice each en croûte in three, then slice each piece in half diagonally and stand them on a dinner plate. Serve hot with the apple gravy. Serve any extra gravy separately.

## PREPARE AHEAD AND FREEZE

*The pork can be prepared up to the end of step 3 up to 12 hours ahead. Not suitable for freezing. The gravy can be made up to 2 days ahead. Freeze for up to 1 month.*

## IN THE AGA

Bake on the second set of runners in the roasting oven for 30 minutes. Slide the baking sheet on to the floor of the roasting oven 8 minutes before the end of cooking.

# PAPRIKA PORK FILLET

*A variation on one of Mary's best-loved pork recipes. Lucy's family adores it and always puts in a request for it on special occasions. Serve with mashed potatoes and green vegetables.*

## SERVES 6

2 tbsp olive oil

900g (2lb) pork fillet, trimmed and cut into 1cm (½in) slices

25g (scant 1oz) butter

1 large onion, roughly chopped

1 level tbsp paprika

2 level tbsp plain flour

300ml (10fl oz) chicken stock

5 tbsp sherry

1 tsp tomato purée

175g (6oz) button chestnut mushrooms, halved

salt and freshly ground black pepper

200g tub full-fat crème fraîche

freshly chopped parsley (optional)

## SERVES 12

4 tbsp olive oil

1.8kg (4lb) pork fillet, trimmed and sliced into 1cm (½in) slices

50g (1¾oz) butter

2 large onions, roughly chopped

2 level tbsp paprika

4 level tbsp plain flour

600ml (1 pint) chicken stock

150ml (5fl oz) sherry

2 tsp tomato purée

350g (12oz) button chestnut mushrooms, halved

salt and freshly ground black pepper

2 x 200g tubs full-fat crème fraîche

freshly chopped parsley (optional)

1. Heat the oil in a large non-stick frying pan or casserole. Add the pork and brown quickly on all sides. Remove with a slotted spoon and set aside. You may need to do this in batches.

2. Add the butter and onion to the pan, cover with a lid, and leave to soften over a low heat for 15 minutes or until tender.

3. Stir in the paprika and flour and fry over a high heat for 1 minute. Add the stock and sherry and bring to the boil, stirring all the time, to thicken slightly. Add the tomato purée and mushrooms.

4. Return the pork to the pan, season with salt and freshly ground black pepper, cover with a lid, and simmer over a low heat for 15 minutes (25–30 minutes for 12) or until the pork is tender.

5. Stir in the crème fraîche and serve piping hot, with some chopped parsley scattered over if you like.

### IN THE AGA

Soften the onion in the simmering oven for 20 minutes. At step 4, cover with a lid and transfer to the simmering oven for 15 minutes (25 minutes for 12).

### PREPARE AHEAD AND FREEZE

*The dish can be prepared up to the end of step 4 up to 1 day ahead. Freeze at the end of step 4 for up to 1 month.*

# PASTA AND MEATBALL BAKE WITH TOMATO AND BASIL SAUCE

*This is a perfect all-in-one dish. You can use rigatoni or penne if you can't get hold of elicoidali. Serve with dressed salad.*

## SERVES 6

**Special equipment** *2 litre (3½ pint) shallow wide-based ovenproof dish*

### For the sauce

1 tbsp olive oil

1 large onion, finely chopped

1 red chilli, halved, deseeded, and finely chopped

2 garlic cloves, crushed

2 x 400g cans chopped tomatoes

2 tbsp tomato purée

salt and freshly ground black pepper

2 tbsp coarsely chopped fresh basil

a dash of caster sugar (optional)

### For the meatballs

450g (1lb) good-quality sausagemeat

25g (scant 1oz) fresh fine breadcrumbs

50g (1¾oz) freshly grated Parmesan cheese

2 tbsp finely chopped fresh basil

50g (1¾oz) mozzarella, cut into about 30 cubes

1 tbsp olive oil

225g (8oz) elicoidali pasta

50g (1¾oz) Parmesan cheese, freshly grated

50g (1¾oz) mozzarella, chopped into small pieces

## SERVES 12

**Special equipment** *2 x 2 litre (3½ pint) shallow wide-based ovenproof dishes or 1 x 4 litre (7 pint) dish*

### For the sauce

2 tbsp olive oil

2 large onions, finely chopped

2 red chillies, halved, deseeded, and finely chopped

4 garlic cloves, crushed

4 x 400g cans chopped tomatoes

3 tbsp tomato purée

salt and freshly ground black pepper

3 tbsp coarsely chopped fresh basil

a dash of caster sugar (optional)

### For the meatballs

900g (2lb) good-quality sausagemeat

50g (1¾oz) fresh fine breadcrumbs

100g (3½oz) freshly grated Parmesan cheese

4 tbsp finely chopped fresh basil

100g (3½oz) mozzarella, cut into about 60 cubes

1 tbsp olive oil

450g (1lb) elicoidali pasta

100g (3½oz) Parmesan cheese, freshly grated

100g (3½oz) mozzarella, chopped into small pieces

1. Preheat the oven to 200°C (180°C fan/400°F/Gas 6). Meanwhile, put the oil for the sauce into a deep saucepan, add the onion, and fry over a high heat for a few minutes or until softened slightly but not coloured.

2. Add the chilli and garlic and fry over a high heat for a few minutes. Add the tomatoes and tomato purée, then season with salt and freshly ground black pepper. Bring to the boil, cover with a lid, then lower the heat and simmer for 15 minutes. Add the basil and taste – if it is a little sharp, add a dash of caster sugar.

3. Meanwhile, make the meatballs. Put the sausagemeat, breadcrumbs, Parmesan, and basil into a mixing bowl. Mix together with your hands, season with salt and freshly ground black pepper, and shape into 30 balls (60 for 12). Using your finger, make a hole in the middle of each meatball, then push a cube of mozzarella into the centre and reshape so the mozzarella is hidden inside.

4. Heat the oil in a large frying pan and fry the meatballs for 4 minutes or until they are golden brown all over and just cooked through. You may need to do this in batches.

5. Meanwhile, cook the pasta in boiling salted water according to the packet instructions until just tender. Drain, refresh in cold water, and dry well with kitchen paper.

6. Stir the pasta into the sauce and season with salt and freshly ground black pepper. Stir in the meatballs, then spoon into the ovenproof dish and sprinkle the Parmesan and mozzarella on top.

7. Bake for 20–25 minutes (45 minutes for 12) or until golden brown on top and piping hot in the centre.

### IN THE AGA

Bake on the second set of runners in the roasting oven for 20 minutes (45 minutes for 12).

## PREPARE AHEAD

*You can make the bake up to the end of step 6 up to 8 hours ahead. Not suitable for freezing.*

# SMOKY SAUSAGE CASSOULET

## SERVES 6

3 tbsp olive oil

12 sausages

4 large onions, sliced

2 tsp paprika

50g (1¾oz) chorizo, very finely chopped

2 x 400g cans chopped tomatoes

2 tbsp tomato purée

2 tbsp Worcestershire sauce

2 tsp balsamic vinegar

salt and freshly ground black pepper

400g can butter beans, drained and rinsed

## SERVES 12

5 tbsp olive oil

24 sausages

7 large onions, sliced

4 tsp paprika

100g (3½oz) chorizo, very finely chopped

4 x 400g cans chopped tomatoes

4 tbsp tomato purée

4 tbsp Worcestershire sauce

1 tbsp balsamic vinegar

salt and freshly ground black pepper

2 x 400g cans butter beans, drained and rinsed

*Use your favourite sausages for this smoky casserole. We like Cumberland or pork and leek. This dish is especially popular with the young. If they are not keen on chorizo, replace it with smoked bacon, cut into small pieces. Serve with a green vegetable.*

1. Heat 1 tablespoon of the oil in a large non-stick frying pan or casserole dish over a high heat, then brown the sausages until golden on all sides. Remove with a slotted spoon and set aside. You may need to do this in batches.

2. Add the remaining oil to the pan and fry the onions for a few minutes or until lightly golden. Add the remaining ingredients (except the butter beans and sausages) and season with salt and freshly ground black pepper.

3. Simmer over a gentle heat for 20–25 minutes or until the onions are nearly soft. Add the butter beans and stir.

4. Arrange the sausages on top, cover with a lid, and cook for 20 minutes (35–40 minutes for 12) or until the sausages are completely cooked.

### IN THE AGA

At step 3, cover with a lid and transfer to the simmering oven for 30 minutes. Add the beans and sausages, cover again, and return to the simmering oven for a further 25 minutes.

## PREPARE AHEAD AND FREEZE

*The cassoulet can be made up to the end of step 3 up to 1 day ahead. Alternatively, cook it completely and reheat to serve. Not suitable for freezing.*

# GLAZED HAM WITH CUMBERLAND SAUCE

**SERVES 6–12**

1.35kg (3lb) joint smoked or unsmoked gammon

½ onion, cut in half

1 small celery stick, cut into three

1 small bay leaf

50g (1¾oz) light or dark muscovado sugar

2 tbsp redcurrant jelly

2 tsp grainy mustard

**SERVES 12–20**

3kg (6½lb) joint smoked or unsmoked gammon

1 onion, quartered

1 celery stick, cut into four

1 bay leaf

100g (3½oz) light or dark muscovado sugar

4 tbsp redcurrant jelly

1 tbsp grainy mustard

*Hot or cold, ham is irresistible and perfect for any buffet table. It feeds twice the number when cold because it's easier to slice thinly. When you're buying the gammon, ask the butcher if it needs soaking to remove any excess saltiness. If you get it from supermarkets, it is usually presoaked, but always check the label. The Cumberland sauce is also very good with cold meats, turkey at Christmas, and game pie.*

1. Weigh the joint and calculate the cooking time based on 20 minutes per 450g (1lb). A 1.35kg (3lb) joint will take 1 hour. A 3kg (6½lb) joint will take 2 hours 10 minutes.

2. Place it skin side down in a large deep saucepan. Add the vegetables, bay leaf, and sugar, then cover with cold water and a lid.

3. Bring to the boil (this takes longer than you may imagine) and, once boiling, start the timing. Simmer very gently until cooked. Check from time to time and top up with boiling water, if needed, to ensure the gammon is covered.

4. Once the ham is cooked through, carefully lift it out of the pan and, using a small sharp knife, remove the skin, leaving a very thin layer of fat on the joint. Preheat the oven to 200°C (180°C fan/400°F/Gas 6).

5. Meanwhile, put the redcurrant jelly and mustard into a bowl and stir until combined. Score the layer of fat on the ham in a lattice pattern with a knife, then spread the mixture over it.

6. Line a large roasting tin with foil and sit the ham in the centre with the glaze at the top. Bring the foil up so the flesh is completely covered and only the glaze is exposed – this prevents the ham drying out.

7. Bake for 15–20 minutes or until the glaze has melted and started to caramelize. If serving hot, rest for a good 10 minutes before carving. If serving cold, set aside until needed.

## FOR THE CUMBERLAND SAUCE

*This sauce is wonderfully rich and vibrantly coloured. To serve 6, use a potato peeler to remove thin strips of peel from an orange. Scrape off any white pith, then cut into needle-thin strips and place in a pan. Cover with water, bring to the boil, and simmer over a low heat for 3–4 minutes or until soft. Drain, refresh in cold water, then dry well with kitchen paper and set aside. Put 340g redcurrant jelly from a jar and 75ml (2½fl oz) Port into a saucepan. Add the juice of the orange to the pan with 1 tsp Dijon mustard and a dash of Worcestershire sauce. Whisk over a high heat until the jelly has melted, then boil rapidly for 4–5 minutes or until reduced by half. Season with salt and freshly ground black pepper, add the juice of ½ lemon to taste, then spoon into a serving dish and sprinkle with the orange strips. Serve warm or cold. To serve 12, double all quantities. The sauce can be made up to 1 week ahead. To serve warm, reheat gently in a pan. Not suitable for freezing.*

## PREPARE AHEAD

*The ham can be prepared up to 5 days ahead. To serve warm, it can be boiled up to 5 days ahead and then glazed on the day. Not suitable for freezing.*

## IN THE AGA

Bring to the boil on the boiling plate, then, with the lid still on, transfer to the simmering oven and start the timing. At step 7, bake at the top of the roasting oven for 10–15 minutes.

# QUICHE LORRAINE

*Some classic recipes are unbeatable, but our quiche Lorraine – with added parsley – has the edge, we think. Serve warm with salad.*

## SERVES 6

**Special equipment** *20cm (8in) round 5cm (2in) deep loose-bottomed tart tin or quiche dish*

*175g (6oz) plain flour, plus a little extra to dust*

*85g (3oz) cold butter, cubed*

*1 egg*

### For the filling
*a knob of butter*

*1 large onion, roughly chopped*

*225g (8oz) unsmoked bacon, snipped into small pieces*

*1 heaped tbsp freshly chopped flat-leaf parsley*

*75g (2½oz) mature Cheddar cheese, grated*

*3 eggs*

*200ml tub full-fat crème fraîche*

*150ml (5fl oz) double cream*

*salt and freshly ground black pepper*

## SERVES 12

**Special equipment** *28cm (11in) round 5cm (2in) deep loose-bottomed tart tin or quiche dish*

*225g (8oz) plain flour, plus a little extra to dust*

*115g (4oz) cold butter, cubed*

*1 egg*

*1–2 tbsp water*

### For the filling
*a knob of butter*

*2 large onions, roughly chopped*

*350g (12oz) unsmoked bacon, snipped into small pieces*

*2 heaped tbsp freshly chopped flat-leaf parsley*

*175g (6oz) mature Cheddar cheese, grated*

*6 eggs*

*300ml (10fl oz) full-fat crème fraîche*

*300ml (10fl oz) double cream*

*salt and freshly ground black pepper*

1. Put the flour and butter into a food processor and whiz until the mixture resembles breadcrumbs. Add the egg (and the water if you're making the larger one) and whiz again until you have a smooth dough. Dust a work surface with flour and knead the dough lightly. Roll the dough out and use to line the flan tin (see page 267). Prick the base all over with a fork and chill for 15 minutes.

2. Preheat the oven to 200°C (180°C fan/400°F/Gas 6). Pop a baking sheet in to get hot. Line the pastry case with baking parchment, fill with dried beans, and bake for 15–20 minutes (see page 311). Remove the beans and paper, lower the temperature to 160°C (140°C fan/325°F/Gas 3), and return the pastry case to the oven to dry out for 5–10 minutes. Set aside to cool. Turn the oven up to 190°C (170°C fan/375°F/Gas 5).

3. To make the filling, melt the butter in a frying pan, add the onion and bacon, and fry over a high heat for 2 minutes or until starting to crisp. Cover with a lid, lower the heat, and cook slowly for 15–20 minutes or until the onion is tender and the bacon cooked. Spoon into the pastry case and spread out evenly. Scatter with half the parsley and half the cheese.

4. Put the eggs, crème fraîche, and double cream into a mixing bowl and whisk by hand until combined. Add the remaining parsley and season with salt and freshly ground black pepper. Pour into the flan case and sprinkle over the remaining cheese.

5. Bake in the oven for 25 minutes (30–35 minutes for 12) or until golden brown and the egg mixture is just set.

### IN THE AGA
Skip step 2. Make the filling and pour into the unbaked pastry case. Bake on the floor of the roasting oven for 25 minutes (35 minutes for 12).

### PREPARE AHEAD AND FREEZE
*The quiche can be made up to 2 days ahead. Freeze for up to 2 months.*

# SUMMER FRITTATA

## SERVES 6

**Special equipment** *20cm (8in) round springform tin, greased and base-lined*

*350g (12oz) potatoes, cut into 3cm (1¼in) cubes*

*1 small onion, roughly chopped*

*salt and freshly ground black pepper*

*8 large eggs*

*1 tsp freshly chopped thyme leaves*

*100g (3½oz) roll goat's cheese, cut into small cubes*

*50g (1¾oz) Parma or Black Forest ham, cut into thin strips*

## SERVES 12

**Special equipment** *2 x 20cm (8in) round springform tins, greased and base-lined*

*700g (1lb 9oz) potatoes, cut into 3cm (1¼in) cubes*

*2 small onions, roughly chopped*

*salt and freshly ground black pepper*

*16 large eggs*

*2 tsp freshly chopped thyme leaves*

*2 x 100g (3½oz) rolls goat's cheese, cut into small cubes*

*100g (3½oz) Parma or Black Forest ham, cut into thin strips*

*A frittata is a baked omelette and this one – cooked in the oven rather than in a frying pan – is ideal for picnics. Black Forest ham is one of the most reasonably priced cured hams. If you can't get hold of it, use Serrano ham or Parma ham. Cut the frittata into wedges and serve warm or cold with a dressed salad and bread.*

1. Preheat the oven to 200°C (180°C fan/400°F/Gas 6). Cook the potatoes and onion in boiling salted water for 5–8 minutes or until tender. Drain and refresh in cold water.

2. Crack the eggs into a large mixing bowl, add the thyme, and season with salt and freshly ground black pepper. Whisk by hand until combined. Add the potatoes and onion and stir in the cheese.

3. Pour into the tin(s) and scatter over the strips of ham.

4. Bake for 12–15 minutes (15–20 minutes for 12) or until slightly risen and just firm. To make slicing easier, leave to cool slightly before serving.

### IN THE AGA
Bake on the second set of runners in the roasting oven for 15 minutes (20 minutes for 12).

### PREPARE AHEAD
*The frittata can be made up to 8 hours ahead. Not suitable for freezing.*

# PAPRIKA PORK GOULASH

*Served with rice, this Hungarian classic is perfect bowl food. We like it made with pork shoulder, but you could also use pork fillet if you prefer. Reduce the cooking time by half if using fillet of pork.*

## SERVES 6

2 tbsp olive oil

900g (2lb) boneless pork shoulder, cut into 4cm (1½in) pieces

2 medium onions, sliced

2 garlic cloves, crushed

2 tbsp paprika

3 tbsp tomato purée

300ml (10fl oz) chicken stock or beef stock

salt and freshly ground black pepper

2 chargrilled red peppers, peeled, deseeded, and sliced

1 tbsp balsamic vinegar

1 tsp brown sugar

2–3 tbsp soured cream or crème fraîche (depending on taste)

2 tbsp freshly chopped flat-leaf parsley

## SERVES 12

4 tbsp olive oil

1.8kg (4lb) boneless pork shoulder, cut into 4cm (1½in) pieces

3 large onions, sliced

4 garlic cloves, crushed

3 heaped tbsp paprika

5 heaped tbsp tomato purée

600ml (1 pint) chicken stock or beef stock

salt and freshly ground black pepper

4 chargrilled red peppers, peeled, deseeded, and sliced

2 tbsp balsamic vinegar

2 tsp brown sugar

6 tbsp soured cream or crème fraîche

4 tbsp freshly chopped flat-leaf parsley

1.  Preheat the oven to 160°C (140°C fan/325°F/Gas 3). Meanwhile, heat the oil in a deep frying pan or casserole. Add the pork and brown quickly on all sides. You may need to do this in batches. Remove with a slotted spoon and set aside.

2.  Add the onions to the pan and fry for 3 minutes or until starting to soften. Stir in the garlic and paprika and fry for 1 minute. Add the tomato purée and stock and return the meat to the pan. Bring to the boil, season with salt and freshly ground black pepper, cover with a lid, and transfer to the oven for 1¼–1½ hours (2 hours for 12) or until the pork is tender.

3.  Meanwhile, blacken the skin of the peppers under the grill, then pop them into a polythene bag and seal. When cold, peel off the charred skin with your fingers, then pull out the core and seeds, and slice the peppers.

4. Add the peppers, vinegar, and sugar to the pan and bring to the boil, then check the seasoning. Stir in the soured cream or crème fraîche to taste and serve garnished with the parsley.

### IN THE AGA
Cook in the simmering oven for 2 hours or until tender.

### PREPARE AHEAD AND FREEZE
*You can make the goulash up to 1 day ahead. The flavour will improve, in fact. Freeze without the cream for up to 2 months.*

# PASTA WITH PANCETTA, BROAD BEANS, AND MASCARPONE

*A delicious creamy pasta dish that's also quick to cook – it takes barely 15 minutes once you've prepared the ingredients. You can use bacon instead of pancetta if you prefer. Serve with salad.*

## SERVES 6

300g (11oz) conchiglie shell pasta

salt and freshly ground black pepper

150g (5½oz) frozen small broad beans

200g (7oz) French beans, trimmed and sliced into three

140g packet pancetta cubes

250g tub full-fat mascarpone cheese

75g (2½oz) freshly grated Parmesan cheese

juice of 1 small lemon

small bunch of basil, roughly chopped

## SERVES 12

600g (1lb 5oz) conchiglie shell pasta

salt and freshly ground black pepper

300g (11oz) frozen small broad beans

400g (14oz) French beans, trimmed and sliced into three

2 x 140g packets pancetta cubes

2 x 250g tubs full-fat mascarpone cheese

175g (6oz) freshly grated Parmesan cheese

juice of 1 large lemon

large bunch of basil, roughly chopped

1. Cook the pasta in boiling salted water according to the packet instructions. Add the broad beans and French beans 5 minutes before the end of cooking.

2. Meanwhile, heat a large frying pan, add the pancetta, and fry until crisp. Stir in the mascarpone and two-thirds of the Parmesan and stir until melted.

3. Drain the pasta and beans, leaving a little of the cooking water in the saucepan. Add the pasta and beans to the frying pan along with 6 tablespoons of the cooking water (10 tablespoons for 12). Add the lemon juice and basil, toss together well, and season with salt and freshly ground black pepper.

4. Sprinkle with the remaining Parmesan and serve at once.

## PREPARE AHEAD

*The pasta and beans can be cooked, drained, and refreshed in cold water up to 6 hours ahead. Remember to reserve a little of the cooking water. Not suitable for freezing.*

# MAIN COURSES
## FISH

*Fish is a favourite for entertaining year round.*
*A whole fillet of salmon, poached, baked, or en croûte,*
*is a classic buffet centrepiece, which guests couldn't fail*
*to be impressed by. We find that cooking fish with the*
*skin on helps keep it from drying out.*

# DOUBLE SALMON FISHCAKES WITH HORSERADISH SAUCE

*So many people love fishcakes, which is why we always invent a new recipe for them for each of our books.*

## SERVES 6

350g (12oz) cooked salmon, skin and bones removed

100g (3½oz) hot-smoked salmon

450g (1lb) mashed potato

3 tbsp mayonnaise

2 tbsp creamed horseradish

2 heaped tbsp freshly snipped chives

2 heaped tbsp freshly chopped parsley

salt and freshly ground black pepper

1 egg, beaten

50g (1¾oz) fresh breadcrumbs

1 tbsp olive oil

1 lemon, cut into 6 wedges, to garnish

### For the horseradish sauce

150ml (5fl oz) soured cream or full-fat crème fraîche

3 tbsp creamed horseradish

2 tbsp mayonnaise

2 tbsp freshly snipped chives

## SERVES 12

700g (1lb 9oz) cooked salmon, skin and bones removed

200g (7oz) hot-smoked salmon

900g (2lb) mashed potato

6 tbsp mayonnaise

4 tbsp creamed horseradish

4 heaped tbsp freshly snipped chives

4 heaped tbsp freshly chopped parsley

salt and freshly ground black pepper

1 egg, beaten

100g (3½oz) fresh breadcrumbs

2 tbsp olive oil

2 lemons, each cut into 6 wedges, to garnish

### For the horseradish sauce

300ml (10fl oz) soured cream or full-fat crème fraîche

6 tbsp creamed horseradish

4 tbsp mayonnaise

4 tbsp freshly snipped chives

1. Put both kinds of salmon, the mashed potato, mayonnaise, horseradish, and herbs into a mixing bowl, season with salt and freshly ground black pepper, and stir well to combine.

2. Divide the mixture into 12 (24 for 12) and shape into fishcakes. They shouldn't be too thick. Brush with beaten egg, coat with breadcrumbs, and chill for a minimum of 1 hour.

3. Meanwhile, make the sauce: put all the ingredients into a bowl, season with salt and freshly ground black pepper, and mix together well. Set aside.

4. Heat the oil in a non-stick frying pan and fry the fishcakes for 3–4 minutes on each side or until golden on the outside and hot in the middle. You may need to do this in batches and keep them warm in the oven.

5. Serve the fishcakes hot with a spoonful of the cold sauce and a lemon wedge.

## PREPARE AHEAD AND FREEZE

*The fishcakes can be made up to the end of step 2 up to 1 day ahead. Alternatively, fry them the day before and reheat. The sauce can be made up to 3 days ahead. Freeze the fishcakes at the end of step 2 for up to 2 months.*

# SALMON AND CRAYFISH PIE

*This recipe is ideal for preparing the day before. Shelled crayfish tails can be bought in all good supermarkets or fishmongers. They come in tubs of brine. Serve the pie with steamed broccoli or salad.*

## SERVES 6

**Special equipment** *2.4 litre (4 pint) shallow wide-based ovenproof dish*

750g (1lb 10oz) King Edward potatoes or other floury potatoes, cut into 5cm (2in) pieces

a knob of butter

150ml (5fl oz) milk

salt and freshly ground black pepper

**For the pie**
75g (2½oz) butter

1 onion, finely chopped

2 leeks, finely sliced

50g (1¾oz) plain flour

600ml (1 pint) hot milk

juice of ½ lemon

2 tbsp freshly chopped dill

2 tbsp freshly chopped parsley

2 tbsp capers, drained

500g (1lb 2oz) skinned salmon fillet, cut into 5cm (2in) cubes

250g (9oz) cooked crayfish tails in brine, drained

75g (2½oz) Cheddar cheese, grated

lemon wedges, to serve

## SERVES 12

**Special equipment** *2 x 2.4 litre (4 pint) shallow wide-based ovenproof dishes or 1 x 4 litre (7 pint) dish*

1.5kg (3lb 3oz) King Edward potatoes or other floury potatoes, cut into 5cm (2in) pieces

a large knob of butter

300ml (10fl oz) milk

salt and freshly ground black pepper

**For the pie**
175g (6oz) butter

2 onions, finely chopped

4 leeks, finely sliced

100g (3½oz) plain flour

1.2 litres (2 pints) hot milk

juice of 1 lemon

4 tbsp freshly chopped dill

4 tbsp freshly chopped parsley

4 tbsp capers, drained

1kg (2¼lb) skinned salmon fillet, cut into 5cm (2in) cubes

500g (1lb 2oz) cooked crayfish tails in brine, drained

175g (6oz) Cheddar cheese, grated

lemon wedges, to serve

1. Preheat the oven to 220°C (200°C fan/425°F/Gas 7). Put the potatoes in a pan of cold salted water, cover with a lid, bring to the boil, and cook for 15 minutes or until tender. Drain, add the butter and milk, season with salt and freshly ground black pepper, and mash until smooth. You may need a little more milk to get the right consistency.

2. Meanwhile, melt the butter for the pie in a large saucepan. Stir in the onion and leeks, cover with a lid, and cook over a low heat for 15 minutes or until the onion is soft. Stir in the flour and, over a high heat, gradually add the milk, stirring all the time until the sauce is smooth and thick.

3. Remove from the heat, add all the remaining ingredients (except the cheese), and season with salt and freshly ground black pepper. Spoon into the ovenproof dish and level the top. Cover with the mash and fluff up the surface with a fork. Sprinkle over the cheese.

4. Bake for 35 minutes (50 minutes for 12) or until golden brown and piping hot. Serve at once with wedges of lemon.

### IN THE AGA
Bake on the second set of runners in the roasting oven for 35 minutes (50 minutes for 12).

---

### PREPARE AHEAD
*The pie can be made up to the end of step 3 up to 1 day ahead. Not suitable for freezing.*

# CLASSIC POACHED SALMON WITH HERB SAUCE

*We find this the best way to poach salmon and over the years we have perfected the method so it's foolproof. If you are cooking a very large salmon and it is too big for the fish kettle, cut off the head before poaching. The timing will be the same. If cooking for a very large crowd, buy extra salmon and poach separately.*

## SERVES 12

**Special equipment** *fish kettle*

2.7–3kg (6–6½lb) salmon (head on), gutted

small handful of salt

12 black peppercorns

cucumber, sliced into thin ribbons, to garnish

24 cooked North Atlantic prawns, shelled but heads left on, to garnish

sprigs of parsley or dill, to garnish

**For the sauce**

2 tbsp fresh dill

2 tbsp fresh chives

2 tbsp fresh mint

2 tbsp fresh flat-leaf parsley

200ml tub full-fat crème fraîche

200g tub full-fat Greek yogurt

300ml (10fl oz) good mayonnaise

1 tbsp caster sugar

juice of 1 lemon

## SERVES 20

**Special equipment** *fish kettle*

5–5.5kg (11–12lb) salmon (head on), gutted

small handful of salt

12 black peppercorns

cucumber, sliced into thin ribbons, to garnish

40 cooked North Atlantic prawns, shelled but heads left on, to garnish

sprigs of parsley or dill, to garnish

**For the sauce**

4 tbsp fresh dill

4 tbsp fresh chives

4 tbsp fresh mint

4 tbsp fresh flat-leaf parsley

400ml tub full-fat crème fraîche

400g tub full-fat Greek yogurt

600ml (1 pint) good mayonnaise

2 tbsp caster sugar

juice of 2 lemons

1. Put the salmon in the fish kettle and pour in enough cold water from the tap to cover it completely. Remove the fish.

2. Add the salt and peppercorns to the water, then bring to a full rolling boil. Carefully lower the salmon into the water, bring back to the boil, and boil for 2 minutes per kilo (1 minute per pound) and no more. Do not cover with a lid.

3. Remove from the heat and cover with a tight-fitting lid. Set in a cool place (not the fridge) and leave undisturbed for about 8 hours – the salmon will continue to cook as it cools.

4. Transfer the salmon to a chopping board or work surface and carefully peel off the skin while it is still lukewarm. Using two fish slices and taking care not to damage the flesh, turn the fish over and peel the skin from the other side, leaving a little over the end of the tail and the head. Cut off the fins with scissors and cut a neat "V" in the tail.

5. To make the sauce, put the herbs into a food processor and whiz until chopped. Add the rest of the ingredients and season well with salt and freshly ground black pepper. Spoon into a serving dish (not silver as the sauce will discolour), cover, and chill until required.

6. To serve, arrange the salmon on a platter and decorate with cucumber ribbons and prawns. Finish with the sprigs of parsley or dill. Serve cold with the lemon and herb sauce.

## PREPARE AHEAD

*The salmon can be poached up to 1 day ahead, then skinned and wrapped tightly in cling film to keep it moist. Garnish to serve. The herb sauce is better made 1 day ahead but can be made up to 3 days ahead. Not suitable for freezing.*

# SALMON SALSA VERDE EN CROÛTE

*The traditional Italian salsa verde sauce gives an amazing flavour and a wonderful green layer.*

## SERVES 6

**For the salsa verde**

3 tbsp flat-leaf parsley

2 tbsp fresh basil leaves

2 tbsp fresh mint leaves

1 garlic clove, halved

3 anchovy fillets

2 tbsp Dijon mustard

1 egg yolk

freshly ground black pepper

2 x 350g (12oz) salmon fillets, skinned and bones removed

375g packet all-butter puff pastry

a little plain flour, to dust

1 egg beaten with 1 tbsp milk

**For the dressing**

2 large firm but ripe tomatoes

salt

2 spring onions, finely chopped

2 tsp caster sugar

2 tbsp white wine vinegar

4 tbsp olive oil

½ tsp Dijon mustard

1 tbsp freshly chopped parsley

## SERVES 12

**For the salsa verde**

75g (2½oz) flat-leaf parsley

25g (scant 1oz) fresh basil leaves

25g (scant 1oz) fresh mint leaves

2 garlic cloves, halved

6 anchovy fillets

4 tbsp Dijon mustard

1 egg

freshly ground black pepper

2 x 750g (1lb 10oz) salmon fillets, skinned and bones removed

500g packet all-butter puff pastry

a little plain flour, to dust

1 egg beaten with 1 tbsp milk

**For the dressing**

4 large firm but ripe tomatoes

salt

3 spring onions, finely chopped

1 tbsp caster sugar

4 tbsp white wine vinegar

8 tbsp olive oil

1 tsp Dijon mustard

2 tbsp freshly chopped parsley

1. To make the salsa verde, put the herbs into a food processor and whiz. Add the garlic, anchovies, mustard, egg yolk (whole egg for 12), and some freshly ground black pepper and whiz until smooth.

2. Arrange one fillet on a chopping board and spread the salsa verde over in an even layer. Sit the other fillet on top to look like a whole fish.

3. Cut two-thirds of the pastry from the block (freeze the rest for later) and place on a piece of lightly floured baking parchment. Roll it out so it is long enough and wide enough to enclose the fillets completely. Sit the fillets in the centre and brush the pastry with the beaten egg (reserving some for later). Fold the ends of the pastry over the fillet and bring the sides up to meet at the top. Pinch the edges together with your fingers. Chill for a minimum of 30 minutes.

4. Preheat the oven to 240°C (220°C fan/475°F/Gas 9) (220°C (200°C fan/425°F/Gas 7) for 12) and put a baking sheet in to get hot. Brush the en croûte with beaten egg, then coarsely grate the frozen pastry and scatter on top.

5. Transfer the en croûte (still on the baking parchment) to the hot baking sheet and bake for 25–30 minutes (35–40 minutes for 12) or until the pastry is golden and cooked at the top and bottom. Allow to rest at room temperature for about 15 minutes.

6. Meanwhile, make the dressing. Plunge the tomatoes into boiling salted water for 1 minute, then remove with a slotted spoon, plunge into cold water, and drain. Remove the skins, then deseed, cut into dice, and tip into a bowl. Add the remaining ingredients, season with salt and freshly ground black pepper, and stir to combine.

7. Carve the en croûte into thick slices and serve the dressing alongside in a bowl.

## IN THE AGA

Bake on a cold baking sheet on the floor of the roasting oven for 25–30 minutes (35–40 minutes for 12). Check after 20 minutes to see if the pastry underneath is getting too brown. If it is, lift the baking sheet onto the grid shelf on the floor of the roasting oven for the remaining time.

## PREPARE AHEAD AND FREEZE

*The en croûte can be made up to the end of step 3 up to 12 hours ahead. The dressing can be made up to 2 days ahead. Freeze the uncooked en croûte for up to 2 months.*

# SALMON FILLET WITH TARRAGON BUTTER SAUCE

## SERVES 6

1 onion, finely chopped

1 carrot, finely chopped

1 celery stick, finely chopped

1 large tomato, cut in half

360ml (12fl oz) water

1 heaped tbsp freshly chopped tarragon (stalks reserved)

a little olive oil, to grease

salt and freshly ground black pepper

750–900g (1lb 10oz–2lb) side of salmon fillet in one piece, skin on

150g (5½oz) cold butter (straight from the fridge), cut into cubes

## SERVES 12

2 onions, finely chopped

2 carrots, finely chopped

2 celery sticks, finely chopped

2 large tomatoes, cut in half

750ml (1¼ pints) water

2 heaped tbsp freshly chopped tarragon (stalks reserved)

a little olive oil, to grease

salt and freshly ground black pepper

1.8kg (4lb) side of salmon or 2 x 750–900g (1lb 10oz–2lb) sides of salmon

300g (11oz) cold butter (straight from the fridge), cut into cubes

*The tomato in the vegetable stock gives the sauce a wonderful colour. To allow the flavours to infuse, prepare it the day before. You can cook individual salmon fillets if you like, but we prefer doing it this way, as the fish doesn't dry out. Serve with new potatoes and fresh green vegetables or salad.*

1. Put the onion, carrot, celery, tomato, and water into a saucepan. Add the reserved tarragon stalks and bring to the boil. Cover with a lid and simmer over a low heat for 10 minutes. Set aside for a minimum of 1 hour (ideally overnight) for the flavours to infuse.

2. Preheat the oven to 180°C (160°C fan/350°F/Gas 4). Line a baking sheet with foil, oil it lightly, and sprinkle with salt and freshly ground black pepper.

3. Lay the salmon skin side down on a board. Using a sharp knife, divide it into equal serving portions, cutting through the flesh until the knife touches the skin, but not cutting through it. Lay skin side up on the foil and bake for 20 minutes (25–30 minutes for 12) or until matt pink and just done. The precise timing will depend on the thickness.

4. To make the sauce, strain the vegetable stock into a saucepan, then boil rapidly until it reduces by half. Put the butter into a heatproof bowl, pour over the boiling stock, and whiz with a hand blender or in a food processor until smooth.

5. Peel the skin from the fish and discard (if it doesn't peel easily, it isn't quite cooked, so pop it back into the oven for a few minutes). Transfer the fish portions to a platter or plates. Add the tarragon to the hot sauce, pour over the fish, and serve.

### IN THE AGA

At step 1, cover with a lid and transfer to the simmering oven for 15 minutes. Bake the salmon on the second set of runners in the roasting oven for 15 minutes (20 minutes for 12).

### PREPARE AHEAD

*The sauce can be made up to 2 days ahead. Add the tarragon while reheating. The salmon can be cooked the day before and served cold. Not suitable for freezing.*

# SALMON AND ASPARAGUS WITH A BASIL SAUCE

*Salmon fillets, cooked simply and slowly, are complemented by a rich sauce of asparagus, cream, and pesto. Don't be tempted to pile the fillets on top of each other to cook them -- bake in a single layer in separate roasting tins. Serve with baby new potatoes or, for a special occasion, Jersey Royals.*

## SERVES 6

6 x 150g (5½oz) centre-cut salmon fillets, skinned

salt and freshly ground black pepper

12 asparagus spears

300ml (10fl oz) double cream

juice of ½ lemon

4 tbsp pesto

## SERVES 12

12 x 150g (5½oz) centre-cut salmon fillets, skinned

salt and freshly ground black pepper

24 asparagus spears

600ml (1 pint) double cream

juice of 1 lemon

8 tbsp pesto

1. Preheat the oven to 140°C (120°C fan/275°F/Gas 1). Line a roasting tin with a large piece of foil and arrange the salmon fillets on top in a single layer. Season with salt and freshly ground black pepper, then scrunch the sides of the foil at the top so the fillets are enclosed.

2. Cook in the oven for 50 minutes (1 hour for 12) or until the salmon is matt pink and just done. Don't let it overcook or it will become dry.

3. Meanwhile, trim the woody ends from the asparagus spears and discard, then cut off 5cm (2in) from each tip and put to one side. Finely shred the stalks, cutting them diagonally into thin slices.

4. Bring a pan of salted water to the boil, add the asparagus tips and shredded stalks, then bring back to the boil and cook for 3 minutes. Drain, separate the tips from the stalks, and keep warm.

5. Heat the cream, lemon juice, and pesto in a pan until hot. Add the cooked shredded stalks and season with salt and freshly ground black pepper.

6. To serve, arrange the hot salmon fillets on a serving plate. Pour over the sauce and garnish each fillet with two asparagus tips. Serve any leftover sauce separately.

### IN THE AGA

Cook the salmon in the simmering oven for 45 minutes (55 minutes for 12).

### PREPARE AHEAD

*The asparagus can be cooked up to 8 hours ahead, then drained, refreshed in cold water, and drained again. Plunge the asparagus tips into boiling water for 30 seconds to warm through. The sauce can be made up 8 hours ahead. Not suitable for freezing.*

# TROUT FILLETS WITH ROASTED VEGETABLES AND HOT LEMON DRESSING

*A wonderful all-in-one dish — new potatoes, onions, and courgettes with lightly cooked trout fillets and a fresh sauce.*

## SERVES 6

750g (1lb 10oz) baby new potatoes, halved lengthways

3 medium onions, peeled and cut into 8 wedges

salt and freshly ground black pepper

3 tbsp olive oil

4 small courgettes, thinly sliced

6 trout fillets, skin on

**For the sauce**

6 tbsp freshly chopped parsley

finely grated zest and juice of 1 large lemon

85g (3oz) butter, melted

## SERVES 12

1.5kg (3lb 3oz) baby new potatoes, halved lengthways

5 large onions, peeled and cut into 8 wedges

salt and freshly ground black pepper

6 tbsp olive oil

8 small courgettes, thinly sliced

12 trout fillets, skin on

**For the sauce**

large bunch of parsley, chopped

finely grated zest and juice of 2 large lemons

175g (6oz) butter, melted

1. Preheat the oven to 200°C (180°C fan/400°F/Gas 6). Put the potatoes and onions in a pan, cover with cold salted water, bring to the boil, and cook for 10 minutes or until just tender.

2. Drain, toss in half the oil, season with black pepper, and arrange in a single layer in a large roasting tin or ovenproof dish (two tins or dishes for 12). Roast for 20 minutes (30 minutes for 12) or until the potatoes and onions are just tender.

3. Toss the courgettes in a bowl with the remaining oil and season with salt and freshly ground black pepper.

4. Season the flesh side of the trout with salt and freshly ground black pepper. Stir the contents of the roasting tin, then lay the trout skin side up in a single layer on top of them. Scatter the courgettes around the fish. Return to the oven and cook for 12–15 minutes (20–30 minutes for 12) or until the fish is tender.

5. Meanwhile, make the sauce: mix the parsley, lemon zest, and lemon juice together in a bowl. Stir in the butter and season with salt and freshly ground black pepper.

6. Peel the skin from the fish and discard. If the skin doesn't come off easily, the trout is not quite cooked, so pop it back into the oven for a few minutes. Transfer the fish to a serving plate with the vegetables, then spoon some of the hot sauce over the top. Serve the rest of the sauce separately.

### IN THE AGA

At step 2, roast on the floor of the roasting oven for 15 minutes (30 minutes for 12). At step 4, cook on the second set of runners in the roasting oven for 12 minutes (15 minutes for 12).

## PREPARE AHEAD

The vegetables can be cooked up to the end of step 2 up to 6 hours ahead. The sauce can be made up to 1 day ahead. Not suitable for freezing.

# HOT BAKED TROUT WITH TOMATO AND BASIL SALSA

*An impressive centrepiece for a dinner party or buffet table. Cooking the trout with the skin on gives it a fresher flavour and keeps it moist.*

**SERVES 6**

a little olive oil

salt and freshly ground black pepper

750g (1lb 10oz) trout fillet, skin on

**For the salsa**

500g (1lb 2oz) tomatoes

½ cucumber

3 spring onions, finely chopped

3 tbsp freshly shredded basil

3 tbsp olive oil

1 tsp caster sugar

a good dash of Tabasco

1 tbsp lemon juice

**SERVES 12**

a little olive oil

salt and freshly ground black pepper

1.35kg (3lb) trout fillet or 2 x 750g (1lb 10oz) trout fillets, skin on

**For the salsa**

1kg (2¼lb) tomatoes

1 cucumber

6 spring onions, finely chopped

6 tbsp freshly shredded basil

6 tbsp olive oil

2 tsp caster sugar

a good dash of Tabasco

2 tbsp lemon juice

1. Preheat the oven to 200°C (180°C fan/400°F/Gas 6). Line a baking sheet with foil, then brush it with a little olive oil and sprinkle with salt and freshly ground black pepper.

2. Lay the trout skin side down on a board. Using a sharp knife, cut it into equal serving portions, taking care not to cut through the skin. Lay it skin side up on the baking sheet and bake for 15–20 minutes (30 minutes for 12) or until just cooked.

3. Meanwhile, make the salsa. To skin the tomatoes, place them in boiling water for 20 seconds or until the skin splits, then remove. When cool enough to handle, carefully peel the skin from the tomato with a paring knife. Slice in half, remove the seeds, and cut the flesh into small dice. Peel the cucumber with a vegetable peeler, then slice in half lengthways. Discard the seeds and cut the flesh into dice the size of the tomatoes.

4. Mix the tomatoes, cucumber, onions, and half the basil in a bowl. Whisk the oil, sugar, Tabasco, lemon juice, and some salt and freshly ground black pepper in a separate bowl, then pour over the tomatoes and stir to combine.

5. Peel the skin from the trout and discard (if it does not peel off easily, it is not quite cooked, so pop it back in the oven for a few minutes). Arrange on a serving platter.

6. Spoon the salsa down the centre of the fish and scatter with the remaining basil. If you have any salsa left over, serve it in a separate bowl. Serve the trout hot or warm with the cold salsa.

### IN THE AGA

Bake on the second set of runners in the roasting oven for 12–15 minutes (20–25 minutes for 12).

### PREPARE AHEAD

*The salsa can be made up to 8 hours ahead. Not suitable for freezing.*

# LOCH FYNE HADDOCK BAKE

*Named after the area of Scotland famous for its fish and seafood, this pie is quick to make. It's unusual in that the potatoes are in the bake and not mashed on top. Make sure you buy undyed smoked haddock – the dyed fillets are bright yellow and very unnatural-looking. Serve with peas or salad.*

## SERVES 6

**Special equipment** *2 litre (3½ pint) shallow wide-based ovenproof dish*

350g (12oz) King Edward potatoes or other floury potatoes, peeled and cut into 2cm (¾in) cubes

salt and freshly ground black pepper

500g (1lb 2oz) baby spinach

1 tbsp olive oil

250g (9oz) small chestnut mushrooms, sliced in half

knob of butter, to grease

3 eggs, hardboiled, peeled, and sliced into quarters

500g (1lb 2oz) undyed smoked haddock, skinned and cut into 5cm (2in) pieces

300ml (10fl oz) double cream

2 tsp grainy mustard

75g (2½oz) mature Cheddar cheese, grated

## SERVES 12

**Special equipment** *2 x 2 litre (3½ pint) shallow wide-based ovenproof dishes or 1 x 4 litre (7 pint) dish*

750g (1lb 10oz) King Edward potatoes or other floury potatoes, peeled and cut into 2cm (¾in) cubes

salt and freshly ground black pepper

1kg (2¼lb) baby spinach

2 tbsp olive oil

500g (1lb 2oz) small chestnut mushrooms, sliced in half

knob of butter, to grease

6 eggs, hardboiled, peeled, and sliced into quarters

1kg (2¼lb) undyed smoked haddock, skinned and cut into 5cm (2in) pieces

600ml (1 pint) double cream

4 tsp grainy mustard

175g (6oz) mature Cheddar cheese, grated

1. Preheat the oven to 200°C (180°C fan/400°F/Gas 6). Meanwhile, put the potatoes into a pan of cold salted water, cover with a lid, bring to the boil, and cook for 10–15 minutes or until just cooked. Drain well and set aside.

2. Heat a large frying pan, add the spinach, and cook for a few minutes or until just wilted but still holding its shape. Drain well in a colander, squeezing to remove excess liquid, then set aside. You may need to do this in batches.

3. Heat the oil in the frying pan, add the mushrooms, and fry for 3 minutes or until just cooked.

4. Grease the ovenproof dish(es) with the butter, then arrange the potatoes, spinach, and mushrooms in the base. Scatter over the eggs and haddock and season with salt and freshly ground black pepper.

5. Mix the cream and mustard in a bowl with some salt and freshly ground black pepper, then pour over the fish mixture, and sprinkle with the cheese.

6. Bake for 20–25 minutes (30–35 minutes for two dishes for 12 or 40–45 minutes for one dish for 12) or until golden on top and cooked through.

### IN THE AGA

Bake on the top set of runners in the roasting oven for 20 minutes (45 minutes for 12) or until golden and cooked through.

### PREPARE AHEAD

*The bake can be made up to the end of step 4 up to 8 hours ahead. Not suitable for freezing.*

# TUNA SALADE NIÇOISE

*This is a great main course for a picnic, but it's also good as a side dish – in which case it will feed more. Serve with fresh crusty bread.*

**SERVES 6**

100g (3½oz) French beans, trimmed

salt and freshly ground black pepper

6 eggs

3 small Baby Gem lettuces

6 tomatoes, quartered

225g (8oz) baby new potatoes, cooked and halved lengthways

2 x 200g cans tuna in oil, drained

12 canned anchovy fillets, drained

100g (3½oz) pitted black olives, halved lengthways

1 red onion, finely sliced

**For the dressing**

4 tbsp good olive oil

2 tbsp grainy mustard

2 tbsp white wine vinegar

2 tsp caster sugar

juice of 1 lemon

**SERVES 12**

200g (7oz) French beans, trimmed

salt and freshly ground black pepper

12 eggs

6 small Baby Gem lettuces

12 tomatoes, quartered

450g (1lb) baby new potatoes, cooked and halved lengthways

2 x 400g cans tuna in oil, drained

24 canned anchovy fillets, drained

225g (8oz) pitted black olives, halved lengthways

2 red onions, finely sliced

**For the dressing**

8 tbsp good olive oil

4 tbsp grainy mustard

4 tbsp white wine vinegar

4 tsp caster sugar

juice of 2 lemons

1.  Cook the beans in boiling salted water for 4 minutes or until just tender. Drain, refresh in cold water, and set aside.

2.  Put the eggs into a saucepan, cover with water, and bring to the boil. Boil for 7 minutes, then drain and cover again with cold water. Peel and slice into quarters.

3.  Cut each lettuce into six wedges. Place in a serving bowl with the beans, eggs, tomatoes, potatoes, tuna, anchovies, olives, and onion and mix together. Season with salt and freshly ground black pepper.

4.  Mix the ingredients for the dressing in a bowl, pour over the salad, toss gently, and serve.

**PREPARE AHEAD**

The salad can be prepared up to the end of step 3 up to 6 hours ahead. Dress just before serving. Not suitable for freezing.

# MACARONI TUNA BAKE

## SERVES 6

**Special equipment** *1.5 litre (2¾ pint) shallow wide-based ovenproof dish*

350g (12oz) macaroni

salt and freshly ground black pepper

150g (5½oz) frozen peas

75g (2½oz) butter

75g (2½oz) plain flour

900ml (1½ pints) hot milk

1 tbsp Dijon mustard

juice of ½ lemon

75g (2½oz) strong Cheddar cheese, grated

75g (2½oz) Parmesan cheese, freshly grated

2 x 185g cans tuna in springwater, drained

4 large tomatoes, cut in quarters, deseeded, and roughly chopped

## SERVES 12

**Special equipment** *2.4 litre (4 pint) shallow wide-based ovenproof dish*

750g (1lb 10oz) macaroni

salt and freshly ground black pepper

300g (10oz) frozen peas

175g (6oz) butter

175g (6oz) plain flour

1.7 litres (3 pints) hot milk

2 tbsp Dijon mustard

juice of 1 lemon

175g (6oz) strong Cheddar cheese, grated

175g (6oz) Parmesan cheese, freshly grated

4 x 185g cans tuna in springwater, drained

8 large tomatoes, cut in quarters, deseeded, and roughly chopped

*Guests of all ages will enjoy this tasty tuna, macaroni, and cheese bake – Mary's grandchildren love it! And it really is extremely economical to make. Serve with crusty bread or dressed salad.*

1. Preheat the oven to 200°C (180°C fan/400°F/Gas 6). Cook the macaroni in boiling salted water according to the packet instructions. Add the peas 3 minutes before the end of cooking. Drain, refresh in cold water, and set aside.

2. Melt the butter in a saucepan, add the flour, and stir over the heat for 1 minute. Add the hot milk slowly, whisking until the sauce is smooth and thick.

3. Add the mustard, lemon juice, and two-thirds of each cheese. Add the pasta and peas and lots of salt and freshly ground black pepper. Stir in the tuna and mix together. Spoon into the ovenproof dish, scatter over the tomatoes, and sprinkle over the remaining cheese.

4. Bake for 20–25 minutes (30–35 minutes for 12) or until lightly golden and crispy.

### IN THE AGA

Bake in the middle of the roasting oven for 20–25 minutes (35–40 minutes for 12) or until golden and crispy.

### PREPARE AHEAD

*The dish can be made up to the end of step 3 up to 1 day ahead. Not suitable for freezing.*

# SEAFOOD LINGUINE

## SERVES 6

225g (8oz) dried linguine

salt and freshly ground
black pepper

150g (5½oz) (shelled
weight) raw tiger prawns

small knob of butter

150g (5½oz) raw squid,
sliced

150g (5½oz) raw queen
scallops, sliced in half
horizontally

1 large shallot, finely
chopped

250ml (8fl oz) dry white wine

200ml (7fl oz) double
cream

juice of 1 large lemon

small bunch of dill,
chopped

## SERVES 12

450g (1lb) dried linguine

salt and freshly ground
black pepper

300g (11oz) (shelled
weight) raw tiger prawns

large knob of butter

300g (11oz) raw squid,
sliced

300g (11oz) raw queen
scallops, sliced in half
horizontally

2 large shallots, finely
chopped

600ml (1 pint) dry white
wine

450ml (15fl oz) double
cream

juice of 2 large lemons

large bunch of dill,
chopped

*We usually buy ready-peeled prawns for this, but if you
can only find them with their shells on, buy a few extra
and do it yourself – they're very easy to shell. Serve
with dressed salad.*

1.  Cook the linguine in boiling salted water according to the packet
instructions. Drain well.

2.  Shell the prawns if needed. Start by pulling off the head of the
prawn, then peel off the shell and legs with your fingers. If the
prawns are large, you may wish to slice along the back and remove
the dark intestinal vein.

3.  Heat the butter in a large frying pan, add the prawns, squid, and
scallops, and fry for 3–4 minutes or until the prawns have turned pink
and the squid and scallops are just cooked. Remove with a slotted
spoon and set aside.

4.  Add the shallot and wine to the pan, bring to the boil, and allow
to bubble over a high heat until the wine has reduced by half. Add
the cream and return to the boil.

5.  Add the cooked seafood and toss together. Season with salt and
freshly ground black pepper, stir in the pasta, lemon juice, and dill,
heat through thoroughly, and serve.

## PREPARE AHEAD

*The dish is best prepared and served straightaway.
Not suitable for freezing.*

# SPAGHETTI WITH KING PRAWNS AND TOMATOES

*This full-flavoured tomato and garlic sauce with a hint of chilli is excellent with spaghetti. The breadcrumbs give a lovely crispy texture – make sure they are very fine. Serve with dressed salad.*

### SERVES 6

300g (11oz) spaghetti

salt and freshly ground black pepper

4 tbsp olive oil

50g (1¾oz) very fine fresh brown breadcrumbs

finely grated zest and juice of 1 lemon

1 large shallot, finely chopped

4 garlic cloves, crushed

1 red chilli, halved, deseeded, and finely diced

300g (11oz) shelled cooked king prawns

6 large ripe tomatoes, halved, deseeded, and roughly chopped

1 large bunch of flat-leaf parsley, chopped

freshly grated Parmesan cheese, to serve

### SERVES 12

600g (1lb 5oz) spaghetti

salt and freshly ground black pepper

7 tbsp olive oil

100g (3½oz) very fine fresh brown breadcrumbs

finely grated zest and juice of 2 lemons

2 large shallots, finely chopped

8 garlic cloves, crushed

2 red chillies, halved, deseeded, and finely diced

600g (1lb 5oz) shelled cooked king prawns

12 large ripe tomatoes, halved, deseeded, and roughly chopped

1 very large bunch of flat-leaf parsley, chopped

freshly grated Parmesan cheese, to serve

1. Cook the spaghetti in boiling salted water according to the packet instructions. Drain well.

2. Heat 1 tablespoon of the oil (1½ tablespoons for 12) in a deep frying pan, add the breadcrumbs and lemon zest, and fry for 1 minute or until crispy. Remove with a slotted spoon and set aside.

3. Add the remaining oil to the pan, stir in the shallot, garlic, and chilli and fry for 3–4 minutes or until starting to soften.

4. Stir in the prawns and tomatoes, then add the parsley and lemon juice.

5. Stir in the spaghetti, season with salt and freshly ground black pepper, and heat through thoroughly. Stir in the breadcrumbs and serve immediately with the Parmesan.

### PREPARE AHEAD

*This is best prepared and served immediately. Not suitable for freezing.*

# TIGER PRAWN BALTI

*Tiger prawns are expensive, but this is a great dish for a special occasion. To cut costs, you could use a mixture of tiger prawns and other cooked seafood, such as mussels and squid. Serve with Pilaf rice (page 247) or, as part of a buffet, with Vegetable korma (page 245) and Aromatic beef curry (page 152).*

## SERVES 6

3 tbsp sunflower oil

2 large onions, finely chopped

2 red peppers, halved, deseeded, and roughly chopped

6cm (2½in) piece fresh root ginger, peeled and finely grated

3 red chillies, halved, deseeded, and roughly chopped

1 tsp turmeric

2 tsp ground coriander

2 tsp garam masala

1 tsp black mustard seeds

2 x 400g cans chopped tomatoes

300ml (10fl oz) water

4 tbsp tomato purée

4 tsp lime pickle

juice of 1 lime

2 tbsp honey

salt and freshly ground black pepper

1kg (2¼lb) raw shelled tiger prawns

1 heaped tbsp freshly chopped coriander, to garnish

## SERVES 12

5 tbsp sunflower oil

4 large onions, finely chopped

4 red peppers, halved, deseeded, and roughly chopped

18cm (7in) piece fresh root ginger, peeled and finely grated

6 red chillies, halved, deseeded, and roughly chopped

2 tsp turmeric

4 tsp ground coriander

4 tsp garam masala

2 tsp black mustard seeds

4 x 400g cans chopped tomatoes

600ml (1 pint) water

8 tbsp tomato purée

2 heaped tbsp lime pickle

juice of 2 limes

4 tbsp honey

salt and freshly ground black pepper

2kg (4½lb) raw shelled tiger prawns

2 heaped tbsp freshly chopped coriander, to garnish

1. Heat the oil in a large frying pan or saucepan, add the onions, peppers, ginger, and chillies and fry over a high heat for 2 minutes or until starting to soften.

2. Cover with a lid, then reduce the heat and cook for 10 minutes or until the onions and peppers are nearly soft. Add the spices and stir over a high heat to coat the vegetables.

3. Add the tomatoes, water, tomato purée, lime pickle, lime juice, and honey. Bring to the boil and simmer for 10 minutes (15 minutes for 12). Season with salt and freshly ground black pepper, add the prawns, and cook for 5 minutes (5–10 minutes for 12) or until they turn pink and are cooked through. Garnish with the coriander and serve straightaway.

### IN THE AGA

At step 2, cover with a lid and transfer to the simmering oven to soften for 30 minutes, then continue on the boiling plate.

### PREPARE AHEAD AND FREEZE

*The sauce can be made up to 1 day ahead. Reheat to serve, adding the prawns at the end. Freeze the sauce without the prawns for up to 1 month.*

# MAIN COURSES VEGETARIAN AND VEGETABLE SIDES

*Whether at a special dinner, on a buffet table, or at a supper party, vegetarians will love these mains. We've also included a selection of potato, rice, and vegetable side dishes, which go down very well served alongside many of the main courses in this book.*

# MUSHROOM AND SPINACH CANNELLONI

*To make the cannelloni easier to serve, arrange them in neat rows in a rectangular dish. Serve with dressed salad and crusty bread.*

### SERVES 6

**Special equipment** *1.7 litre (3 pint) wide-based ovenproof dish*

1 tbsp olive oil

500g (1lb 2oz) mixed mushrooms, such as shiitake, chestnut, and button, roughly chopped

3 garlic cloves, crushed

225g (8oz) baby spinach, roughly chopped

salt and freshly ground black pepper

400g can tomatoes, drained and juice discarded

2 tbsp pesto

75g (2½oz) freshly grated Parmesan cheese or vegetarian alternative

12–14 cannelloni tubes

**For the sauce**

75g (2½oz) butter

75g (2½oz) plain flour

900ml (1½ pints) hot milk

100ml (3½fl oz) double cream

2 heaped tbsp pesto

### SERVES 12

**Special equipment** *2 x 1.7 litre (3 pint) wide-based ovenproof dishes or 1 x 3 litre (5¼ pint) dish*

2 tbsp olive oil

1kg (2¼lb) mixed mushrooms, such as shiitake, chestnut, and button, roughly chopped

6 garlic cloves, crushed

500g (1lb 2oz) baby spinach, roughly chopped

salt and freshly ground black pepper

2 x 400g cans tomatoes, drained and juice discarded

4 tbsp pesto

175g (6oz) freshly grated Parmesan cheese or vegetarian alternative

24–28 cannelloni tubes

**For the sauce**

175g (6oz) butter

175g (6oz) plain flour

1.7 litres (3 pints) hot milk

200ml (7fl oz) double cream

4 heaped tbsp pesto

1.  Heat the oil in a frying pan, add the mushrooms, and fry over a high heat for 2 minutes or until just cooked. Add the garlic and spinach and toss together until the spinach is just wilted. Season with salt and freshly ground black pepper and set aside to cool.

2.  To make the sauce, melt the butter in a saucepan, whisk in the flour, and cook for 1 minute. Whisking all the time, gradually blend in the hot milk and the cream and bring to the boil. Season with salt and freshly ground black pepper, remove from the heat, and stir in the pesto.

3.  Put the tomatoes into a mixing bowl, add the cooled mushroom mixture, the pesto, and one-third of the cheese. Stir to combine.

4.  Preheat the oven to 200°C (180°C fan/400°F/Gas 6). Meanwhile, fill the cannelloni tubes with the mushroom and spinach filling, dividing it equally among them.

5.  Spoon one-third of the sauce into the base of the ovenproof dish and arrange the filled cannelloni on top in neat rows. Pour the remaining sauce over the top and sprinkle with the rest of the cheese.

6.  Bake for 30–35 minutes (45 minutes for 12) or until golden brown and bubbling.

### IN THE AGA

Bake the cannelloni on the grid shelf on the floor of the roasting oven for 15 minutes (25 minutes for 12), transfer to the top set of runners, and cook for a further 20 minutes (30 minutes for 12).

### PREPARE AHEAD

*The cannelloni can be made up to the end of step 5 up to 8 hours ahead. Not suitable for freezing.*

# MUSHROOMS AND SPINACH EN CROÛTE

*Whether it's on a buffet table or at a supper party, vegetarians will love this. Be sure to buy all-butter puff pastry, as it has a much better flavour than other kinds and is a little softer to handle. If you are serving large numbers, make multiple en croûtes – never make an en croûte larger than for 12, as the pastry may split. Serve with dressed salad leaves.*

**SERVES 6**

1 tbsp olive oil

½ large onion, chopped

1 garlic clove, crushed

150g (5½oz) chestnut mushrooms, sliced

225g (8oz) baby spinach

125g (4½oz) ricotta

75g (2½oz) Gruyère, grated

1 egg yolk

dash of Tabasco

salt and freshly ground black pepper

a little plain flour, to dust

½ x 500g packet ready-rolled all-butter puff pastry (freeze the other half for another occasion)

1 egg beaten with 1 tbsp milk

**SERVES 12**

1 tbsp olive oil

1 large onion, chopped

2 garlic cloves, crushed

250g (9oz) chestnut mushrooms, sliced

450g (1lb) baby spinach

200g (7oz) ricotta

175g (6oz) Gruyère, grated

1 egg

dash of Tabasco

salt and freshly ground black pepper

a little plain flour, to dust

375g packet ready-rolled all-butter puff pastry

1 egg beaten with 1 tbsp milk

1. Preheat the oven to 220°C (200°C fan/425°F/Gas 7) and put a baking sheet in the oven to get hot. Meanwhile, heat the oil in a non-stick frying pan, add the onion, and fry for 2 minutes. Lower the heat, cover with a lid, and cook for 15 minutes or until soft.

2. Add the garlic, mushrooms, and spinach and cook over a high heat for 3 minutes or until the spinach has wilted and the mushrooms have softened. Set aside to cool.

3. Meanwhile, put the ricotta, Gruyère, egg yolk (whole egg for 12), and Tabasco into a bowl, season with salt and freshly ground black pepper, and mix until combined. Stir into the cold spinach mixture.

4. Lay the sheet of pastry on a lightly floured work surface and roll it out into a 28 x 33cm (11 x 13in) rectangle (33 x 38cm/13 x 15in rectangle for 12).

5. Pile the spinach mixture into the middle, leaving a 4cm (1½in) gap around the edge. Brush the pastry with the egg mixture, then fold the ends over the filling and bring the sides up so they meet at the top. Crimp the ends together to seal, then brush the pastry with egg.

6. Transfer to the hot baking sheet and bake for 30 minutes (45 minutes for 12) or until golden all over. Leave to rest at room temperature for 5 minutes, then slice and serve hot.

### IN THE AGA

Sit the en croûte on a cold baking sheet and bake on the floor of the roasting oven for 25–30 minutes.

### PREPARE AHEAD

*The en croûte can be made up to the end of step 5 up to 8 hours ahead. Not suitable for freezing.*

# MUSHROOM STROGANOFF

## SERVES 6

25g (scant 1oz) butter

1 large onion, thinly sliced

2 garlic cloves, crushed

1 tbsp paprika

1 tbsp plain flour

100ml (3½fl oz) Marsala

200g tub full-fat crème fraîche

650g (1lb 7oz) mixed mushrooms, such as oyster, chestnut, and portabella, sliced

salt and freshly ground black pepper

juice of ½ lemon

1 tsp tomato purée

1 tsp caster sugar

50g (1¾oz) cornichons, chopped

## SERVES 12

50g (1¾oz) butter

2 large onions, thinly sliced

4 garlic cloves, crushed

2 tbsp paprika

2 tbsp plain flour

200ml (7fl oz) Marsala

2 x 200g tubs full-fat crème fraîche

1.1kg (2½lb) mixed mushrooms, such as oyster, chestnut, and portabella, sliced

salt and freshly ground black pepper

juice of 1 lemon

2 tsp tomato purée

2 tsp caster sugar

100g (3½oz) cornichons, chopped

*This is great for vegetarians and meat-eaters alike – the mass of tasty mushrooms is delicious and the cornichons (baby gherkins) give a lovely texture and sweetness. If you don't have any Marsala, you can use another fortified wine such as medium sherry or Port. Serve with rice.*

1. Melt the butter in a deep frying pan, add the onion, and fry for 1 minute. Lower the heat, cover with a lid, and simmer for 15 minutes or until soft.

2. Stir in the garlic, then sprinkle in the paprika and flour and mix well. Add the Marsala and crème fraîche and stir until thickened slightly.

3. Add the mushrooms, season with salt and freshly ground black pepper, and simmer over a low heat for 4 minutes (5–10 minutes for 12) or until the mushrooms are just cooked.

4. Stir in the lemon juice, tomato purée, and sugar and check the seasoning. Scatter over the cornichons and serve hot.

### IN THE AGA

Soften the onion in the simmering oven for 15 minutes, then continue on the boiling plate.

### PREPARE AHEAD

*This is best made and served immediately. Not suitable for freezing.*

# BUTTERNUT SQUASH LASAGNE

*A lasagne with wow factor. The star ingredient is butternut squash. Prepare the dish the day before if you can, so the lasagne sheets have time to soften in the sauce. Serve with salad and crusty bread.*

## SERVES 6

**Special equipment** *2.4 litre (4 pint) shallow wide-based ovenproof dish*

1 tbsp olive oil

225g (8oz) butternut squash (peeled weight), chopped into small cubes (see page 223)

1 red pepper, halved, deseeded, and diced

1 onion, roughly chopped

2 garlic cloves, crushed

225g (8oz) chestnut mushrooms, sliced

2 x 400g cans chopped tomatoes

1 tbsp tomato purée

2 tsp sugar

1 tbsp freshly chopped thyme

salt and freshly ground black pepper

100g (3½oz) spinach, chopped

6–8 sheets lasagne

### For the white sauce

75g (2½oz) butter

75g (2½oz) plain flour

900ml (1½ pints) hot milk

2 tsp Dijon mustard

100g (3½oz) Gruyère cheese, grated

250g (9oz) mozzarella, chopped into small cubes

## SERVES 12

**Special equipment** *2 x 2.4 litre (4 pint) shallow wide-based ovenproof dishes or 1 x 4 litre (7 pint) shallow wide-based ovenproof dish*

2 tbsp olive oil

500g (1lb 2oz) butternut squash (peeled weight), chopped into small cubes (see page 223)

2 red peppers, halved, deseeded, and diced

2 onions, roughly chopped

4 garlic cloves, crushed

500g (1lb 2oz) chestnut mushrooms, sliced

4 x 400g cans chopped tomatoes

2 tbsp tomato purée

1 heaped tbsp sugar

2 tbsp freshly chopped thyme

salt and freshly ground black pepper

200g (7oz) spinach, chopped

12–16 sheets lasagne

### For the white sauce

175g (6oz) butter

175g (6oz) plain flour

1.7 litres (3 pints) hot milk

1 heaped tbsp Dijon mustard

200g (7oz) Gruyère cheese, grated

500g (1lb 2oz) mozzarella, chopped into small cubes

1. Heat the oil in a large deep frying pan. Add the squash, pepper, onion, and garlic and fry over a moderate heat for 4–5 minutes or until the onion is starting to soften. Add the mushrooms, tomatoes, tomato purée, sugar, thyme, and some salt and freshly ground black pepper. Cover with a lid and simmer over a low heat for 20–30 minutes (35–40 minutes for 12) or until the vegetables are tender. Add the spinach and toss together until just wilted.

2. Meanwhile, make the white sauce. Melt the butter in a saucepan, add the flour, and stir over the heat for 1 minute. Slowly whisk in the hot milk until the sauce is smooth and thick. Season with salt and freshly ground black pepper, then stir in the mustard and half the Gruyère.

3. Spoon one-third of the tomato sauce over the base of the ovenproof dish, then spoon one-third of the white sauce on top. Arrange a single layer of lasagne over the white sauce and scatter over half the mozzarella. Spoon half the remaining tomato sauce on top, followed by half the remaining white sauce. Arrange another layer of lasagne on top and scatter over the remaining mozzarella. Spread the rest of the tomato sauce on top, followed by the rest of the white sauce, then sprinkle with the remaining Gruyère.

4. Transfer to the fridge for at least 6 hours or overnight so the lasagne starts to soften.

5. To serve, preheat the oven to 200°C (180°C fan/400°F/Gas 6), then bake the lasagne for 45 minutes (1–1¼ hours for 12) or until golden brown and bubbling around the edges.

### IN THE AGA

Cook the tomato sauce in the simmering oven for 20–30 minutes. Bake the lasagne in the middle of the roasting oven for 40–45 minutes (1 hour for 12).

### PREPARE AHEAD AND FREEZE

*The lasagne can be made up to the end of step 3 up to 2 days ahead. Freeze for up to 2 months.*

# SPICY ROAST SQUASH AND FETA SALAD

*This unusual salad goes well with barbecued meat or fish. To allow the flavours to infuse, make it up to six hours ahead.*

### SERVES 6

1 large butternut squash

1 red onion, thinly sliced

2 tbsp olive oil

salt and freshly ground black pepper

1 tsp ground cumin

100g (3½oz) feta cheese, crumbled

2 tbsp freshly chopped parsley

**For the dressing**

1 tbsp white wine vinegar

2 tbsp olive oil

1 tsp honey

½ garlic clove, crushed

### SERVES 12

2 large butternut squash

2 red onions, thinly sliced

4 tbsp olive oil

salt and freshly ground black pepper

1 tbsp ground cumin

200g (7oz) feta cheese, crumbled

4 tbsp freshly chopped parsley

**For the dressing**

2 tbsp white wine vinegar

4 tbsp olive oil

2 tsp honey

1 garlic clove, crushed

1. Preheat the oven to 220°C (200°C fan/425°F/Gas 7). Cut the squash in half lengthways, then scoop out the seeds and fibres with a spoon and discard. Then cut into sections and use a peeler to remove the skin. You may need a knife for larger squash. Cut the flesh into thin half-moon slices.

2. Scatter the squash and onion over the base of a roasting tin. Drizzle with the oil, season with salt and freshly ground black pepper, and toss to combine.

3. Roast for 25–30 minutes (30–35 minutes for 12) or until pale golden and just tender. Transfer to a mixing bowl with a slotted spoon, scatter over the cumin, and toss together. Set aside to cool.

4. When completely cool, stir in the feta and parsley. Put the ingredients for the dressing into a clean jam jar, tighten the lid, and shake well.

5. Pour the dressing over the salad and mix together. Transfer to a salad bowl and chill for up to 6 hours before serving.

### IN THE AGA

Roast the squash on the floor of the roasting oven for 20–25 minutes (25–30 minutes for 12).

### PREPARE AHEAD

*The salad can be made up to 6 hours ahead.*
*Not suitable for freezing.*

# BUTTERNUT SQUASH WITH SPINACH AND MUSHROOMS

*Half a small butternut squash per person is ideal at lunchtime or even as a main meal. Choose the smallest squash you can find – somewhere between 400–700g (14oz–1½lb) works well. Serve with dressed salad and bread.*

## SERVES 6

3 x 400g (14oz) butternut squash, halved lengthways through the stalk and seeds and fibres discarded

2 tbsp olive oil

150ml (5fl oz) water

salt and freshly ground black pepper

2 leeks, sliced

250g (9oz) chestnut mushrooms, quartered

100g (3½oz) baby spinach

100ml (3½fl oz) double cream

75g (2½oz) Parmesan cheese or vegetarian alternative, freshly grated

freshly chopped parsley, to garnish

## SERVES 12

6 x 400g (14oz) butternut squash, halved lengthways through the stalk and seeds and fibres discarded

4 tbsp olive oil

150ml (5fl oz) water

salt and freshly ground black pepper

4 leeks, sliced

500g (1lb 2oz) chestnut mushrooms, quartered

200g (7oz) baby spinach

200ml (7fl oz) double cream

175g (6oz) Parmesan cheese or vegetarian alternative, freshly grated

freshly chopped parsley, to garnish

1. Preheat the oven to 200°C (180°C fan/400°F/Gas 6). Put the squash cut side up in a large roasting tin (two tins for 12) and drizzle over the oil. Pour the water around them, season with salt and freshly ground black pepper, and roast in the oven for 45 minutes (1 hour for 12) or until the flesh is soft. Set aside and allow to cool slightly.

2. Meanwhile, put the leeks into a frying pan and cook slowly over a medium heat for 10 minutes or until soft. Add the mushrooms and spinach and stir together over a high heat for 10 minutes or until the spinach has wilted and the mushrooms are nearly cooked.

3. Remove the pan from the heat and stir in the cream, some salt and freshly ground black pepper, and half the cheese. Scoop out some of the cooked squash, leaving a 2cm (¾in) border inside each squash case, and stir into the spinach mixture. Spoon the mixture into the squash cases and sprinkle over the remaining cheese.

4. Bake for 20–25 minutes (55 minutes for 12) or until golden on top and heated through. Garnish with a sprinkle of parsley and serve.

### IN THE AGA
Roast the squash on the grid shelf on the floor of the roasting oven for 40–45 minutes. At step 4, bake on the highest set of runners in the roasting oven for 20–25 minutes (55 minutes for 12).

### PREPARE AHEAD
*The squash can be prepared up to the end of step 3 up to 1 day ahead. Not suitable for freezing.*

# RED PEPPER AND AUBERGINE SALAD WITH BASIL DRESSING

*Buy the freshest peppers and aubergines you can find, with smooth skins, not wrinkly. Toast the pine nuts in a dry frying pan until golden. Watch them carefully, as they burn quickly. Serve with crusty bread.*

### SERVES 6

2 red peppers, cut in half and deseeded

2 large aubergines, sliced in half lengthways and cut into 5mm (¼in) slices

2 tbsp olive oil

salt and freshly ground black pepper

100g (3½oz) baby spinach

**For the dressing**

2 tbsp olive oil

2 tbsp balsamic vinegar

1½ tbsp fresh basil pesto

50g (1¾oz) pine nuts, toasted

1 tbsp chopped basil

### SERVES 12

4 red peppers, cut in half and deseeded

4 large aubergines, sliced in half lengthways and cut into 5mm (¼in) slices

4 tbsp olive oil

salt and freshly ground black pepper

200g (7oz) baby spinach

**For the dressing**

4 tbsp olive oil

4 tbsp balsamic vinegar

3 tbsp fresh basil pesto

75g (2½oz) pine nuts, toasted

2 tbsp chopped basil

1.  Preheat the oven to 220°C (200°C fan/425°F/Gas 7). Arrange the pepper halves cut side down in a single layer on one end of a baking sheet, then lay the aubergine slices in a single layer at the other. (For 12, lay the peppers on one sheet and the aubergines on another sheet.) Drizzle over the oil and season with salt and freshly ground black pepper.

2.  Roast for 25–30 minutes or until the peppers are chargrilled and the aubergines tender and golden. Put the hot peppers into a polythene bag, seal tightly, and set aside until cold. This allows them to sweat, which makes it easier to remove the skins.

3.  Peel the skin from the peppers and discard. Cut the flesh into thin slices and transfer to a serving bowl. Add the aubergines and spinach and season with salt and freshly ground black pepper.

4.  To make the dressing, put the oil, vinegar, and pesto into a jam jar, seal with a lid, and shake vigorously.

5.  To serve, pour the dressing over the salad, toss well, then scatter with the pine nuts and the basil. For the flavours to infuse, it is best to do this about an hour before serving.

### IN THE AGA

Roast the peppers and aubergines on the top set of runners in the roasting oven for 30 minutes.

**PREPARE AHEAD**

*The salad can be made up to the end of step 2 up to 12 hours ahead. The dressing can be made up to 4 days ahead. Not suitable for freezing.*

# GLOBE ARTICHOKE AND PUY LENTIL SALAD

*Packed with lentils, herbs, and vegetables, this side salad makes a fantastic accompaniment to barbecued meats and fish.*

### SERVES 6

200g (7oz) dried Puy lentils

2 large celery sticks, finely diced

½ small red onion, finely diced

100g tub chargrilled artichokes in oil, drained and sliced into large pieces

2 tbsp freshly chopped flat-leaf parsley

2 tbsp freshly chopped mint

225g (8oz) cherry tomatoes, quartered

**For the dressing**

2 tbsp white wine vinegar

4 tbsp olive oil

1 garlic clove, crushed

2 tbsp sun-dried tomato paste

1 tbsp balsamic vinegar

salt and freshly ground black pepper

### SERVES 12

400g (11oz) dried Puy lentils

4 large celery sticks, finely diced

1 small red onion, finely diced

195g tub chargrilled artichokes in oil, drained and sliced into large pieces

small bunch of flat-leaf parsley, chopped

small bunch of mint, chopped

500g (1lb 2oz) cherry tomatoes, quartered

**For the dressing**

4 tbsp white wine vinegar

8 tbsp olive oil

2 garlic cloves, crushed

4 tbsp sun-dried tomato paste

2 tbsp balsamic vinegar

salt and freshly ground black pepper

1. Cook the lentils in boiling water for 15–20 minutes or until tender. Don't add salt or they might not soften. Drain and refresh in cold water.

2. Put the celery, onion, artichokes, herbs, and tomatoes into a large mixing bowl and stir in the lentils.

3. Mix the ingredients for the dressing in a small bowl and pour over the salad.

4. Season well with salt and freshly ground black pepper and chill in the fridge for 1 hour before serving.

### PREPARE AHEAD

The salad can be made up to the end of step 2 up to 12 hours ahead. Add the dressing up to 3 hours ahead. Not suitable for freezing.

# CHARGRILLED VEGETABLE AND HALLOUMI SKEWERS

*The sweet marinade for these kebabs helps the vegetables and cheese turn golden. Serve with salad and jacket potatoes.*

## SERVES 6

**Special equipment** *6 metal or wooden skewers (soak wooden skewers in water for 12 hours beforehand to prevent them burning)*

*2 medium red onions*

*salt*

*1 yellow pepper, halved, deseeded, and cut into 12 large pieces*

*1 red pepper, halved, deseeded, and cut into 12 large pieces*

*250g (9oz) halloumi cheese, cut into 18 cubes*

*12 small cherry tomatoes*

*2 tbsp olive oil, for frying*

**For the marinade**

*2 tbsp soy sauce*

*1 tbsp runny honey*

*1 red chilli, halved, deseeded, and finely chopped*

*1 large garlic clove, crushed*

## SERVES 12

**Special equipment** *12 metal or wooden skewers (soak wooden skewers in water for 12 hours beforehand to prevent them burning)*

*4 medium red onions*

*salt*

*2 yellow peppers, halved, deseeded, and cut into 12 large pieces each*

*2 red peppers, halved, deseeded, and cut into 24 large pieces*

*450g (1lb) halloumi cheese, cut into 36 cubes*

*24 small cherry tomatoes*

*4 tbsp olive oil, for frying*

**For the marinade**

*4 tbsp soy sauce*

*2 tbsp runny honey*

*2 red chillies, halved, deseeded, and finely chopped*

*2 large garlic cloves, crushed*

1. Slice each onion into six wedges, leaving the root end intact on each wedge so that the layers stay together during cooking. Bring a pan of salted water to the boil, add the onion wedges, the pieces of yellow pepper and the pieces of red pepper, and bring back to the boil. Boil for 5 minutes, then drain, refresh in cold water, and drain again.

2. In the order of your choice, thread two onion wedges, two pieces of yellow pepper, two pieces of red pepper, three cubes of cheese, and two tomatoes on to each skewer. Place in a shallow dish.

3. Put all the ingredients for the marinade into a small bowl and mix well. Pour over the kebabs and leave to marinate for at least 1 hour and up to 8 hours.

4. Heat the oil in a large frying pan or griddle pan, add the kebabs, and fry for 2–3 minutes on each side or until chargrilled and brown and the cheese is just soft. You may need to do this in batches. Alternatively, cook under the grill or on a barbecue. Serve hot on the skewers.

**PREPARE AHEAD**

*The kebabs can be made up to the end of step 2 up to 1 day ahead. They can be marinated for up to 8 hours. Not suitable for freezing.*

# AUBERGINES BAKED WITH FETA AND CHICKPEAS

*This is a winning recipe for vegetarians and perfect for a summer lunch with a green salad and crusty bread.*

## SERVES 6

3 medium aubergines, sliced in half lengthways

2 tbsp olive oil

salt and freshly ground black pepper

1 large onion, roughly chopped

2 garlic cloves, crushed

400g can chopped tomatoes

400g can chickpeas, drained and rinsed

2 tbsp sun-dried tomato paste

50g (1¾oz) pitted black or green olives, sliced in half

small bunch of fresh mint, chopped

100g (3½oz) feta cheese, crumbled

## SERVES 12

6 medium aubergines, sliced in half lengthways

4 tbsp olive oil

salt and freshly ground black pepper

2 large onions, roughly chopped

4 garlic cloves, crushed

2 x 400g cans chopped tomatoes

2 x 400g cans chickpeas, drained and rinsed

4 tbsp sun-dried tomato paste

100g (3½oz) pitted black or green olives, sliced in half

large bunch of fresh mint, chopped

200g (7oz) feta cheese, crumbled

1. Preheat the oven to 200°C (180°C fan/400°F/Gas 6). Put the aubergines cut side up in a roasting tin. Drizzle over half the oil, season with salt and freshly ground black pepper, and bake for 25 minutes (40 minutes for 12) or until the flesh is tender. Remove from the oven and leave to cool.

2. Heat the remaining oil in a frying pan. Add the onion and garlic and cook for 10 minutes or until soft. Add the tomatoes, chickpeas, tomato paste, and olives, and simmer for 5 minutes.

3. Meanwhile, scoop out a little of the flesh from the aubergine halves, leaving a 1cm (½in) border inside the aubergine cases. Add the flesh to the chickpea mixture and mix together. Add the mint and half the feta and season with salt and freshly ground black pepper. Spoon the mixture into the aubergine cases and top with the remaining feta.

4. Bake in the oven for 20 minutes (35 minutes for 12) or until the feta is tinged brown and the aubergines are hot.

### IN THE AGA

Bake the aubergines on the grid shelf on the floor of the roasting oven for 20–25 minutes. To serve, slide the roasting tin on the highest set of runners in the roasting oven and cook for 20–35 minutes or until golden.

### PREPARE AHEAD

*The dish can be assembled up to the end of step 3 up to 1 day ahead. Not suitable for freezing.*

# MINI AUBERGINE AND ROCKET PIZZAS

*These look so lovely and the soft-yolked quail's eggs on top are an extra treat. You'll find pizza bases in most supermarkets. The uncooked dough comes in packets ready for you to add your choice of topping. Marinated and grilled aubergines are available from the deli counter of the supermarket.*

## SERVES 6

**Special equipment** *10cm (4in) scone cutter*

2 x 150g (5½oz) pizza bases

100ml (3½fl oz) passata

2 tbsp sun-dried tomato paste

salt and freshly ground black pepper

200g tub marinated and grilled aubergines, drained (oil reserved) and sliced

100g (3½oz) Gruyère cheese, grated

6 quail's eggs

50g (1¾oz) rocket

## SERVES 12

**Special equipment** *10cm (4in) scone cutter*

4 x 150g (5½oz) pizza bases

200ml (7fl oz) passata

4 tbsp sun-dried tomato paste

salt and freshly ground black pepper

2 x 200g tubs marinated and grilled aubergines, drained (oil reserved) and sliced

225g (8oz) Gruyère cheese, grated

12 quail's eggs

100g (3½oz) rocket

1. Preheat the oven to 200°C (180°C fan/400°F/Gas 6). Using a 10cm (4in) scone cutter, cut three circles from each pizza base and arrange on a baking sheet (two baking sheets for 12).

2. Put the passata into a bowl, add the sun-dried tomato paste, season with salt and freshly ground black pepper, and mix well. Spread over the base of each dough circle.

3. Arrange the aubergine slices over the tomato and sprinkle with the cheese. Using the back of a tablespoon, make a well in the centre of each pizza, ready for the egg to sit in.

4. Bake for 8 minutes (10 minutes for 12) or until the pizzas are very hot, then carefully crack an egg into the well in each one, keeping the yolk intact. Return to the oven for 3 minutes or until the pizza is lightly golden, the egg white completely cooked, and the yolk just set.

5. Transfer to serving plates, arrange some rocket on top of each pizza, and drizzle with a little of the reserved aubergine oil. Serve at once.

### IN THE AGA
Bake on the grid shelf on the floor of the roasting oven for 8 minutes (8–10 minutes for 12), add the eggs, then bake for a further 3 minutes.

### PREPARE AHEAD AND FREEZE
*The pizzas can be made up to the end of step 3 up to 8 hours ahead. Freeze at the end of step 3 for up to 2 months.*

# GOAT'S CHEESE, THYME, AND ONION MARMALADE GALETTE

*A fantastic vegetarian lunch. Make two separate galettes for 12. If you don't have time to roast the peppers and make the onion marmalade, use shop-bought, but buy the best you can. Allow to cool slightly before slicing and serving warm with salad.*

## SERVES 6

2 red peppers, halved and deseeded

1 tbsp olive oil

salt and freshly ground black pepper

a little plain flour, to dust

320g packet ready-rolled puff pastry

2 x 150g tubs soft goat's cheese

1 tbsp fresh thyme leaves, plus a few sprigs to garnish

1 egg, beaten

**For the onion marmalade**

2 tbsp olive oil

3 large onions, sliced

1 tbsp caster sugar

1 tbsp balsamic vinegar

## SERVES 12

4 red peppers, halved and deseeded

2 tbsp olive oil

salt and freshly ground black pepper

a little plain flour, to dust

2 x 320g packets ready-rolled puff pastry

4 x 150g tubs soft goat's cheese

2 tbsp fresh thyme leaves, plus a few sprigs to garnish

1 egg, beaten

**For the onion marmalade**

3 tbsp olive oil

6 large onions, sliced

2 tbsp caster sugar

2 tbsp balsamic vinegar

1. Preheat the oven to 200°C (180°C fan/400°F/Gas 6). Arrange the peppers cut side down on a baking sheet, drizzle over the oil, and season with salt and freshly ground black pepper. Roast for 25–30 minutes or until blackened. Transfer to a polythene bag, seal, and set aside.

2. Meanwhile, make the onion marmalade. Heat the oil in a non-stick frying pan over a high heat, add the onions, and fry for 3 minutes or until starting to soften. Sprinkle in the sugar and vinegar and season with salt and freshly ground black pepper. Cover with a lid, lower the heat, and cook for 20–30 minutes or until the onions are soft. Set aside to cool.

3. Pop a baking sheet in the oven to get hot (two sheets for 12). Lightly flour a piece of baking parchment (two pieces for 12) and roll the pastry out into a 23 x 33cm (9 x 13in) rectangle (two rectangles for 12). Prick the base with a fork, leaving a border of 5cm (2in). Spread the cheese inside the border, scatter over the thyme, and spoon the onion marmalade on top. Peel the peppers, cut into strips, and scatter over the top. Brush the border with beaten egg.

4. Transfer the baking parchment and galette(s) to the baking sheet and bake for 20–25 minutes (30–35 minutes for 12) or until the pastry is golden. Garnish with thyme sprigs.

### IN THE AGA
Roast the peppers on the second set of runners in the roasting oven for 15–20 minutes. At step 2, transfer to the simmering oven for 20 minutes. Bake the galette on the floor of the roasting oven for 25–30 minutes. Bake two galettes individually.

### PREPARE AHEAD
*The galette can be made up to the end of step 3 up to 8 hours ahead. Not suitable for freezing.*

# PENNE ALLA PARMIGIANA

*This is a budget recipe. A sort of upmarket macaroni cheese – perfect for a crowd of hungry teenagers – and one they could very easily cook for themselves. Serve with dressed salad.*

**Special equipment**
1.5 litre (2¾ pint) shallow ovenproof dish

350g (12oz) penne

salt and freshly ground black pepper

50g (1¾oz) butter

50g (1¾oz) plain flour

1.2 litres (2 pints) hot milk

1 tbsp Dijon mustard

100g (3½oz) strong Cheddar cheese, grated

100g (3½oz) Parmesan cheese or vegetarian alternative, freshly grated

6 tomatoes

**Special equipment**
2.4 litre (4 pint) shallow ovenproof dish

600g (1lb 5oz) penne

salt and freshly ground black pepper

100g (3½oz) butter

100g (3½oz) plain flour

1.7 litres (3 pints) hot milk

2 tbsp Dijon mustard

175g (6oz) strong Cheddar cheese, grated

175g (6oz) Parmesan cheese or vegetarian alternative, freshly grated

8 large tomatoes

1. Preheat the oven to 200°C (180°C fan/400°F/Gas 6). Cook the penne in boiling salted water according to the packet instructions. Drain and refresh in cold water.

2. Melt the butter in a large saucepan, add the flour, and stir over the heat for 1 minute. Gradually add the hot milk, whisking all the time, until the sauce is smooth and thick.

3. Add the mustard and two-thirds of the Cheddar and Parmesan, then add the penne and some salt and freshly ground black pepper.

4. Spoon into the ovenproof dish. To prepare the tomatoes, halve them, loosen the seeds with a teaspoon, then gently squeeze them out into a bowl. Place the deseeded tomatoes cut side down on a board and chop. Arrange the chopped tomatoes on top of the pasta, and sprinkle over the remaining cheese.

5. Bake for 20–25 minutes (35–40 minutes for 12) or until lightly golden and crispy.

### IN THE AGA
Bake in the middle of the roasting oven for 20–25 minutes (30–35 minutes for 12) or until golden and crispy.

### PREPARE AHEAD
The dish can be made up to the end of step 4 up to 1 day ahead. Not suitable for freezing.

# PENNE WITH ASPARAGUS AND DOLCELATTE

*Penne is one of our favourite kinds of pasta because sauces cling really well to the quill shape. But you can use spaghetti if you prefer. Serve with dressed salad.*

## SERVES 6

350g (12oz) asparagus spears

350g (12oz) penne

salt and freshly ground black pepper

1 tbsp olive oil

250g (9oz) small portabella mushrooms, sliced

1 garlic clove, crushed

150ml (5fl oz) double cream

100g (3½oz) dolcelatte cheese, cut into small cubes

small bunch of basil, chopped

## SERVES 12

600g (1lb 5oz) asparagus spears

600g (1lb 5oz) penne

salt and freshly ground black pepper

2 tbsp olive oil

500g (1lb 2oz) small portabella mushrooms, sliced

2 garlic cloves, crushed

300ml (10fl oz) double cream

225g (8oz) dolcelatte cheese, cut into small cubes

large bunch of basil, chopped

1. Cut off the tips of the asparagus about 5cm (2in) from the top and set aside. Cut the rest of the spears into small slices.

2. Cook the penne in boiling salted water according to the packet instructions. Add the sliced asparagus 5 minutes before the end of cooking. Add the asparagus tips 3 minutes before the end of cooking. Drain and refresh in cold water.

3. Heat the oil in a large frying pan, add the mushrooms and garlic, and fry for 2 minutes. Add the cream and cheese, season with salt and freshly ground black pepper, and stir well.

4. Add the pasta and asparagus to the pan, bring to the boil, and reheat until piping hot. Stir in half the basil and transfer to a serving bowl.

5. Garnish with the remaining basil and serve at once.

## PREPARE AHEAD

*The penne and asparagus can be cooked up to the end of step 2 up to 6 hours ahead and kept in a colander covered in cling film. Not suitable for freezing.*

# ROASTED VEGETABLE RISOTTO

*Risottos are popular with everyone, and this version, full of flavour and bright healthy vegetables, is great for vegetarians. Serve hot with fresh salad leaves.*

## SERVES 6

225g (8oz) butternut squash, peeled and cut into 2cm (¾in) cubes

1 onion, coarsely chopped

1 small aubergine, cut into 1cm (½in) cubes

1 small red pepper, halved, deseeded, and cut into 1cm (½in) cubes

3 tbsp olive oil

salt and freshly ground black pepper

2 tsp freshly chopped thyme leaves

300g (11oz) risotto rice

225g (8oz) chestnut mushrooms, sliced

1.2 litres (2 pints) hot vegetable stock

50g (1¾oz) Parmesan cheese or vegetarian alternative, made into small shavings with a vegetable peeler

2 tbsp freshly snipped chives

## SERVES 12

450g (1lb) butternut squash, peeled and cut into 2cm (¾in) cubes

2 onions, coarsely chopped

2 small aubergines, cut into 1cm (½in) cubes

2 small red peppers, halved, deseeded, and cut into 1cm (½in) cubes

6 tbsp olive oil

salt and freshly ground black pepper

1 heaped tbsp freshly chopped thyme leaves

600g (1lb 5oz) risotto rice

450g (1lb) chestnut mushrooms, sliced

2.4 litres (4 pints) hot vegetable stock

100g (3½oz) Parmesan cheese or vegetarian alternative, made into small shavings with a vegetable peeler

4 tbsp freshly snipped chives

1. Preheat the oven to 200°C (180°C fan/400°F/Gas 6). Put the squash, onion, aubergine, and pepper into a large roasting tin (two tins for 12) in a single layer.

2. Pour over one-third of the oil and toss well with your hands. Season with salt and freshly ground black pepper, then sprinkle over the thyme.

3. Roast for 30 minutes (35 minutes for 12) or until tender and golden.

4. Heat the remaining oil in a deep saucepan over a high heat, add the rice, and stir to coat. Stir in the mushrooms, then gradually add the stock, a ladleful at a time. Stir continuously and only add more when it's been absorbed.

5. When all the stock has been absorbed and the rice is cooked, stir in the roasted vegetables and half the cheese. Transfer to a serving dish and sprinkle with the remaining cheese and the chives.

### IN THE AGA

At step 3, roast on the floor of the roasting oven for 20–30 minutes.

### PREPARE AHEAD

*The vegetables can be roasted up to 8 hours ahead. Not suitable for freezing.*

# VEGETABLE KORMA

*We always try to keep the number of ingredients to a minimum, but by nature a curry has many – it's the blend of spices that give it flavour. Sorry! Serve with naan breads and Pilaf rice (pages 246–247).*

### SERVES 6

100g (3½oz) French beans, sliced into three

salt and freshly ground black pepper

2 tbsp olive oil

1 large onion, roughly chopped

2cm (¾in) piece fresh root ginger, peeled and grated

1 tsp cardamom seeds, crushed

1½ tbsp ground cumin

1½ tbsp ground coriander

1½ tbsp garam masala

450g (1lb) potatoes, peeled and chopped into 1½cm (⅝in) cubes

350g (12oz) carrots, peeled and chopped into 1½cm (⅜in) cubes

350g (12oz) cauliflower, cut into even-sized florets

400g can coconut milk

450ml (15fl oz) vegetable stock

100g (3½oz) ground almonds

juice of 1 lemon

2 tbsp mango chutney

### SERVES 12

175g (6oz) French beans, sliced into three

salt and freshly ground black pepper

3 tbsp olive oil

2 large onions, roughly chopped

5cm (2in) piece fresh root ginger, peeled and grated

2 tsp cardamom seeds, crushed

3 tbsp ground cumin

3 tbsp ground coriander

3 tbsp garam masala

900g (2lb) potatoes, peeled and chopped into 1½cm (⅝in) cubes

700g (1lb 9oz) carrots, peeled and chopped into 1½cm (⅜in) cubes

700g (1lb 9oz) cauliflower, cut into even-sized florets

2 x 400g cans coconut milk

900ml (1½ pints) vegetable stock

225g (8oz) ground almonds

juice of 2 lemons

4 tbsp mango chutney

1. Cook the beans in boiling salted water for 4 minutes or until just cooked. Drain, refresh in cold water, and set aside.

2. Heat the oil in a deep frying pan or casserole, add the onion, and fry over a high heat for 2 minutes.

3. Add the ginger and spices, stir to coat the onions, and fry for 1 minute. Add all the vegetables except the beans, then stir in the coconut milk and stock. Season well with salt and freshly ground black pepper and bring to the boil.

4. Cover with a lid and simmer over a low heat for 25–35 minutes (45 minutes for 12) or until the vegetables are tender.

5. Stir in the ground almonds (they will thicken the sauce), then add the reserved beans, the lemon juice, and chutney. Check the seasoning and serve.

### IN THE AGA

At step 3, bring to the boil on the boiling plate, cover with a lid, and transfer to the simmering oven for 35 minutes.

### PREPARE AHEAD

*The korma can be made up to the end of step 4 up to 12 hours ahead. Not suitable for freezing.*

# GARLIC AND CORIANDER NAAN BREADS

## SERVES 6

3 large or 6 small plain
naan breads

25g (scant 1oz) butter,
at room temperature

2 garlic cloves, crushed

3 tbsp freshly chopped
coriander

salt and freshly ground
black pepper

## SERVES 12

6 large or 12 small plain
naan breads

50g (1¾oz) butter, at room
temperature

4 garlic cloves, crushed

6 tbsp freshly chopped
coriander

salt and freshly ground
black pepper

*True naan breads are rather a palaver to make, so these are a bit of a cheat – but a really delicious one! Serve them with any of the curries on pages 121, 152, 210, and 245.*

1.  Preheat the oven to 200°C (180°C fan/400°F/Gas 6). Arrange the naan breads on a baking sheet without overlapping them.

2.  Put the butter, garlic, and coriander into a bowl and mix until combined. Season with salt and freshly ground black pepper and mix again.

3.  Spread evenly over the naan breads so the whole of each bread is covered.

4.  Bake for 5–8 minutes (8 minutes for 12) or until the butter has melted and the bread is crisp.

### IN THE AGA
Bake on the top set of runners in the roasting oven for 6 minutes.

### PREPARE AHEAD AND FREEZE
*The naan breads can be prepared up to the end of step 3 up to 12 hours ahead. Freeze for up to 3 months.*

# PILAF RICE

## SERVES 6

225g (8oz) basmati rice

salt and freshly ground
black pepper

50g (1¾oz) butter

1 onion, roughly chopped

4 garlic cloves, crushed

1 red chilli, halved,
deseeded, and finely
chopped

225g (8oz) chestnut
mushrooms, sliced

1 tsp paprika

juice of 1 lemon

50g (1¾oz) sultanas

25g (scant 1oz) flaked
almonds

100g (3½oz) cooked
petits pois

## SERVES 12

450g (1lb) basmati rice

salt and freshly ground
black pepper

75g (2½oz) butter

2 onions, roughly chopped

6 garlic cloves, crushed

2 red chillies, halved,
deseeded, and finely
chopped

350g (12oz) chestnut
mushrooms, sliced

2 tsp paprika

juice of 2 small lemons

100g (3½oz) sultanas

50g (1¾oz) flaked almonds

225g (8oz) cooked
petits pois

*Pilaf (sometimes called pilaff or pilau) rice is a dish that originates from the near East. It's the perfect accompaniment to any of the curries on pages 121, 152, 210, and 245.*

1. Cook the rice in boiling salted water according to the packet instructions. Drain, refresh in cold water, and set aside.

2. Meanwhile, melt the butter in a large saucepan, add the onion, garlic, and chilli and fry for 2 minutes. Lower the heat, cover with a lid, and simmer for 20 minutes or until the onion is soft.

3. Add the mushrooms, turn up the heat, and fry for 3 minutes or until soft. Sprinkle in the paprika, lemon juice, sultanas, almonds, and petits pois and fry for a few minutes, stirring. Add the rice and stir until it is piping hot. Season with salt and freshly ground black pepper and serve.

### IN THE AGA
At step 2, cover with a lid and transfer to the simmering oven for 20 minutes. Return to the boiling plate at step 3.

### PREPARE AHEAD

*The pilaf can be cooked up to 12 hours ahead. To reheat, transfer to a buttered, wide-based ovenproof dish, cover with buttered foil, and place in an oven preheated to 200°C (180°C fan/ 400°F/Gas 6) for 15 minutes (25 minutes for 12) or until piping hot. Not suitable for freezing.*

# THAI GREEN RICE

## SERVES 6

24 asparagus spears

100g (3½oz) baby corn

salt

225g (8oz) frozen petits pois

100g (3½oz) easy cook
long-grain rice

4 spring onions, finely
sliced

2 tbsp soy sauce

2 tbsp sweet chilli dipping
sauce

a little olive oil, to fry

## SERVES 12

48 asparagus spears

200g (7oz) baby corn

salt

450g (1lb) frozen petits pois

200g (7oz) easy cook
long-grain rice

8 spring onions, finely
sliced

4 tbsp soy sauce

4 tbsp sweet chilli dipping
sauce

a little olive oil, to fry

*This brightly coloured side dish is full of flavour. It is the perfect accompaniment to our Thai beef with lime and chilli on page 138.*

1. Trim the tough ends from the asparagus spears diagonally and discard, then cut the stalks into diagonal slices and set the tips to one side. Cut the corn into 3–4 diagonal slices, depending on their size.

2. Cook the asparagus stalks and corn in boiling salted water for 4 minutes or until just cooked, then drain and refresh in cold water.

3. Cook the asparagus tips and petits pois in boiling salted water for 2 minutes, then drain and refresh in cold water. Cook the rice in boiling salted water according to the packet instructions, then drain.

4. Mix the rice with the cooked vegetables and spring onions, then toss with the soy sauce and sweet chilli dipping sauce.

5. Heat the olive oil in a wok or non-stick frying pan and stir-fry the rice for 5 minutes or until hot. Serve at once – if kept hot, the vegetables will lose their vibrant green colour.

### IN THE AGA
Cook the rice on the lowest set of runners in the roasting oven for 15 minutes (25 minutes for 12).

### PREPARE AHEAD
*The rice can be prepared up to the end of step 4 up to 12 hours ahead. Not suitable for freezing.*

# ROAST POTATOES WITH CHILLI AND THYME

*These are great all year round, but are especially good in the summer months when the flavour of fresh thyme is at its best. Serve with barbecued meats or fish.*

## SERVES 6

6 large old potatoes, peeled and cut into 5cm (2in) cubes

salt and freshly ground black pepper

3 tbsp olive oil

juice of ½ lemon

2 tsp freshly chopped thyme leaves

2–3 garlic cloves, crushed

1–2 red chillies (depending on preference), deseeded and finely chopped

2 tbsp freshly chopped parsley

## SERVES 12

12 large old potatoes, peeled and cut into 5cm (2in) cubes

salt and freshly ground black pepper

6 tbsp olive oil

juice of 1 lemon

4 tsp freshly chopped thyme leaves

5 fat garlic cloves, crushed

2–3 red chillies (depending on preference), deseeded and finely chopped

4 tbsp freshly chopped parsley

1. Preheat the oven to 220°C (200°C fan/425°F/Gas 7). Meanwhile, cook the potatoes in boiling salted water for 4–5 minutes or until they are just soft around the edges but still have a little bite in the middle. Drain and transfer to a bowl.

2. Put all the other ingredients except the parsley into a small bowl and lightly whisk to combine. Pour over the potatoes and season with salt and freshly ground black pepper.

3. Pop a roasting tin (two tins for 12) into the oven for a few minutes to get very hot. Spoon the potatoes and dressing into the tin(s) and roast for 25–30 minutes (45–55 minutes for 12) or until golden and crispy. Garnish with the parsley and serve.

### IN THE AGA
Roast on the floor of the roasting oven for 25 minutes (50 minutes for 12).

### PREPARE AHEAD
*The potatoes can be prepared up to the end of step 2 up to 1 day ahead. Not suitable for freezing.*

# HEAVENLY POTATO GRATIN

*This is one Mary's favourite ways of serving potatoes. She's been cooking them for over 25 years and they're as popular now as they were then. Make sure you use an ovenproof dish that's wide and shallow, so you get more of the delicious crispy golden crust. Serve with chops, grilled meat, or fish.*

### SERVES 6

**Special equipment** *1 litre (1¾ pint) shallow ovenproof dish, buttered*

900g (2lb) even-sized waxy potatoes, such as Désirée

1 tsp salt

freshly ground black pepper

45g (1½oz) butter, melted, plus a little extra to grease

150ml (5fl oz) single cream

### SERVES 12

**Special equipment** *2 litre (3½ pint) shallow ovenproof dish, buttered*

1.8kg (4lb) even-sized waxy potatoes, such as Désirée

1 tsp salt

freshly ground black pepper

75g (2½oz) butter, melted, plus a little extra to grease

300ml (10fl oz) single cream

1. Preheat the oven to 220°C (200°C fan/400°F/Gas 7). Rub off any excess dirt from the potatoes and put them unpeeled into a pan. Cover with cold water and add the salt. Cover with a lid, bring to the boil, and cook until just tender. The timing will depend on their size, but they should be soft around the edges and slightly firm in the centre. Set aside for them to cool completely.

2. Peel the skins from the potatoes and discard. Using a coarse grater, grate the potatoes into the buttered dish, seasoning between the layers with salt and freshly ground black pepper. Do not press down – they should be light and fluffy.

3. Pour over the melted butter and cream and bake for 20–25 minutes (40 minutes for 12) or until crisp and golden brown.

### IN THE AGA

Bake on the second set of runners in the roasting oven for 20–25 minutes (35 minutes for 12).

### PREPARE AHEAD

*The potatoes can be made up to the end of step 2 up to 1 day ahead. Not suitable for freezing.*

# CHEESE-TOPPED DAUPHINOIS POTATOES

*These are best prepared a day ahead. Make more than you need and freeze them for another occasion – they're great when there are just two or four of you. Serve with chops, grilled meat, or fish.*

## SERVES 6

**Special equipment** *18cm (7in) square shallow metal tin lined with baking parchment and greased*

*750g (1lb 10oz) large King Edward potatoes or other floury potatoes*

*150ml (5fl oz) chicken stock or vegetable stock*

*100ml (3½fl oz) double cream*

*salt and freshly ground black pepper*

*knob of butter*

*25g (scant 1oz) mature Cheddar cheese, grated*

## SERVES 12

**Special equipment** *23 x 30cm (9 x 12in) roasting tin lined with baking parchment and greased*

*1.35kg (3lb) large King Edward potatoes or other floury potatoes*

*300ml (10fl oz) chicken stock or vegetable stock*

*150ml (5fl oz) double cream*

*salt and freshly ground black pepper*

*25g (scant 1oz) butter*

*50g (1¾oz) mature Cheddar cheese, grated*

1. Preheat the oven to 220°C (200°C fan/425°F/Gas 7). Peel the potatoes and rinse under cold water, then dry and slice very thinly by hand or with the slicer attachment on a food processor. Put the stock into a large jug and mix with the cream.

2. Arrange a layer of potato over the base of the tin, season with salt and freshly ground black pepper, then pour over a little of the stock mixture. Continue in the same way until the potato and liquid are used up. Dot the butter over the top and cover tightly with foil.

3. Bake for 30 minutes (45 minutes for 12) or until soft around the edges but still firm in the middle. Remove the foil and cook for a further 25–30 minutes (35–45 minutes for 12) or until golden and tender. Leave to cool, then chill – overnight is best.

4. Choose a lipped board or tray that's bigger than the roasting tin (so it will catch any juices). Place on top of the tin and carefully turn it upside down so that the board is on the bottom. Remove the tin and baking parchment. Cut the potatoes into even-sized servings, arrange on a paper-lined baking tray, and sprinkle the cheese on top.

5. Reheat in an oven preheated to 200°C (180°C fan/400°F/Gas 6) for 25–30 minutes (35 minutes for 12) or until golden and piping hot.

### IN THE AGA
At step 3, cook on the second set of runners in the roasting oven.
At step 5, reheat on the second set of runners in the roasting oven.

### PREPARE AHEAD AND FREEZE
*The dish can be made up to the end of step 3 up to 1 day ahead or up to the end of step 4 up to 8 hours ahead. Freeze for up to 2 months.*

# ORANGE-GLAZED CARROTS

*We love recipes that you can do much of the preparation for up to a day ahead and that require little last-minute attention. These carrots can be popped into the oven while you're doing the roast.*

## SERVES 6

1kg (2¼lb) carrots, sliced thickly diagonally

salt and freshly ground black pepper

25g (scant 1oz) butter, melted

½ orange

freshly chopped parsley, to garnish

## SERVES 12

2kg (4½lb) carrots, sliced thickly diagonally

salt and freshly ground black pepper

50g (1¾oz) butter, melted

1 orange

freshly chopped parsley, to garnish

1. Preheat the oven to 200°C (180°C fan/400°F/Gas 6). Immerse the carrots in a pan of boiling salted water for 4 minutes to blanch them, then drain and refresh in cold water.

2. Pour over the melted butter, season with salt and freshly ground black pepper, and stir to coat well.

3. Arrange in a roasting tin or ovenproof dish. Squeeze over the juice from the orange and pop the shell in the tin for extra flavour.

4. Cover with foil and bake for 30 minutes (40 minutes for 12) or until tender.

5. To serve, remove the orange shell and discard. Sprinkle over the parsley and toss lightly.

### IN THE AGA

Bake on the lowest set of runners in the roasting oven for 25 minutes (35 minutes for 12).

### PREPARE AHEAD

*The carrots can be blanched up to 1 day ahead. Coat in the butter and orange juice and roast to serve. Not suitable for freezing.*

# ROASTED CHICORY
# WITH GARLIC BUTTER

*This is an unusual vegetable dish, best served alongside more conventional vegetables such as broccoli or runner beans. Serve as an accompaniment to meat or fish.*

| SERVES 6 | SERVES 12 |
|---|---|
| salt and freshly ground black pepper | salt and freshly ground black pepper |
| 12 chicory heads, sliced in half lengthways | 24 chicory heads, sliced in half lengthways |
| 25g (scant 1oz) butter | 50g (1¾oz) butter |
| 2 garlic cloves, crushed | 4 garlic cloves, crushed |
| 50g (1¾oz) mature Cheddar cheese, grated | 100g (3½oz) mature Cheddar cheese, grated |
| a little paprika, to dust | a little paprika, to dust |

1. Preheat the oven to 220°C (200°C fan/425°F/Gas 7). Bring a pan of cold salted water to the boil, add the chicory, and bring back up to a rolling boil. Cook for 3 minutes, then drain. Arrange the chicory in a single layer in an ovenproof dish.

2. Add the butter and garlic to the empty pan and melt over the heat. Spoon over the chicory in the dish and season with salt and freshly ground black pepper. Sprinkle over the cheese and a light dusting of paprika.

3. Bake for 15–20 minutes (25–30 minutes for 12) or until lightly golden.

### IN THE AGA
Bake on the top set of runners in the roasting oven for 15 minutes (30 minutes for 12).

### PREPARE AHEAD
*The chicory can be prepared up to the end of step 1 up to 6 hours ahead. Not suitable for freezing.*

# ROASTED CAULIFLOWER AND CARROTS

## SERVES 4

1 large cauliflower

2 tbsp olive oil

500g large carrots, peeled and sliced into thick batons

salt and freshly ground black pepper

juice and zest of ½ lemon

2 tbsp parsley, chopped

*This is a wonderful change to the more traditional roasted potatoes or root vegetables. It makes a great accompaniment for the Highland game pie on page 130.*

1.  Preheat the oven to 220° (180°C fan/400°F/Gas 7). To prepare the cauliflower, remove the leaves and discard. Break the florets from the stalk into small pieces.

2.  Pour the oil into a large roasting tin and place in the oven for 5 minutes to get hot. Add the carrots and cauliflower and season with salt and freshly ground black pepper. Toss in the hot fat to coat, then roast in the oven for about 15 minutes or until nearly tender.

3.  Add the lemon juice and zest and return to the oven for another 5 minutes or until golden.

4.  Sprinkle with the parsley and serve piping hot.

### IN THE AGA

Roast on the floor of the roasting oven for 15–20 minutes, turning halfway through.

# SWEET CHILLI COLESLAW

*Coleslaw should be light and fresh rather than rich and sloppy. This recipe comes from our lovely friend Joanna. Look for sweet chilli dipping sauce in the world food section of the supermarket. It gives coleslaw a sweet kick and stops the sauce being too thick.*

## SERVES 6

300g (11oz) white cabbage

1 small white onion

2 celery sticks

2 carrots, coarsely grated

salt and freshly ground black pepper

3 tbsp cider vinegar

2 tsp Dijon mustard

8 tbsp mayonnaise

5 tbsp sweet chilli dipping sauce

## SERVES 12

600g (1lb 5oz) white cabbage

1 large white onion

4 celery sticks

4 carrots, coarsely grated

salt and freshly ground black pepper

6 tbsp cider vinegar

1 heaped tbsp Dijon mustard

250ml (8fl oz) mayonnaise

150ml (5fl oz) sweet chilli dipping sauce

1. Slice the cabbage, onion, and celery in a food processor, using the slicing blade. If you have a mandolin, use the thin blade. Alternatively, slice them very finely by hand.

2. Transfer to a bowl, add the carrots, and season with salt and freshly ground black pepper.

3. Put the vinegar, mustard, mayonnaise, and sweet chilli dipping sauce into a jam jar. Seal with a lid and shake vigorously to combine.

4. Pour over the dressing and toss well. Transfer to the fridge for a minimum of 3 hours. Serve chilled or at room temperature.

## PREPARE AHEAD

*The dressing can be made and kept in the jar for up to 4 days. The coleslaw can be made up to 1 day ahead. The flavours improve, in fact. Not suitable for freezing.*

# ROASTED MEDITERRANEAN VEGETABLES

*Roasted vegetables make a wonderful side dish for so many meats and fish. The secret is to cook the vegetables in a single layer, so they chargrill rather than steaming and becoming soggy. If you have any vegetables left over, toss them with a little balsamic vinegar and some olive oil and serve them as a salad.*

### SERVES 6

2 tbsp olive oil

1 small aubergine, sliced into 5cm (2in) chunks

2 small courgettes, thickly sliced

1 red pepper, halved, deseeded, and cut into 5cm (2in) chunks

1 onion, quartered

3 garlic cloves (unpeeled)

2 sprigs of fresh rosemary

3 sprigs of fresh thyme

salt and freshly ground black pepper

### SERVES 12

4 tbsp olive oil

2 small aubergines, sliced into 5cm (2in) chunks

4 small courgettes, thickly sliced

2 red peppers, halved, deseeded, and cut into 5cm (2in) chunks

2 onions, quartered

6 garlic cloves (unpeeled)

4 sprigs of fresh rosemary

6 sprigs of fresh thyme

salt and freshly ground black pepper

1. Preheat the oven to 220°C (200°C fan/425°F/Gas 7). Put the oil into a large roasting tin (two tins for 12) and pop in the oven for a few minutes to get hot.

2. Add the vegetables and toss in the hot oil. Scatter over the garlic and herbs.

3. Roast for 40–45 minutes (1 hour for 12) or until tender and golden. Turn halfway through cooking.

4. Transfer to a serving bowl with a slotted spoon. Squeeze the garlic from their skins and mix in with the vegetables. Discard the herbs if woody. Season with salt and freshly ground black pepper, toss, and serve.

### IN THE AGA

Roast on the floor of the roasting oven for 35 minutes (1 hour for 12), stirring halfway through.

### PREPARE AHEAD

*The vegetables can be prepared up to the end of step 4 up to 1 day ahead. Not suitable for freezing.*

# OUR FAVOURITE PUDDINGS

*Even if it's only one sumptuous dessert plus a fruit salad,
we always serve a choice of puddings at any gathering of
eight people or more. In general, we'll serve one pudding
that's rich and indulgent, and another that's light and
fruity – fruit compotes are always popular.*

# APRICOT AND ALMOND GALETTE

## MAKES 1 (SERVES 6)

a little plain flour, to dust

½ x 375g packet all-butter puff pastry

a little milk

400g can apricots in natural juices, drained

150g (5½oz) golden marzipan, coarsely grated

1 tbsp apricot jam

1 tsp water

## MAKES 2 (SERVES 12)

a little plain flour, to dust

375g packet all-butter puff pastry

a little milk

2 x 400g cans apricots in natural juices, drained

250g (9oz) golden marzipan, coarsely grated

2 tbsp apricot jam

2 tsp water

*This is also very good made with thinly sliced unpeeled eating apples instead of apricots. Use about three per galette. Take the pastry and marzipan straight from the fridge – they are easier to handle when cold. If you're not using all the pastry immediately, freeze any left over until needed. Serve the pudding warm with cream.*

1.  Preheat the oven to 220°C (200°C fan/425°F/Gas 7). Pop a baking sheet in the oven to get hot. Lightly flour a piece of baking parchment and roll the pastry out into a 12.5 x 30cm (5 x 12in) rectangle. For 12, roll it out into a 25 x 30cm (10 x 12in) rectangle, cut it in half lengthways to make two strips, then arrange them neatly side by side.

2.  With a knife, score a 1cm (½in) border around the rectangle(s), taking care not to cut all the way through – this allows the strip to rise up around the apricots and stops any liquid or fruit leaking out. Brush the border(s) with a little milk.

3.  Slice each apricot into four slices and arrange them in rows inside the borders. Sprinkle over the marzipan.

4.  Slide the paper on to the hot baking sheet and bake for 20 minutes (20–25 minutes for two galettes) or until golden brown. Check halfway through cooking and, if they are getting too brown, cover loosely with foil.

5.  Heat the apricot jam in a pan with the water, whisking until smooth. Brush the apricots with a thin layer to glaze them. Serve warm.

### IN THE AGA

Bake the galette on the grid shelf on the floor of the roasting oven for 15–20 minutes (20–25 minutes for two galettes).

### PREPARE AHEAD AND FREEZE

*The galette(s) can be made up to 2 days ahead. Freeze for up to 1 month.*

# MINI APPLE, APRICOT, AND HAZELNUT CRUMBLES

## SERVES 6

**Special equipment** *6 x size 1 (150ml/5fl oz) ramekins*

*900g (2lb) Bramley apples, peeled and cut into 1cm (½in) cubes*

*175g (6oz) ready-to-eat dried apricots, snipped into small pieces*

*100ml (3½fl oz) apple juice*

*100g (3½oz) demerara sugar*

*100g (3½oz) plain flour*

*50g (1¾oz) cold butter, cubed*

*30g (1oz) hazelnuts, chopped*

## SERVES 12

**Special equipment** *12 x size 1 (150ml/5fl oz) ramekins*

*1.8kg (4lb) Bramley apples, peeled and cut into 1cm (½in) cubes*

*350g (12oz) ready-to-eat dried apricots, snipped into small pieces*

*200ml (7fl oz) apple juice*

*200g (7oz) demerara sugar*

*200g (7oz) plain flour*

*100g (3½oz) cold butter, cubed*

*50g (1¾oz) hazelnuts, chopped*

*These individual crumbles are scrumptious and so easy to make. You could equally make one large crumble – use a 1.2 litre (2 pint) ovenproof dish for six or a 2.4 litre (4 pint) dish for 12, and bake for 30 minutes (45 minutes for 12). Serve with cream, crème fraîche, or warm custard.*

1. Preheat the oven to 200°C (180°C fan/400°F/Gas 6). Put the apples, apricots, apple juice, and all but 1 heaped tablespoon (3 level tablespoons for 12) of the demerara sugar into a saucepan. Bring to the boil, cover with a lid, and simmer for 5–7 minutes or until the apples are just soft. Remove from the heat and divide among the ramekins.

2. Put the flour and butter into a mixing bowl. Using the tips of your fingers, rub the cold butter into the flour until the mixture resembles breadcrumbs. Add the remaining sugar and the hazelnuts and mix together.

3. Sprinkle the crumble topping over the apples in the ramekins, then place on a baking sheet and bake for 15 minutes or until the crumble is light golden brown and the fruit is bubbling around the edges.

### IN THE AGA

Bake the crumbles in the middle of the roasting oven for 15 minutes or until golden.

### PREPARE AHEAD AND FREEZE

*The crumbles can be made up to 2 days ahead. Freeze for up to 1 month.*

# APRICOT CUSTARD CRUMBLE PIE

MAKES A 28CM (11IN)
PIE (SERVES 8–10)

**Special equipment** *28cm
(11in) round tart tin with
a removable base*

*175g (6oz) plain flour,
plus a little extra to dust*

*75g (2½oz) butter*

*2 tbsp caster sugar*

*1 egg*

**For the filling**

*150ml (5fl oz) full-fat soured
cream*

*3 egg yolks*

*1 tsp vanilla extract*

*200g (7oz) caster sugar*

*25g (scant 1oz) plain flour*

*2 x 400g cans apricot
halves in natural juices,
drained and each apricot
cut into three*

**For the crumble topping**

*50g (1¾oz) butter*

*75g (2½oz) plain flour*

*50g (1¾oz) caster sugar*

*What makes this crumble so unusual is the layer of
creamy custard in the middle. Serve it as it is or with
a little more cream.*

1. Preheat the oven to 200°C (180°C fan/400°F/Gas 6). Put a baking
sheet in to get hot. Meanwhile, make the pastry. Put the flour and
butter into a processor and whiz until the mixture resembles
breadcrumbs. Add the sugar and egg and whiz again to form a ball.

2. Place the base of the tart tin on a work surface. Lightly dust the
base of the tart tin and the work surface with flour. To line the tart
tin, place the ball of pastry in the middle of the base of the tin and
roll into a circle 5cm (2in) bigger than the base. Carefully fold in
the edges all around. Return the base of the tin to the surround,
then unfold the edge of the pastry and neaten. Prick the disc of
pastry all over with a fork.

3. Line the pastry with baking paper and fill with dried beans or
baking beans, then bake for 15 minutes. Remove the beans and
paper and bake for a further 5 minutes.

4. To make the filling, put the soured cream, egg yolks, vanilla extract,
sugar, and flour into a mixing bowl and whisk by hand until smooth.

5. Arrange the apricots over the base of the pastry case and pour
the custard filling over the top. Sit the pie on the hot baking sheet
and bake for 35–40 minutes or until the filling is just beginning to set.

6. Meanwhile, make the crumble topping. Put the butter, flour,
and sugar into a mixing bowl and rub with your fingertips until the
mixture resembles coarse breadcrumbs.

7. Sprinkle the crumble topping over the just-set custard. Return
to the oven and bake for a further 15 minutes or until golden and
the custard is completely set. If the crumble topping starts to get
too brown, cover with foil. Serve warm or cold.

### IN THE AGA

At step 4, bake on the floor of the roasting oven for 20 minutes.
Add the topping and return to the floor of the oven for 15 minutes.
If the pastry is getting too brown, slide onto the grid shelf on the
floor. If the topping is getting too brown, slide the cold sheet on
to the second set of runners.

### PREPARE AHEAD

*The pie can be made the day before and gently
reheated. Not suitable for freezing.*

# MELT-IN-THE-MOUTH APPLE PIE

**MAKES A 24CM
(9½IN) PIE (SERVES 8)**

**Special equipment** *5cm
(2in) deep round pie dish
with a 19cm (7½in) base
and a 24cm (9½in) top*

*225g (8oz) plain flour,
plus a little extra to dust*

*150g (5½oz) cold butter,
cubed*

*25g (scant 1oz) caster
sugar, plus a little extra
to decorate*

*1 egg, beaten*

*1–2 tbsp water*

**For the filling**

*1.35kg (3lb) Bramley apples,
peeled, cored, and thinly
sliced*

*175g (6oz) caster sugar*

*½ tsp ground cinnamon*

*1 egg, beaten, to glaze*

*Crisp, short pastry packed with fruit – this apple pie
is perfect for a special Sunday lunch. Serve warm
with custard, cream, or ice cream.*

1. Preheat the oven to 200°C (180°C fan/400°F/Gas 6). Meanwhile,
put the flour, butter, and sugar into a food processor and whiz until
the mixture resembles breadcrumbs. Add the egg and water and
whiz again until it forms a ball. The dough will weigh about 450g
(1lb). Divide it into a 250g (9oz) piece and a 200g (7oz) piece.

2. Lightly flour a work surface and roll the larger piece out very
thinly, then use it to line the inside of the dish, leaving a little hanging
over at the sides.

3. To make the filling, put the apples, sugar, and cinnamon into
a bowl, mix well, then spoon into the base of the dish. The apples
will be higher than the pastry, but they will sink down as they cook.

4. Lightly flour the work surface and roll the remaining pastry out
slightly larger than the surface of the dish. Brush the top of the
pastry rim in the dish with water, then sit the pastry circle on top
and gently push down to seal the edges. Using a small sharp knife,
trim off any excess pastry and crimp the edges together with your
fingertips. Brush the pie with the beaten egg.

5. Bake for 45–50 minutes or until golden brown and crisp. Allow to
cool slightly, then sprinkle with a little extra caster sugar and serve.

## IN THE AGA

Bake on the floor of the roasting oven for 15 minutes, then slide the
grid shelf on the floor underneath the pie and bake for 30 minutes.
If the pie is getting too brown, slide the cold sheet onto the second
set of runners.

**PREPARE AHEAD AND FREEZE**

*The pie can be made up to the end of step 4
up to 1 day ahead. Freeze for up to 2 months.*

# TWICE-BAKED LEMON SOUFFLÉS

*These individual soufflés look impressive and, despite their rather complicated-sounding name, are extremely simple to make.*

## SERVES 6

**Special equipment** *6 x size 1 (150ml/5fl oz) ramekins, greased and base-lined with a disc of baking parchment*

*3 eggs, separated*

*175g (6oz) caster sugar*

*25g (scant 1oz) cornflour*

*finely grated zest of 2 large lemons*

*juice of 1 large lemon*

*250g (9oz) half-fat cream cheese*

*1 large tbsp luxury lemon curd*

### For the lemon sauce
*300ml (10fl oz) double cream*

*1 tbsp luxury lemon curd*

*finely grated zest and juice of 1 lemon*

## SERVES 12

**Special equipment** *12 x size 1 (150ml/5fl oz) ramekins, greased and base-lined with a disc of baking parchment*

*6 eggs, separated*

*350g (12oz) caster sugar*

*50g (1¾oz) cornflour*

*finely grated zest of 4 large lemons*

*juice of 2 large lemons*

*500g (1lb 2oz) half-fat cream cheese*

*2 large tbsp luxury lemon curd*

### For the lemon sauce
*600ml (1 pint) double cream*

*2 tbsp luxury lemon curd*

*finely grated zest and juice of 2 lemons*

1. Preheat the oven to 190°C (170°C fan/375°F/Gas 5). Put the egg yolks and half the sugar into a mixing bowl and whisk with an electric whisk until pale, thick, and frothy.

2. Mix the cornflour, lemon zest, and lemon juice in a bowl until smooth. Fold in the egg-yolk mixture, then beat in the cream cheese and lemon curd with a spatula.

3. Whisk the egg whites with an electric whisk until they resemble clouds. Whisking constantly, add the remaining sugar a teaspoon at a time until the whites are stiff and shiny.

4. Carefully fold the egg-white mixture into the mixing bowl, then spoon into the ramekins. Run a knife around the edge of each one to ensure they rise evenly. Sit the ramekins snugly in a roasting tin, then pour in enough boiling water to come halfway up the sides of the tin.

5. Bake for 15–20 minutes or until the soufflés have risen well and are just cooked. Set aside to cool completely.

6. Turn the soufflés out of the ramekins, remove the paper bases, and arrange snugly in one layer in an ovenproof dish.

7. To make the sauce, put all the ingredients into a mixing bowl and whisk until smooth. Pour the sauce around the soufflés in the dish, then bake in an oven preheated to 200°C (180°C fan/400°F/Gas 6) for 10 minutes (20–25 minutes for 12). Serve at once.

### IN THE AGA
At step 5, bake on the second set of runners in the roasting oven for 15 minutes. At step 7, bake on the second set of runners in the roasting oven for 8–10 minutes.

### PREPARE AHEAD
*The soufflés can be made up to the end of step 6 and the sauce poured around them up to 8 hours ahead. Not suitable for freezing.*

# LEMON MERINGUE PIE

**MAKES A 28CM (11IN) PIE (SERVES 8–10)**

**Special equipment** *2 8cm (11in) fluted loose-bottomed tart tin*

*225g (8oz) plain flour, plus a little extra to dust*

*175g (6oz) cold butter, cubed*

*45g (1½oz) icing sugar*

*1 large egg, beaten*

*1 tbsp water*

**For the lemon filling**

*finely grated zest and juice of 6 lemons*

*65g (2¼oz) cornflour*

*450ml (15fl oz) water*

*250g (9oz) caster sugar*

*6 egg yolks*

**For the topping**

*4 egg whites*

*225g (8oz) caster sugar*

*2 level tsp cornflour*

*This is a truly wonderful LMP. It takes a bit of time to make but, for a really special occasion, it's worth it. Serve warm or cold, but not hot, as the pie will be too soft to cut.*

1. Put the flour and butter into a food processor and whiz until the mixture resembles breadcrumbs. Add the icing sugar, egg, and water and whiz until it forms a ball. Transfer to a lightly floured work surface and roll the dough out thinly until slightly larger than the tin, then use to line the tin. Cover with cling film and chill for about an hour.

2. Preheat the oven to 200°C (180°C fan/400°F/Gas 6). Line the pastry case with baking parchment, fill with dried beans or baking beans, and bake for 15 minutes (see page 311). Remove the beans and parchment and return to the oven for 5 minutes to dry out, then remove from the oven and set aside. Reduce the oven temperature to 180°C (160°C fan/350°F/Gas 4).

3. To make the filling, mix the lemon zest, lemon juice, and cornflour to a smooth paste in a small bowl. Bring the water to the boil in a pan, add the lemon mixture, and stir over the heat until thickened, then boil for 1 minute. Mix the sugar and yolks in a bowl and carefully add to the pan. Stir over a medium heat until you have a thick custard. Set aside to cool slightly, then pour into the pastry case.

4. To make the topping, whisk the egg whites with an electric whisk until they look like clouds. Gradually add the caster sugar, whisking on maximum speed until the whites are stiff and glossy. Add the cornflour and whisk to combine.

5. Spoon the meringue on top of the lemon filling, spreading to cover it completely and swirling the top. Bake for 30 minutes or until the filling is completely set and the meringue is lightly golden and crisp.

## IN THE AGA

Skip step 2. At the end of step 3, bake the pie on the floor of the roasting oven, with the cold sheet on the second set of runners, for 20 minutes or until the filling is just set. At step 5, bake on a grid shelf on the floor of the roasting oven, with the cold sheet on the second set of runners, for 5–10 minutes.

## PREPARE AHEAD

*The pastry case can be made up to 2 days ahead. The pie can be made completely up to 1 day ahead. Not suitable for freezing.*

# TOFFEE PUDDING WITH WARM TOFFEE SAUCE

*This is similar to sticky toffee pudding and it's truly scrumptious. If you're serving 12–16, bake the pudding in two tins.*

## SERVES 6–8

**Special equipment** *23 x 33cm (9 x 13in) traybake tin, greased, lined with baking parchment, and greased*

100g (3½oz) butter, at room temperature

175g (6oz) light muscovado sugar

2 eggs

225g (8oz) self-raising flour

2 tbsp black treacle

150ml (5fl oz) milk

50g (1¾oz) walnuts, chopped

### For the toffee sauce

150g (5½oz) light muscovado sugar

150g (5½oz) golden syrup

50g (1¾oz) butter

170g can evaporated milk

## SERVES 12–16

**Special equipment** *Two 23 x 33cm (9 x 13in) traybake tins, greased, lined with baking parchment, and greased*

225g (8oz) butter, at room temperature

350g (12oz) light muscovado sugar

4 eggs

450g (1lb) self-raising flour

4 tbsp black treacle

300ml (10fl oz) milk

100g (3½oz) walnuts, chopped

### For the toffee sauce

300g (11oz) light muscovado sugar

300g (11oz) golden syrup

100g (3½oz) butter

2 x 170g cans evaporated milk

1. Preheat the oven to 180°C (160°C fan/350°F/Gas 4). Put the butter, sugar, eggs, flour, and treacle into a bowl and whisk with an electric whisk until combined. Slowly add the milk, whisking until smooth. Pour into the lined tin and sprinkle with the walnuts.

2. Bake for 30–35 minutes (40 minutes for two puddings) or until well risen, just firm in the middle, and lightly golden brown. Keep warm.

3. To make the sauce, put the sugar, golden syrup, and butter into a saucepan and stir over a low heat until the sugar has dissolved, the butter has melted, and all the ingredients are combined. Simmer for 5 minutes, then remove from the heat and stir in the evaporated milk.

4. Cut the pudding into squares and serve warm with the warm toffee sauce.

### IN THE AGA

Bake on the grid shelf on the floor of the roasting oven, with the cold sheet on the second set of runners, for 25–30 minutes (30–35 minutes for two puddings).

### PREPARE AHEAD AND FREEZE

*The pudding can be made up to 1 day ahead. Freeze for up to 2 months. The sauce can be made up to 3 days ahead. Not suitable for freezing.*

# WHITE CHOCOLATE AND ORANGE MOUSSES

*This recipe was given to us by Becca, a great friend of ours. She has her own catering company and has given us invaluable advice on cooking for numbers. If you don't have cooking rings, you can make one large mousse – follow the recipe for 12 and spoon the mousse into a 20cm (8in) round springform tin.*

## SERVES 6

**Special equipment** *6 x 7cm (2¾in) round metal cooking rings*

*75g (2½oz) HobNobs, crushed*

*45g (1½oz) butter, melted*

*1 tbsp demerara sugar*

**For the mousse**

*100g (3½oz) full-fat cream cheese*

*150ml (5fl oz) double cream*

*150g (5½oz) Belgian or continental 100 per cent white chocolate*

*1 tbsp Cointreau*

*1 large orange*

## SERVES 12

**Special equipment** *12 x 7cm (2 ¾in) round metal cooking rings*

*175g (6oz) HobNobs, crushed*

*75g (2½oz) butter, melted*

*1½ tbsp demerara sugar*

**For the mousse**

*250g (9oz) full-fat cream cheese*

*300ml (10fl oz) double cream*

*300g (11oz) Belgian or continental 100 per cent white chocolate*

*3 tbsp Cointreau*

*2 large oranges*

1. Put the HobNobs into a mixing bowl, add the butter and sugar, and mix to combine.

2. Line a baking sheet with cling film and sit the rings on top. Spoon the biscuit mixture evenly into the rings and level the tops with the back of a teaspoon. Transfer to the fridge to chill while you make the mousse.

3. Put the cream cheese and cream into a mixing bowl and whisk with an electric whisk until thick and holding its shape.

4. Gently melt the chocolate in a bowl set over a pan of just-simmering water until smooth. Allow to cool.

5. Add the chocolate to the cream mixture and stir in the Cointreau. Finely grate the zest of the orange and add to the mousse.

6. Spoon the mousse into the rings and level the tops. Chill for a minimum of 4 hours to firm up. Meanwhile, peel the orange with a small knife. Cut the segments free and place in a bowl. Squeeze over the juice from the peel.

7. Remove the rings and serve the mousses with the orange segments arranged on top. Garnish with grated white chocolate.

### ON THE AGA
To melt the chocolate, break it up into a bowl and place on the back of the Aga until melted.

### PREPARE AHEAD

*You can make the mousses up to 12 hours ahead. Not suitable for freezing.*

# CRÈME BRÛLÉE AND CHOCOLATE POTS

**SERVES 12**

**For the crème brûlée**

**Special equipment**
*18cm (7in) square cake tin, greased*

*600ml (1 pint) double cream*

*4 egg yolks*

*25g (scant 1oz) caster sugar*

*½ tsp vanilla extract*

*100g (3½oz) demerara sugar*

**For the chocolate pots**

**Special equipment** *12 shot glasses, about 75ml (2½fl oz) in capacity*

*300g (11oz) Bournville chocolate*

*300ml (10fl oz) double cream*

*200ml (7fl oz) full-fat crème fraîche*

---

**FOR THE GLAZED SUMMER BERRIES**

*Place 250g (9oz) small strawberries (hulled and halved), 250g (9oz) raspberries, and 100g (3½oz) blueberries in a large mixing bowl and mix gently. Sift 3 tsp icing sugar over the top and gently combine. Cover and chill in the fridge for up to 4 hours. The sugar will dissolve in the strawberry juices to form a shimmering glaze.*

---

**PREPARE AHEAD AND FREEZE**

*The custard for the crème brûlée can be made up to 2 days ahead. Add the topping up to 5 hours before serving. The chocolate pots can be made up to 2 days ahead. The berries can be prepared up to 4 hours ahead. Not suitable for freezing.*

*This is so impressive – two small puddings on one plate, served with some glazed summer berries. To serve fewer than 12 people, make just one of these special puddings – cut the crème brûlée into six servings, and make the chocolate pots in six 150ml (5fl oz) ramekins or glasses. Serve with or without the glazed berries.*

1. **To make the crème brûlée,** preheat the oven to 140°C (120°C fan/275°F/Gas 1). Heat the double cream gently in a saucepan until hand hot. Put the egg yolks, caster sugar, and vanilla extract into a bowl and whisk until combined. Pour the hot cream onto the mixture and whisk until smooth. Transfer to a jug, then strain into the cake tin.

2. Sit the cake tin in a roasting tin, pour enough boiling water into the roasting tin to come halfway up the sides of the cake tin, then transfer to the oven and bake for 35–40 minutes or until the cream mixture has just set. Set aside to cool.

3. Once cold, sprinkle the demerara sugar on top and slide under a hot grill until the sugar dissolves and becomes caramel-coloured. Set aside to firm up in the fridge for at least 1 hour and up to 5 hours.

4. **To make the chocolate pots,** reserve two squares of chocolate for decoration, then put the rest in a bowl set over a pan of simmering water. Add 200ml (7fl oz) of the cream and stir until the chocolate has melted. Set aside to cool slightly.

5. Stir in the crème fraîche, then pour into the shot glasses. Leave to set in the fridge for at least 2 hours.

6. Once set, pour the remaining double cream over the top. Coarsely grate the reserved chocolate and sprinkle on top.

7. When ready to serve, cut the crème brûlée into even-sized squares with a fish slice. Arrange a crème brûlée, a chocolate pot, and a few of the glazed summer berries on a plate and dust with icing sugar.

**IN THE AGA**

Bake the custard for the crème brûlée on the grid shelf on the lowest set of runners in the roasting oven for 8 minutes. Transfer to the simmering oven and cook for 40 minutes or until just set.

# RHUBARB AND LEMON POTS

**SERVES 6**

750g (1lb 10oz) rhubarb, sliced into 4cm (1¾in) pieces

finely grated zest of ½ orange, plus 2 tbsp orange juice

25g (scant 1oz) caster sugar

**For the lemon topping**

300ml (10fl oz) double cream

50g (1¾oz) caster sugar

finely grated zest and juice of 1½ lemons

6 mint leaves, to decorate

**SERVES 12**

1.5kg (3lb 3oz) rhubarb, sliced into 4cm (1¾in) pieces

finely grated zest of 1 orange, plus 4 tbsp orange juice

50g (1¾oz) caster sugar

**For the lemon topping**

600ml (1 pint) double cream

100g (3½oz) caster sugar

finely grated zest and juice of 3 lemons

12 mint leaves, to decorate

*The combination of rhubarb and lemon is delicious. This pudding looks particularly pretty made with young pink rhubarb, which is available in the shops towards the end of the winter.*

1. Put the rhubarb, orange zest, orange juice, and sugar into a saucepan. Stir over a high heat for 2 minutes, cover with a lid, lower the heat, and simmer for 10 minutes (15 minutes for 12) or until the rhubarb is just tender. Set aside to cool.

2. To make the topping, put the cream, sugar, and lemon zest into a pan. Heat gently over a low heat until the sugar dissolves and the mixture reaches simmering point. Remove from the heat, stir in the lemon juice, and set aside to cool slightly.

3. Spoon the rhubarb and a little of the liquid into the base of some pretty glasses or tumblers. Pour the lemon topping on top, then transfer to the fridge for a minimum of 4 hours to set.

4. Serve chilled, decorated with mint leaves.

**PREPARE AHEAD**

*The pots can be made up to 12 hours ahead. Not suitable for freezing.*

# INDIVIDUAL TIRAMISUS

**SERVES 6**

1½ tsp instant coffee granules

120ml (4fl oz) boiling water

3 tbsp Baileys Irish Cream

2 eggs

75g (2½oz) caster sugar

300ml (10fl oz) double cream

250g tub full-fat mascarpone

3 squares from a packet of trifle sponges

75g (2½oz) plain chocolate, coarsely grated

**SERVES 12**

1 tbsp instant coffee granules

300ml (10fl oz) boiling water

6 tbsp Baileys Irish Cream

4 eggs

150g (5½oz) caster sugar

600ml (1 pint) double cream

2 x 250g tubs full-fat mascarpone

6 squares from a packet of trifle sponges

150g (5½oz) plain chocolate, coarsely grated

*We all love tiramisu. This version is served individually, with the added decadence of a splash of Baileys Irish Cream – if you don't have any, you can replace it with the same quantity of brandy. Serve the tiramisu in tumblers or wine, martini, or champagne glasses.*

1. Put the coffee granules and boiling water into a jug and stir to dissolve. Allow to cool slightly, then stir in the Baileys.

2. Break the eggs into a mixing bowl, add the sugar, and whisk with an electric whisk until pale, thick, and frothy and the whisk leaves a trail on the surface when lifted.

3. Whip the cream till just lightly whipped and holding its shape.

4. Put the mascarpone into a bowl, stir in 2 tablespoons of the whipped cream, and mix with a spatula. Gently fold in the rest of the whipped cream, followed by the egg mixture, taking care not to knock out any of the air.

5. Cut the trifle sponges in half horizontally and then in half crossways. Push a piece into the base of each tumbler or glass, drizzle over half the coffee mixture, then spoon over half the cream mixture. Repeat to give another layer of sponge, coffee, and cream. Finish with a sprinkling of the grated chocolate.

6. Cover and chill in the fridge for a minimum of 4 hours.

**PREPARE AHEAD AND FREEZE**

*The tiramisus can be made up to 12 hours ahead. Freeze for up to 1 month.*

# CHOCOLATE TRUFFLE CHEESECAKE

SERVES 12

**Special equipment** 19cm
(7½in) square tin or an 18cm
(7in) round springform tin,
lined with cling film

200g (7oz) Bournville
chocolate

2 eggs, separated

50g (1¾oz) caster sugar

175g (6oz) full-fat cream
cheese

½ tsp vanilla extract

150ml (5fl oz) double
cream, lightly whipped

175g (6oz) chocolate
digestive biscuits, crushed

75g (2½oz) butter, melted

*A rich, indulgent cheesecake that requires no gelatine –
ideal for vegetarians. Serve on its own or with pouring
cream and fresh summer fruits such as raspberries
and strawberries.*

1.  Break the chocolate into small pieces into a bowl. Sit the bowl over a pan of hot water on a low heat and stir until melted. Take care not to allow the chocolate to get too hot or it will lose its shine and become too thick.

2.  Put the egg yolks and sugar into a large bowl and whisk with an electric whisk until light and thick and a trail is left when the whisks are lifted from the bowl.

3.  Mix the cream cheese and vanilla extract in a bowl, then stir in the melted chocolate. Fold in the whisked egg yolks and sugar, taking care not to knock out any air. Fold in the whipped cream.

4.  Whisk the egg whites with an electric hand whisk until like clouds. Fold a spoonful of egg whites into the chocolate mixture with a spatula. Cut and fold (but do not mix) until no whites are visible. Add the rest of the egg white and fold in until smooth.

5.  Spoon into the prepared tin and level the top. Transfer to the fridge for 1 hour or until just set.

6.  Mix the biscuits and butter together until combined. Carefully press on top of the cheesecake in an even layer. Return to the fridge for a minimum of 6 hours.

7.  To serve, turn the cheesecake upside-down onto a board or plate and cut into 12 fingers or wedges. Dust with cocoa powder.

## ON THE AGA
To melt the chocolate, break it up into a bowl and place on the back of the Aga until melted.

## PREPARE AHEAD AND FREEZE
*The cheesecake can be made up to the end of step 6 up to 2 days ahead. Freeze for up to 3 months.*

# CHOCOLATE AND HAZELNUT BOOZY ROULADE

MAKES A 33CM (13IN) ROULADE (SERVES 8-10)

**Special equipment** *23 x 33cm (9 x 13in) Swiss roll tin, greased and lined with non-stick baking paper*

*175g (6oz) plain chocolate, broken into pieces*

*6 eggs, separated*

*175g (6oz) caster sugar*

*2 level tbsp cocoa, sieved*

*50g (1¾ oz) chopped and roasted hazelnuts*

**For the filling**
*300ml (10fl oz) double cream*

*2–3 tbsp Baileys Irish Cream*

**For the hazelnut praline**
*100g (3½ oz) granulated sugar*

*50g (1¾ oz) whole blanched hazelnuts, halved*

*icing sugar, to dust*

**PREPARE AHEAD AND FREEZE**

*The roulade can be assembled up to 6 hours ahead. Freezes well filled.*

*The perfect celebratory dessert for any special occasion, especially Christmas. If you haven't time to make praline, top with a coarsely crushed bought praline bar.*

1.  Preheat the oven to 180°C (160°C fan/350°F/Gas 4). Melt the chocolate slowly in a bowl over a pan of hot water. Allow to cool slightly until warm but still runny.

2.  Whisk the egg whites in a large mixing bowl until stiff but not dry. Put the sugar and egg yolks into a separate large bowl and whisk until light, thick, and creamy.  Add the melted chocolate and stir until blended.

3.  Gently stir two large spoonfuls of the egg whites into the mixture, then fold in the remaining egg whites, followed by the cocoa. Stir in the hazelnuts. Pour into the prepared tin and gently level the surface. Bake for 20–25 minutes or until risen.

4.  Remove the cake from the oven and set aside to cool in the tin.

5.  Whip the cream into soft peaks and stir in the Baileys. Dust a large piece of non-stick baking parchment with icing sugar. Turn the cake out onto the paper and peel off the lining paper, then spread with the whipped cream. Make a cut part way through the roulade along the short edge nearest to you, about 2cm (¾ inch) in. Roll up the cake, tightly to start with and using the paper to help. Don't worry if it cracks – that is quite normal and part of its charm! Place on a long plate.

6.  To make the praline, put the sugar and 3 tablespoons of water into a stainless steel saucepan. Stir over a low heat until the sugar has dissolved. When clear, bring up to the boil. Boil until a medium straw colour. Add the hazelnuts, then pour quickly onto a baking sheet lined with non-stick paper. Leave to cool slightly, then use a teaspoon to carefully group together small clusters of nuts. Leave to cool and become hard. When set, break into pieces and arrange on the top of the roulade. Sprinkle with icing sugar to serve.

## IN THE AGA

Bake the roulade on the grid shelf on the floor of the roasting oven, with the cold sheet on the second set of runners for about 18 minutes – turn round half way through.

# HEAVENLY LEMON CHEESECAKE ON A GINGER CRUST

**MAKES A 20CM (8IN) CHEESECAKE (SERVES 8)**

**Special equipment** *20cm (8in) round loose-bottomed cake tin, greased and base-lined with baking parchment*

100g (3½oz) ginger biscuits, crushed

50g (1¾oz) butter, melted

2 x 250g tubs full-fat mascarpone

325g jar luxury lemon curd

juice of 1 small lemon

fresh raspberries and blueberries, to decorate

icing sugar, to dust

*This was the favourite pudding at a charity buffet for 40 that Mary was a guest at – it went like lightning. The other good news is that once you've collected the ingredients together, it only takes 10 minutes to make. You can make up to three of these cheesecakes in one go (but take care not to overbeat the mixture at step 2). If you're making more cheesecakes than that, prepare them in separate batches.*

1. Mix the biscuits with the butter in a bowl, then press into the base of the tin (but not up the sides).

2. Put the mascarpone, lemon curd, and lemon juice in a bowl and beat with a spatula until smooth.

3. Spoon onto the biscuit base and level the top. Chill in the fridge for at least 4 hours and up to 24 hours to firm up.

4. To serve, remove the cheesecake from the tin, peel off the baking parchment, and arrange on a platter. Decorate with the fruit and dust with icing sugar.

**PREPARE AHEAD**

*The cheesecake can be made up to the end of step 3 up to 1 day ahead. Not suitable for freezing.*

# CHILLED MARBLED RASPBERRY CHEESECAKE

MAKES A 23CM (9IN)
CHEESECAKE
(SERVES 8)

**Special equipment** *23cm (9in) round springform tin, greased and base-lined with baking parchment*

*100g (3½oz) digestive biscuits, crushed*

*50g (1¾oz) butter, melted*

*25g (scant 1oz) demerara sugar*

**For the raspberry filling**
*500g (1lb 2oz) fresh raspberries*

*2 tsp powdered gelatine*

*2 tbsp water*

*2 tbsp framboise liqueur*

**For the creamy filling**
*3 tsp powdered gelatine*

*3 tbsp water*

*250g (9oz) full-fat cream cheese, at room temperature*

*2 eggs, separated*

*200g (7oz) half-fat crème fraîche*

*100g (3½oz) caster sugar*

*This unusual chilled cheesecake has a delicious raspberry-ripple filling. If we don't have any framboise raspberry liqueur to hand, we make a cherry-ripple cheesecake, using kirsch instead.*

1. Mix the biscuits, butter, and sugar together in a bowl and press into the base of the tin. Transfer to the fridge to chill.

2. Meanwhile, make the raspberry filling. Whiz the raspberries in a food processor until smooth, then push through a sieve into a bowl. Put the gelatine into another bowl and add the water. Allow to soak until the gelatine becomes spongy, then stand the bowl in a saucepan of hot water until it dissolves. Once dissolved, add the framboise liqueur, then pour into the raspberry purée. Stir and set aside.

3. To make the creamy filling, prepare the gelatine and water as above. Put the cream cheese, egg yolks, and crème fraîche into a bowl and stir to combine.

4. Spoon 2 tablespoons of the creamy mixture into the liquid gelatine and mix, then pour the whole lot into the creamy mixture and stir until smooth.

5. Whisk the egg whites with an electric hand whisk until they look like clouds, then add the sugar a teaspoon at a time, whisking constantly until the mixture is stiff and glossy. Fold the egg whites into the creamy mixture until smooth.

6. Carefully fold the raspberry filling into the creamy mixture to give a ripple effect.

7. Spoon into the tin and chill in the fridge for a minimum of 6 hours or until firm.

8. To serve, remove from the tin, discard the disc of paper, and cut into slices.

**PREPARE AHEAD AND FREEZE**
*The cheesecake can be made up to the end of step 7 up to 2 days ahead. Freeze for up to 3 months.*

# RUM AND RAISIN ICE CREAM

SERVES 10–12

**Special equipment** *1.5 litre (2¾ pint) freezerproof container*

*175g (6oz) lexia raisins*

*5 tbsp dark rum*

*4 eggs, separated*

*100g (3½oz) caster sugar*

*300ml (10fl oz) double cream*

*One of the great things about this ice cream (apart from its flavour) is that you don't need an ice-cream maker. It's made with raw meringue, which means it doesn't need whisking as it freezes. Large, plump lexia raisins are lovely in ice cream – if you can't find them, you can use any other kind of raisin.*

1. Put the raisins into a bowl and add the rum. Leave to soak – ideally overnight.

2. Put the egg yolks into a small bowl and whisk with a fork until blended.

3. Whisk the egg whites with an electric whisk until they look like clouds. Whisking on maximum speed, add the sugar a teaspoon at a time until the mixture is stiff and glossy.

4. Whip the cream until soft peaks form, then fold into the egg-white mixture until smooth. Stir in the egg yolks and soaked raisins. If there is any rum left in the bowl, add this too.

5. Transfer to the freezerproof container and freeze for a minimum of 24 hours.

6. Remove from the freezer 10 minutes before serving to make scooping easier.

**PREPARE AHEAD AND FREEZE**

*Freeze for up to 2 months.*

# EXOTIC FRUIT SALAD

½ large cantaloupe melon

1 large mango, stone removed and flesh cut into cubes

3 passion fruit

3 oranges

1 grapefruit

225g (8oz) black seedless grapes

4 tbsp Cointreau or Grand Marnier (optional)

SERVES 12

1 large cantaloupe melon, cut in half

2 large mangoes, stones removed and flesh cut into cubes

6 passion fruit

6 oranges

2 grapefruits

500g (1lb 2oz) black seedless grapes

8 tbsp Cointreau or Grand Marnier (optional)

*This is a lovely refreshing fruit salad and any left over is a real treat for breakfast the next day. Raspberries and strawberries are also good in a fruit salad, but add them at the last minute or they will bleed into the other fruits and turn mushy. Bananas will go soft after a while, too. Avoid apples, pears, and peaches, as they discolour. Serve the fruit salad on its own or with cream.*

1. Scoop the seeds from the melon and discard. Using a sharp knife, cut into wedges and remove the skin. Slice the flesh into 2.5cm (1in) chunks and put into a serving bowl with the mango cubes.

2. Slice the passion fruit in half and scoop the seeds into the bowl.

3. Segment the oranges and grapefruit by cutting a piece from the top and base, then slicing down around the flesh, removing skin and pith. Slide the knife down one side of each segment, then cut down the other side and pull it free, making sure you catch the juices. Add to the bowl.

4. Slice the grapes in half and add to the bowl.

5. Add the Cointreau or Grand Marnier, if using, and mix lightly together, then chill in the fridge until you are ready to serve.

## PREPARE AHEAD

*The salad can be made up to 12 hours ahead.
Not suitable for freezing.*

# POACHED PEARS WITH BLACKBERRY SAUCE

*A fruit-based pudding is so welcome after a rich main course and these poached pears make a great change from fruit salad. The sauce for them is vivid and vibrant in colour. Make the pudding extra special by adding 1 tablespoon of crème de cassis to the purée.*

350g (12oz) granulated sugar

1.2 litres (2 pints) water

a few strips of lemon zest

6 pears, peeled, but stalk left on

**For the blackberry sauce**

450g (1lb) blackberries

100g (3½oz) granulated sugar

SERVES 12

700g (1lb 9oz) granulated sugar

2.5 litres (4¼ pints) water

a few strips of lemon zest

12 pears, peeled, but stalk left on

**For the blackberry sauce**

900g (2lb) blackberries

200g (7oz) granulated sugar

1. Put the sugar, water, and lemon peel into a saucepan just large enough to take the pears upright in a single layer.

2. Heat gently, stirring until the sugar has dissolved, then boil rapidly for 2 minutes.

3. Place the pears in the hot syrup, cover with a wet sheet of greaseproof paper (this ensures the top of the pears do not dry out), and bring to the boil. Cover with a lid and simmer gently for 30–45 minutes (50 minutes for 12) or until the pears are just tender. Set aside to cool.

4. To make the sauce, put the blackberries and sugar into a pan and cook for 5 minutes or until the juices start to run. Push through a sieve into a bowl to get a thickish purée.

5. When the pears are cold, remove them from the syrup and pat dry with kitchen paper.

6. Serve one pear per person or cut each one in half lengthways through the stem, remove the core, and serve two halves. Drizzle over the sauce.

### IN THE AGA

At step 3, bring to the boil, cover with a lid, and transfer to the simmering oven for 40 minutes (50 minutes for 12).

### PREPARE AHEAD AND FREEZE

*The pears can be poached up to 12 hours ahead and kept in the syrup until ready to serve. The sauce can be made up to 3 days ahead. Freeze the sauce for up to 2 months.*

# MAGENTA FRUIT COMPOTE WITH WHITE CHOCOLATE SAUCE

*One of the quickest, most delicious puddings you'll ever make! Serve with shortbread biscuits to make it extra special.*

## SERVES 6

30g (1oz) caster sugar

2 tbsp crème de cassis or blackcurrant liqueur

2 tbsp water

225g (8oz) blueberries

150g (5½oz) raspberries

225g (8oz) strawberries, quartered

100g (3½oz) Belgian or continental 100 per cent white chocolate

200ml (7fl oz) double cream

## SERVES 12

50g (1¾oz) caster sugar

4 tbsp crème de cassis or blackcurrant liqueur

4 tbsp water

500g (1lb 2oz) blueberries

300g (10oz) raspberries

500g (1lb 2oz) strawberries, quartered

200g (7oz) Belgian or continental 100 per cent white chocolate

400ml (14fl oz) double cream

1. Put the sugar, crème de cassis, and water into a shallow saucepan. Gently heat, then add the blueberries and simmer for a few minutes or until just starting to soften. Remove from the heat and add the raspberries and strawberries. Mix together and leave in the pan to cool completely.

2. Put the chocolate and cream into a bowl set over a pan of just-simmering water and stir until runny. Take care not to overheat the chocolate or it will lose its shine and split. Leave to cool and thicken slightly.

3. Divide the fruit among wine or cocktail glasses. Pour the white chocolate sauce over the top, then place in the fridge for 2 hours to set slightly.

## PREPARE AHEAD

*The fruit can be prepared up to 2 days ahead and the puddings assembled up to 12 hours ahead. Not suitable for freezing.*

# PARTY CRÈME BRÛLÉE

SERVES 12–16

**Special equipment** *2.4 litre (4 pint) shallow wide-based ovenproof dish, greased*

*85g (3oz) caster sugar*

*12 egg yolks*

*3 tsp vanilla extract*

*1.2 litres (2 pints) double cream*

*300ml (10fl oz) single cream*

*225g (8oz) demerara sugar*

*100g (3½oz) raspberries, to decorate*

*mint leaves, to decorate*

*A classic dessert that's brilliant for serving numbers. For a recipe for six, turn to page 278. This is delicious served with soft summer fruits such as raspberries or a fruit coulis.*

1. Preheat the oven to 160°C (140°C fan/325°F/Gas 3). Meanwhile, put the caster sugar, egg yolks, and vanilla extract into a large mixing bowl and whisk together by hand.

2. Put the double cream and single cream into a saucepan and heat until just below boiling point (just hot enough to put your finger in).

3. Pour the hot cream into the egg yolk mixture, whisking quickly until combined.

4. Pour the custard through a sieve into the prepared ovenproof dish.

5. Put the dish into a large roasting tin and pour enough boiling water into the tin so that it comes halfway up the sides of the dish.

6. Carefully slide into the oven and cook for 35–45 minutes or until set but with a slight wobble in the middle. Check after 30 minutes to see how it's doing.

7. Remove from the oven and leave to cool in the roasting tin, then place in the fridge and chill until stone cold.

8. Sprinkle over the demerara sugar, then pop under a hot grill, watching it very carefully, for 20–25 minutes or until melted and golden brown. You could also use a blowtorch to do this. To give the topping time to soften slightly, chill in the fridge for at least 5 hours and up to 10 hours, but no more or it will turn to liquid.

9. To serve, cut into portions with a fish slice and decorate with raspberries and mint leaves.

### IN THE AGA

Slide the tin onto the lowest set of runners in the roasting oven, with the cold sheet on the second set of runners, and bake for 15 minutes or until just set around the edges, then transfer to the simmering oven for 45 minutes. At step 8, add the demerara sugar and brown with a blowtorch.

### PREPARE AHEAD

*The custard can be made up to the end of step 7 up to 2 days ahead. Not suitable for freezing.*

# PEAR AND GINGER PAVLOVA

*Pear and ginger is one of our all-time favourite combinations. This pavlova is sprinkled with pomegranate seeds just before serving – they look so pretty and glisten like little gems.*

## SERVES 6

3 egg whites

175g (6oz) caster sugar

1 level tsp cornflour

1 tsp white wine vinegar

### For the topping

5 fairly ripe pears, peeled, cored, and chopped into chunky slices

juice of ½ lemon

50g (1¾oz) caster sugar

300ml (10fl oz) double cream, whipped

6 bulbs stem ginger (from a jar), drained and coarsely chopped

1 small pomegranate

icing sugar, to dust

## SERVES 12

6 egg whites

350g (12oz) caster sugar

2 level tsp cornflour

2 tsp white wine vinegar

### For the topping

10 fairly ripe pears, peeled, cored, and chopped into chunky slices

juice of 1 lemon

100g (3½oz) caster sugar

600ml (1 pint) double cream, whipped

12 bulbs stem ginger (from a jar), drained and coarsely chopped

2 small pomegranates

icing sugar, to dust

1. Preheat the oven to 160°C (140°C fan/325°F/Gas 3). Whisk the egg whites with an electric whisk until they look like clouds. Gradually add the sugar a little at a time, whisking on maximum speed until the whites are stiff and glossy. Mix the cornflour and vinegar in a cup until smooth, then stir into the meringue mixture.

2. Line a baking sheet with baking parchment and draw a 20 x 30cm (8 x 12in) rectangle on it (two rectangles side by side for 12). Spread the meringue mixture out into the rectangle(s) with a knife, then create a well in the middle by building up the sides.

3. Slide the baking sheet into the oven, immediately reduce the temperature to 150°C (130°C fan/300°F/Gas 2), and bake for 1 hour. Turn the oven off and leave the meringue in the oven for a further hour to dry out.

4. To make the topping, put the pears, lemon juice, and sugar into a small pan and barely cover with water from the tap. Simmer gently over a low heat for 10 minutes or until the pears are just tender. Leave in the liquid until needed, then drain. Slice half of the pears into thin slices and reserve for decoration. Chop the remaining pears and stir into the whipped cream with the ginger.

5. Arrange the pavlova on a serving plate, spoon the cream into the well, and decorate with the reserved pears. Cut the pomegranate in half, pick out the seeds, and sprinkle over the top. Serve at room temperature, dusted with icing sugar.

### IN THE AGA

Bake the meringue in the simmering oven for 2–2½ hours, then sit it by the side of the Aga until cold.

### PREPARE AHEAD AND FREEZE

*The pavlova can be made up to the end of step 3 up to 1 month ahead. Wrap in cling film and then foil and keep in a cool place. The pears can be poached up to 8 hours ahead. The pavlova can be assembled up to 4 hours ahead. Freeze the meringue without the topping for up to 6 months.*

# PARTY PAVLOVA PYRAMID

## SERVES 35-40

2 x 6 egg whites

2 x 350g (12oz) caster sugar

2 x 1 tsp white wine vinegar

2 x 1 tsp cornflour

### For the filling

1.7 litres (3 pints) double cream

500g tub full-fat Greek yogurt

900g (2lb) strawberries, hulled

750g (1lb 10oz) raspberries

450g (1lb) blueberries

a few mint leaves, to decorate (optional)

*You don't get successful meringues if you use more than six egg whites at a time, which is why we make them in two batches for this party pyramid. It is the most spectacular dessert you'll ever make. To make a larger pyramid, add another layer as opposed to making larger meringues.*

1. Preheat the oven to 160°C (140°C fan/325°F/Gas 3). To make the first batch of meringue, put six egg whites into a bowl and whisk with an electric whisk until they look like clouds. Add the sugar a little at a time, whisking on maximum speed until the mixture is stiff and glossy. Mix the vinegar and cornflour in a cup until smooth, then stir into the bowl.

2. Line a baking sheet with baking parchment and spread the meringue mixture out – it should be about 30cm (12in) in diameter and about 5cm (2in) thick. This will be the base for the pyramid.

3. Slide into the oven, then immediately reduce the temperature to 150°C (130°C fan/300°F/Gas 2) and bake for 1 hour. Turn the oven off and leave the meringue inside for 1 hour or overnight to dry.

4. Prepare a second batch of mixture. Use to make one meringue measuring 25cm (10in) in diameter, another measuring 20cm (8in) in diameter, and a third that is 12cm (5in) in diameter. The smallest can be fairly thin and should fit on a baking sheet with the 20cm (8in) one.

5. Cook in the same way: put the 25cm (10in) meringue in the oven and bake for 15 minutes, then pop the two smaller meringues in as well and bake for a further 45 minutes. Switch off the oven and leave to dry out for 1 hour or overnight.

6. To assemble, whip the cream until stiff and mix with the yogurt. Put the largest meringue on a sturdy foil-covered board or tray. Cover with cream and half the fruit, ensuring the fruit can be seen at the edges.

7. Place the next-largest meringue on top and cover with cream and fruit. Continue in the same way with the other meringues. Finish with the last of the cream and a pretty arrangement of fruit and mint leaves on top, if using. To serve, cut in wedges, starting from the top.

## PREPARE AHEAD AND FREEZE

*The meringues can be made up to 1 month ahead and stored (see page 302). Freeze for up to 6 months. The pyramid can be assembled up to 4 hours ahead. This is best done in situ, so you don't need to move it.*

## IN THE AGA

Bake the largest meringue in the simmering oven for 2½ hours. Bake the 25cm (10in) meringue for 1 hour, add the two smaller ones, and bake for a further hour. Sit the meringues by the Aga until cold.

# HAZELNUT MERINGUE ROULADE WITH RASPBERRIES

MAKES A 33CM (13IN)
ROULADE (SERVES
8–10)

**Special equipment** *23 x 33cm (9 x 13in) Swiss roll tin, greased and lined with baking parchment*

*4 egg whites*

*225g (8oz) caster sugar*

*50g (1¾oz) roasted hazelnuts, chopped*

*300ml (10fl oz) double cream, whipped*

*200g (7oz) fresh raspberries*

*Meringue roulade is such a classic pudding. As a twist, we've added chopped roasted hazelnuts to give a lovely nutty flavour that goes sublimely well with raspberries and cream. If you are serving a larger crowd, prepare individual roulades rather than multiplying the quantities and making a big one, and bake one at a time. If your meringues crumble beyond repair, make Eton mess instead – see below left.*

1. Preheat the oven to 200°C (180°C fan/400°F/Gas 6). Meanwhile, put the egg whites into a large clean bowl and whisk with an electric whisk until very stiff. With the whisk still on full speed, gradually add the sugar a teaspoon at a time, whisking well between each addition. The meringue is ready when it is glossy and very, very stiff.

2. Spread the mixture into the prepared tin and sprinkle with the hazelnuts. Bake for 8 minutes or until lightly golden. Reduce the temperature to 160°C (140°C fan/325°F/Gas 3) and bake for a further 20 minutes.

3. Remove the meringue from the oven and turn hazelnut side down onto a sheet of baking parchment. Remove the paper from the base of the meringue and allow to cool for 10 minutes.

4. Spread the whipped cream over the meringue and scatter over the raspberries. Using the parchment to help you, roll the meringue up fairly tightly from one of the long ends to form a roulade. Wrap in baking parchment and chill well before serving.

5. To serve, unwrap and cut into slices.

## ETON MESS

*To serve six, crush 100g (3½oz) meringue into grape-sized pieces. Whip 300ml (10fl oz) double cream until it just holds its shape, and whiz 100g (3½oz) of your chosen fruit in a food processor to make a smooth purée. Carefully fold the fruit purée, 100g (3½oz) chopped fruit, 25g (scant 1oz) icing sugar, and the crushed meringue into the whipped cream. Serve chilled. For 12, double all the quantities. The cream can be whipped and folded with all the ingredients except the meringues up to 12 hours ahead. Fold in the meringues a maximum of 6 hours ahead. Not suitable for freezing.*

### IN THE AGA

Bake on the grid shelf on the floor of the roasting oven, with the cold sheet on the second set of runners, for 12–15 minutes. Transfer to the simmering oven for 15 minutes until firm to the touch.

## PREPARE AHEAD AND FREEZE

*The roulade can be made up to 12 hours ahead. Freeze without the raspberries for up to 2 months. Serve with the raspberries on the side.*

# LEMON AND LIME POSSETS

## SERVES 6

600ml (1 pint) double cream

150g (5½oz) caster sugar

finely grated zest and juice of 2 lemons

finely grated zest and juice of 2 limes

lime zest, sprigs of mint, or borage flowers, to decorate

## SERVES 12

1.2 litres (2 pints) double cream

300g (11oz) caster sugar

finely grated zest and juice of 4 lemons

finely grated zest and juice of 4 limes

lime zest, sprigs of mint, or borage flowers, to decorate

*These creamy desserts are one of those foolproof puds you'll go back to time and again and all your friends will ask for the recipe.*

1. Put the cream, sugar, lemon zest, and lime zest into a wide-based saucepan.

2. Heat gently over a low heat, stirring until the sugar has dissolved and the cream is just under scalding point (just hot enough to touch).

3. Remove from the heat and stir in the lemon juice and lime juice.

4. Pour into small coffee cups or shot glasses and leave to set in the fridge for at least 6 hours.

5. Serve chilled, decorated with lime zest, sprigs of mint, or borage flowers.

## PREPARE AHEAD

The possets can be made up to the end of step 4 up to 2 days ahead. Not suitable for freezing.

# SUMMER BERRY TART

MAKES A 28CM (11IN)
TART (SERVES 8-10)

**Special equipment** *28cm
(11in) loose-bottomed
fluted tart tin*

*225g (8oz) plain flour, plus
a little extra to dust*

*100g (3½oz) cold butter,
cubed*

*25g (scant 1oz) icing sugar*

*1 egg*

*2 tbsp water*

**For the crème pâtissière**

*3 eggs*

*75g (2½oz) caster sugar*

*1 tsp vanilla extract*

*50g (1¾oz) plain flour*

*400ml (14fl oz) milk*

**For the topping**

*300g (10oz) strawberries,
hulled and quartered*

*125g (4½oz) raspberries*

*125g (4½oz) blueberries*

*6–8 tbsp redcurrant jelly*

*1 tbsp water*

*This looks stunning and makes the most of all the lovely
summer fruits. It's a top favourite of Lucy's.*

1. Preheat the oven to 200°C (180°C fan/400°F/Gas 6). Put the flour, butter, and icing sugar into a food processer and whiz until the mixture resembles breadcrumbs. Add the egg and water and whiz again until it forms a smooth dough. Lightly dust a work surface with flour and knead the dough for a few minutes or until it forms a smooth ball. Roll it out and use to line the tart tin (see page 267). Chill while you make the crème pâtissière.

2. Put the eggs, sugar, vanilla extract, and flour into a mixing bowl and mix with a wooden spoon until smooth. Add 2 tablespoons of the milk and stir again. Heat the remaining milk until just below boiling, then pour into the mixing bowl and whisk until smooth. Return to the pan and gently heat, whisking until thick and nearly simmering, but don't let it boil. Set aside to cool.

3. Cut a circle of baking parchment just larger than the tin, then fold into a triangle and snip the edge. Line the pastry case with the baking parchment, pushing it into the rim, and fill with dried beans or baking beans. Bake the pastry case blind for 20 minutes, then remove the beans and paper. The pastry will be partially cooked and won't go soggy when the filling is added. Lower the oven temperature to 160°C (140°C fan/325°F/Gas 3) and return the tart case to the oven for 10 minutes to dry out. Set aside to cool.

4. Pour the crème pâtissière into the tart case and arrange the fruit in circles on top – strawberries on the outside, then a circle of raspberries, and the blueberries in the centre.

5. Heat the redcurrant jelly and water together in a pan over a gentle heat, whisking until smooth. Brush this glaze over the fruit, then place the tart in the fridge and serve chilled.

## IN THE AGA

Skip step 3. Fill the uncooked pastry case and bake on the grid shelf on the floor of the roasting oven, with the cold sheet on the second set of runners, for 25 minutes, then transfer to the simmering oven for 15 minutes.

## PREPARE AHEAD

*The pastry case can be baked up to 2 days ahead.
The crème pâtissière can be made up to 1 day
ahead. The tart can be assembled up to 8 hours
ahead. Not suitable for freezing.*

# TEA FOR A CROWD

*Plates of neatly cut sandwiches, tiers of home-made cakes – it's everyone's idea of a traditional English tea. Keep the food small, and offer a selection of individual items such as cupcakes and muffins, biscuits and scones, which are simple to eat as you stand and chat.*

# SANDWICHES

*At teatime, sandwiches should be small. Some fillings can be added up to 10 hours ahead. Others can be added up to one day ahead with no compromise on freshness or taste. Fillings containing cucumber or tomato should only ever be added on the day. To stop the bread going soggy, you also need to remove the seeds from the vegetables. Slice the cucumber in half lengthways and scoop out the seeds with a teaspoon. To deseed tomatoes, see page 238.*

**MAKES 24 (SERVES 6)**

soft butter

12 slices bread from a thin-cut or medium-cut white or brown loaf

the filling(s) of your choice (see below)

salt and freshly ground black pepper

**Fillings you can add 1 day ahead**

Rare roast beef with horseradish sauce and rocket

Egg mayonnaise with lots of mustard cress

Smoked salmon and cream cheese

Hummus, olive, and grated carrot

Ham and English mustard

Cream cheese, mango chutney, and watercress

Gravadlax and mustard mayonnaise (see page 72)

Mature Cheddar, pickle, and watercress

Goat's cheese, rocket, and sun-dried tomato paste

Thin strips of pan-fried steak and mustard

Crispy bacon with egg mayonnaise

**Fillings to add on the day**

Prawns with lemon mayonnaise

Feta cheese, sun-dried tomato paste, and cucumber

Cucumber and black pepper

Sardine, mayonnaise, and lemon

Fresh salmon and cucumber

Avocado and bacon

Crab and avocado with lime mayonnaise

Pastrami and sweet dill pickle with cream cheese and horseradish sauce

Tomato, basil, and mozzarella

Smoked mackerel, tomato, and aïoli

1. Butter the bread on one side, top half the slices with the filling(s) of your choice, and sandwich together. Leave the crusts on.

2. Arrange the sandwiches in piles of four on a large tray (check first that it will fit in your fridge). Cover with a layer of damp kitchen paper, then cover tightly with cling film, and place the tray in the fridge.

3. Two hours before serving, slice off the crusts and cut the sandwiches into fingers or quarters – either triangles or squares. Cover with cling film and keep at room temperature until ready to serve. They will taste as fresh as the moment you made them.

# LIME MARMALADE TRAYBAKE

**CUTS INTO 12 SQUARES**

**Special equipment** *23 x 30cm (9 x 12in) traybake tin, lined with foil and greased*

*225g (8oz) butter, at room temperature*

*225g (8oz) caster sugar*

*300g (11oz) self-raising flour*

*4 eggs*

*1 tsp baking powder*

*finely grated zest of 1 lime, plus 2 tbsp lime juice*

*2 tbsp lime marmalade*

**For the icing**

*350g (12oz) icing sugar*

*100g (3½oz) full-fat cream cheese*

*50g (1¾oz) butter, at room temperature*

*2 tbsp lime marmalade*

*juice and finely grated zest of 1 small lime*

*Cut into squares, traybakes are great at large gatherings. This unusual recipe has a wonderful zesty taste. See the variation below for another deliciously citrusy cake.*

1. Preheat the oven to 180°C (160°C fan/350°F/Gas 4). Put all the ingredients for the cake into a mixing bowl and beat by hand or with an electric whisk until combined and smooth.

2. Spoon into the traybake tin and level the top.

3. Bake for 30–35 minutes or until risen and golden. Set aside to cool completely.

4. To make the icing, sift the icing sugar into a mixing bowl, add all the other ingredients, and beat with a wooden spoon or an electric whisk until well combined and smooth.

5. Spread the icing over the cake, making a pretty pattern on it with a palette knife. Cut into 12 squares and serve.

## IN THE AGA

Bake on the grid shelf on the floor of the roasting oven, with the cold sheet on the second set of runners, for 30 minutes.

## ICED ORANGE AND LEMON TRAYBAKE

*For orange and lemon traybake, follow the recipe above, omitting the lime zest, juice, and marmalade, and adding 4 tbsp milk to the cake mixture. Stir the grated zest of ½ lemon and ½ small orange into the mixture at the end of step 1, then bake for the same length of time. To make the icing, mix 225g (8oz) icing sugar, 1 tbsp lemon juice, and 2 tbsp orange juice. Sprinkle over the grated zest of ½ lemon and ½ small orange.*

## PREPARE AHEAD AND FREEZE

*The cake can be made up to 1 day ahead and iced on the day. Freeze without the icing for up to 3 months.*

# ALMOND BISCUITS

**MAKES 30–35**

**Special equipment** 5cm (2in) fluted scone cutter

100g (3½oz) butter, at room temperature

75g (2½oz) caster sugar

100g (3½oz) plain flour, plus a little extra to dust

75g (2½oz) ground almonds

½ tsp almond extract

25g (scant 1oz) flaked almonds

*These are as delicious with a cup of coffee as they are at teatime. If you're preparing them ahead, stop them going soggy by storing them in a tin with pieces of kitchen paper between the layers.*

1. Put the butter and sugar into a mixing bowl and whisk with an electric whisk until light and fluffy. Add the flour, ground almonds, and almond extract and whisk again until smooth.

2. Lightly dust a work surface with flour and knead the dough for a few minutes until smooth.

3. Preheat the oven to 180°C (160°C fan/325°F/Gas 4). Grease two baking sheets or line with baking parchment. Lightly flour the work surface again and roll the dough out until it is 5mm (¼in) thick. Using a 5cm (2in) fluted scone cutter, cut out 30–35 rounds.

4. Transfer to the baking sheets with a palette knife. Sprinkle a few flaked almonds on top of each biscuit and press them down gently so they stick to the dough. Chill for 30 minutes.

5. Bake for 12–15 minutes (checking after 10 minutes) or until lightly golden. Leave to cool slightly, then transfer to a wire rack to cool completely.

### IN THE AGA
Bake on the grid shelf on the floor of the roasting oven, with the cold sheet on the second set of runners, for 10 minutes.

### PREPARE AHEAD AND FREEZE
*The biscuits can be made up to 4 days ahead and stored, layered with kitchen paper, in a biscuit tin. Freeze for up to 3 months.*

# PECAN AND CHOCOLATE CHIP COOKIES

## MAKES 24

100g (3½oz) butter, at room temperature

50g (1¾oz) caster sugar

150g (5½oz) self-raising flour, plus a little extra to dust

½ tsp vanilla extract

50g (1¾oz) milk chocolate chips

50g (1¾oz) pecan nuts, chopped

*Everyone loves cookies. And no one will be able to resist this deliciously gooey combination of pecan nuts and chocolate. The cookies keep well in a tin for a couple of days.*

1. Preheat the oven to 180°C (160°C fan/350°F/Gas 4). Put the butter and sugar into a bowl and mix together with a wooden spoon until light and fluffy. Stir in the flour, then add the vanilla extract, chocolate chips, and pecans and mix to a soft dough.

2. Knead the dough lightly on a floured work surface, then divide into 24 balls. Flatten the balls with the palm of your hand and arrange on two baking sheets lined with baking parchment. Space them out so they have room to spread.

3. Bake for 20–25 minutes or until lightly golden. Transfer to a wire rack to cool.

### IN THE AGA

Bake on the grid shelf on the floor of the roasting oven, with the cold sheet on the second set of runners, for 15 minutes.

### PREPARE AHEAD AND FREEZE

*The cookies can be made up to 2 days ahead and kept in a sealed container. Freeze the raw mixture or the cooked cookies for up to 2 months.*

# COFFEE AND WALNUT CUPCAKES

MAKES 12

**Special equipment** *12-hole muffin tin lined with 12 paper muffin cases*

1 tbsp instant coffee granules

1 tbsp boiling water

115g (4oz) butter, softened

140g (5oz) self-raising flour

140g (5oz) caster sugar

2 tbsp milk

2 large eggs

25g (scant 1oz) walnuts, chopped

**For the coffee icing**

2 tsp instant coffee granules

2 tsp boiling water

100g (3½oz) butter, at room temperature

225g (8oz) icing sugar

12 walnut halves, to decorate

*Cupcakes are the cake of the moment, with some shops specializing in just them. These are made in muffin tins, which are fairly large, but make them in bun tins if you wish – you should get 18 fairy cakes. A dozen cupcakes arranged on a tiered cakestand make a spectacular centrepiece for any tea party.*

1. Preheat the oven to 180°C (160°C fan/350°F/Gas 4). Put the coffee granules and water into a mixing bowl and stir until smooth. Add the butter, flour, sugar, milk, and eggs to the mixing bowl and mix with an electric whisk until smooth. Stir in the walnuts, then spoon into the muffin cases.

2. Bake in the centre of the oven for 20–25 minutes or until risen and golden brown. Transfer to a wire rack until stone cold.

3. To make the icing, put the coffee granules and boiling water into a bowl and stir until smooth. Add the butter, sift in the icing sugar, and stir until smooth and free of streaks.

4. Spoon onto the cupcakes, then decorate each one with a walnut half.

### IN THE AGA
Bake on the grid shelf on the floor of the roasting oven, with the cold sheet on the second set of runners, for 15–20 minutes.

### PREPARE AHEAD AND FREEZE
*The cupcakes can be made and iced up to 1 day ahead. Freeze without the icing for up to 1 month.*

# FAIRY CAKES

MAKES 24

**Special equipment** *2 x 12-hole bun tins, greased or lined with paper cases*

*150g (5½oz) butter, softened*

*150g (5½oz) caster sugar*

*150g (5½oz) self-raising flour*

*1½ tsp baking powder*

*1½ tsp vanilla extract*

*3 eggs*

**For the icing**

*150g (5½oz) icing sugar*

*about 3 tbsp lemon juice*

**To decorate**

*sweets of your choice*

*Fairy cakes are always so popular. These are a basic vanilla sponge mix with lemon icing, but you can make whichever flavour you like – see our variations, below left. Decorate them with creative flair. We like to use Jelly Babies, Jelly Tots, and Maltesers.*

1. Preheat the oven to 180°C (160°C fan/350°F/Gas 4). Put all the ingredients for the cakes into a large mixing bowl and beat with an electric whisk until smooth. Spoon evenly into the tins.

2. Bake for 12–15 minutes or until risen and pale golden brown. Set aside to cool, then remove the cakes from the tins.

3. To make the icing, sift the icing sugar into a bowl and add enough lemon juice to make a fairly stiff paste. Spoon a circle of the icing on the top of each cake. While the icing is still soft, decorate with the sweets of your choice.

### IN THE AGA

Bake on the grid shelf on the floor of the roasting oven for 10–12 minutes or until well risen and golden. If the cakes are getting too brown, slide the cold sheet onto the second set of runners.

### FAIRY CAKE VARIATIONS

*For chocolate chip fairy cakes, add 25g (scant 1oz) dark chocolate chips to the basic sponge mix. For lemon fairy cakes, add the grated zest of 1 lemon to the basic mix. For orange fairy cakes, add the grated zest of 1 orange to the basic sponge mix, and for the icing, use orange juice or orange blossom water instead of lemon juice. For rosewater fairy cakes, make the icing with 2 tbsp rosewater and 1 tbsp water instead of the lemon juice.*

### PREPARE AHEAD AND FREEZE

*The cakes can be made and iced up to 1 day ahead. Freeze for up to 2 months.*

# CHOCOLATE AND ORANGE MOUSSE CAKE

**MAKES 24**

**Special equipment** *23cm (9in) springform tin, greased and base-lined*

*180g (6oz) Bournville chocolate*

*6 eggs, separated*

*75g (2½oz) caster sugar*

*2–3 tbsp Cointreau*

*2 level tbsp cocoa powder*

**For the topping**

*100g (3½oz) orange milk chocolate, coarsely grated*

*1–2 tbsp Cointreau*

*200ml (7fl oz) double cream, lightly whipped*

*cocoa powder, to dust*

*This lovely cake has no flour – just cocoa powder – so it is as light as a feather. For children, replace the Cointreau with orange juice. Bake it at Easter and decorate with mini eggs.*

1. Preheat the oven to 180°C (160°C fan/350°F/Gas 4). Meanwhile, break the chocolate into pieces and place in a small heatproof bowl. Sit the bowl over a pan of hot water and stir until the chocolate has melted. Set aside to cool slightly. To base-line the tin, put baking parchment over the base of the tin, clip the ring in place, and trim the parchment with scissors.

2. Whisk the egg whites with an electric whisk until stiff. Put the egg yolks and sugar into a separate bowl and whisk until light and creamy.

3. Pour the melted chocolate into the egg-yolk mixture, add the Cointreau, and gently fold together, taking care not to knock out any of the air. Add the egg whites and gently fold to combine. Sift in the cocoa powder and fold until combined. Spoon evenly into the tin.

4. Bake for 40 minutes or until risen, shrinking away from the sides of the tin, and just firm to the touch in the centre. Leave to cool, then remove from the tin.

5. For the topping, stir half the chocolate and the Cointreau into the cream. Spread over the top of the cake and sprinkle with the remaining chocolate. Sift the cocoa powder on top.

### IN THE AGA

Bake the cake in two 23cm (9in) sandwich tins on the grid shelf on the floor of the roasting oven, with the cold sheet on the second set of runners, for 25 minutes. Use just under half the topping to sandwich the cakes together.

**PREPARE AHEAD AND FREEZE**

*The cake can be made up to the end of step 4 up to 1 day ahead. Add the topping on the day of serving. Freeze without the topping for up to 2 months.*

# FIGGY SEEDED BITES

MAKES 12 BARS
OR 24 BITES

**Special equipment** *18cm
(7in) square shallow tin,
lined with baking
parchment and greased*

*75g (2½oz) butter*

*50g (1¾oz) golden syrup*

*100g (3½oz) caster sugar*

*175g (6oz) porridge oats*

*25g (scant 1oz) sunflower
seeds*

*25g (scant 1oz) pumpkin
seeds*

*25g (scant 1oz) desiccated
coconut*

*100g (3½oz) dried figs,
snipped into tiny pieces*

*50g (1¾oz) dried apricots,
snipped into tiny pieces*

*Seeded bars are extremely popular in the shops. They
are also healthier than a slice of cake, so why not make
your own. When we were testing these, the whole lot
went in one go!*

1.  Preheat the oven to 180°C (160°C fan/350°F/Gas 4). Heat the
butter, golden syrup, and sugar in a saucepan over a gentle heat,
stirring until melted and dissolved.

2.  Put the remaining ingredients into a large mixing bowl, add
the melted butter mixture, and stir well. Pour into the tin and
level the top.

3.  Bake for 30–35 minutes or until lightly golden and firm in the
middle. Leave to cool slightly, then cut into 12 rectangles or 24
squares. Leave in the tin to harden, then transfer to a wire rack
to cool completely.

### IN THE AGA

Bake on the grid shelf on the floor of the roasting oven, with
the cold sheet on the second set of runners, for 15–20 minutes.

### PREPARE AHEAD

*The bites can be made up to 3 days ahead and
kept in a cool place. Not suitable for freezing.*

# WHITE CHOCOLATE AND STRAWBERRY MUFFINS

MAKES 12

**Special equipment** *Deep 12-hole muffin tin lined with paper muffin cases*

*300g (11oz) self-raising flour*

*1 tsp baking powder*

*175g (6oz) caster sugar*

*2 eggs*

*225ml (7½fl oz) milk*

*100g (3½oz) butter, melted*

*2 tsp vanilla extract*

*100g (3½oz) white chocolate chips*

*12 tsp strawberry jam*

*icing sugar, to dust*

*These are perfect for a children's tea party. For a slightly more sophisticated touch, replace the white chocolate chips with dark chocolate chips.*

1. Preheat the oven to 200°C (180°C fan/400°F/Gas 6). Put all the ingredients except the chocolate chips and jam into a large bowl and whisk with an electric whisk until smooth. Stir in the chocolate chips.

2. Divide half the mixture evenly between the cases, spoon 1 teaspoon of jam on top of each one, then spoon the remaining mixture on top.

3. Bake for 25–30 minutes or until well risen and lightly golden brown.

4. Dust with a little icing sugar and serve warm or cold.

### IN THE AGA
Bake on the grid shelf on the floor of the roasting oven, with the cold sheet on the second set of runners, for 20–25 minutes.

### PREPARE AHEAD AND FREEZE
*The muffins can be made up to 2 days ahead. Freeze for up to 1 month.*

# MINCEMEAT BUNS

## MAKES 21

**Special equipment** *2 x 12-hole bun tins, lined with paper cases*

*150g (5½oz) butter, softened*

*150g (5½oz) caster sugar*

*225g (8oz) self-raising flour*

*2 eggs*

*2 tbsp milk*

*100g (3½oz) currants*

*100g (3½oz) mincemeat*

*25g (scant 1oz) flaked almonds*

*Mincemeat buns are traditional at Christmas, but there's no reason why you shouldn't make them at any time of year. Use vegetarian mincemeat if you don't eat meat.*

1. Preheat the oven to 180°C (160°C fan/350°F/Gas 4). Put all the ingredients except the almonds into a bowl and beat well with a wooden spoon to combine.

2. Spoon the mixture into the paper cases, level the tops, and make sure there are no drips over the sides of the cases. Sprinkle with the almonds.

3. Bake for 15 minutes or until well risen and lightly golden.

4. Leave the buns in the tins for a few minutes, then transfer them to a cooling rack and leave to cool completely.

### IN THE AGA
Bake on the grid shelf on the floor of the roasting oven, with the cold sheet on the second set of runners, for 15 minutes or until golden.

### PREPARE AHEAD AND FREEZE
*The buns can be made up to 1 day ahead and kept in the fridge. Freeze for up to 2 months.*

# ALMOND CRUMBLE-TOPPED MINCE PIES

**MAKES 24**

**Special equipment** 2 x 12-hole bun tins

7.5cm (3in) fluted pastry cutter

175g (6oz) plain flour, plus extra to dust

100g (3½oz) chilled butter

2 tbsp icing sugar, plus extra to dust

1 egg, beaten

410g (14¼oz) luxury mincemeat

**For the almond crumble topping**

75g (2½oz) plain flour

25g (scant 1oz) porridge oats

25g (scant 1oz) demerara sugar

25g (scant 1oz) chopped blanched almonds

50g (1¾oz) butter, at room temperature, cubed

*Classic mince pies with a delicious almond crumble topping. They are best served warm.*

1. Preheat the oven to 200°C (180°C fan/400°F/Gas 6). Measure the flour and butter into a food processor and whiz for a few minutes until the mixture resembles breadcrumbs. Add the icing sugar and egg and whiz again until the mixture forms a smooth ball.

2. Roll the pastry out on a floured work surface until thin. Using the fluted cutter, cut out 24 discs. You may need to gather and re-roll the pastry.

3. Line the bun tins with the discs of pastry. Prick the bases with a fork and chill for 10 minutes.

4. To make the almond crumble topping, measure all the ingredients into a bowl and use your fingers to rub them together to make a crumble mixture.

5. Spoon mincemeat into the base of each pastry case, then top with the crumble topping.

6. Bake for 20–25 minutes until golden. Serve warm, dusted with icing sugar.

### AGA

Cook on the grid shelf on the floor of the roasting oven for 15–20 minutes.

**PREPARE AHEAD AND FREEZE**

*The mince pies freeze well. Wrap well once cooked and reheat to serve.*

# APRICOT AND CHERRY LOAF CAKES

*Small loaf cakes are always lovely to make and are quicker to bake than large ones. This recipes makes two. If you don't need both straightaway, you can eat one and freeze the other.*

## MAKES 2

**Special equipment** *2 x 450g (1lb) loaf tins, greased and the bases and sides lined with baking parchment*

*175g (6oz) self-raising flour*

*115g (4oz) butter, softened*

*115g (4oz) caster sugar*

*3 large eggs, beaten*

*150g (5½oz) ready-to-eat apricots, snipped into small pieces*

*50g (1½oz) raisins*

*50g (1½oz) glacé cherries, snipped into small pieces*

1. Preheat the oven to 180°C (160°C fan/350°F/Gas 4). Put the flour, butter, sugar, and eggs into a mixing bowl and whisk with an electric whisk until combined. Stir in the dried fruit and cherries, then spoon into the tins and level the tops.

2. Bake for 45–50 minutes or until golden brown and well risen. Transfer to a wire rack to cool completely.

### IN THE AGA

Sit the loaf tins in a roasting tin (the sides of it will prevent the cake burning) and bake on the lowest set of runners, with the cold sheet on the second set of runners, for 45 minutes.

### PREPARE AHEAD AND FREEZE

*The cakes can be baked up to 2 days ahead, although they are best made and eaten on the same day. Freeze for up to 3 months.*

# ASHBURTON CARROT CAKE

**MAKES A 23CM (9IN) CAKE (SERVES 8)**

**Special equipment** *2 x 23cm (9in) sandwich tins, greased and lined with a disc of baking parchment*

200g (7oz) self-raising flour

300g (11oz) granulated sugar

1 tsp baking powder

1½ tsp ground cinnamon

175ml (6fl oz) sunflower oil

2 eggs, lightly beaten

1 tsp vanilla extract

100g (3½ oz) raw carrots, grated

100g (3½ oz) chopped walnuts

60g (2oz) desiccated coconut

220g can pineapple slices, drained, chopped, and dried thoroughly

**For the icing**

200g (7oz) full-fat cream cheese

100g (3½ oz) butter, softened

200g (7oz) icing sugar

1 tsp vanilla extract

*Passing through the village of Ashburton, in Devon, Mary stopped at a tea shop and had a piece of wonderful carrot cake. The owner kindly gave Mary the recipe and it's loved by one and all.*

1.  Preheat the oven to 180°C (160°C fan/350°F/Gas 4). To base-line the tins, stand each on baking parchment, draw around the base with a pencil, then cut the disc out and place it in the bottom of the greased tin. Put the flour into a large mixing bowl, add the sugar, baking powder, and cinnamon and stir together.

2.  Add the oil, eggs, and vanilla extract and beat well with a wooden spoon or spatula. Fold in the carrots, walnuts, coconut, and pineapple and beat until smooth.

3.  Spoon evenly into the sandwich tins and bake for 45–50 minutes or until well risen and golden brown. To check that the cakes are cooked in the middle, insert a skewer into the centre – if it comes out clean, they are done. Transfer to a wire rack and leave to cool.

4.  To make the icing, put the cream cheese and butter into a bowl, sift in the icing sugar, add the vanilla extract, and whisk with an electric whisk until smooth.

5.  Remove the cakes from the tins and peel off the baking parchment. Turn one cake upside down onto a serving plate and spread with half the icing. Sit the other cake on top and spread the remaining icing over the top.

### IN THE AGA

Bake on the grid shelf on the floor of the roasting oven, with the cold sheet on the second set of runners, for 30 minutes. Keep an eye on it – you may need to replace the cold sheet halfway through cooking to stop it getting too brown.

### PREPARE AHEAD AND FREEZE

*The cake can be made up to 1 day ahead, although it is best made on the day. Freeze without the icing for up to 2 months.*

# BUTTERY SCONES

MAKES 12

**Special equipment** 7.5cm
(3in) scone cutter

225g (8oz) self-raising flour,
plus a little extra to dust

2 tsp baking powder

45g (1½oz) butter, at room
temperature

25g (scant 1oz) caster sugar

1 egg

about 150ml (5fl oz) milk

*Scones are so quintessentially English and a traditional part of tea. For success every time, make sure the dough is good and sticky rather than dry. Be careful not to twist the cutter when cutting the scones out or they won't rise evenly during baking. Serve warm with clotted cream and strawberry jam.*

1. Preheat the oven to 200°C (180°C fan/400°F/Gas 6). Put the flour, baking powder, and butter into a food processor and whiz until the mixture resembles breadcrumbs. Add the sugar.

2. Break the egg into a measuring jug and beat with a fork, then pour in enough of the milk to make just over 150ml (5fl oz). Beat again to mix.

3. Switch the processor on and gradually pour in the milk and egg mixture, leaving about 1 tablespoon in the jug for glazing. Whiz until combined – the mixture should be slightly sticky. Add a little more milk if it isn't.

4. Transfer the dough to a lightly floured work surface and knead until smooth, then roll it out until it is 1cm (½in) thick. Using a 7.5cm (3in) scone cutter, cut out 12 scones, re-rolling the dough until it is all used up.

5. Arrange on a greased baking sheet and brush the tops with the remaining milk and egg mixture to glaze.

6. Bake for 15–20 minutes or until well risen and golden.

### IN THE AGA
Bake on the grid shelf on the floor of the roasting oven, with the cold sheet on the second set of runners, for 45 minutes or until well risen and cooked in the middle.

### PREPARE AHEAD AND FREEZE
*The scones can be made up to 1 day ahead.
Freeze for up to 3 months.*

# BEST-EVER BROWNIES

**MAKES 12**

**Special equipment** *23 x 33cm (9 x 13in) traybake tin, lined with baking parchment and well greased*

*225g (8oz) butter, softened*

*350g (12oz) milk chocolate*

*4 eggs*

*450g (1lb) light muscovado sugar*

*150ml (5fl oz) milk*

*225g (8oz) self-raising flour*

*Most brownies are dense and dark, but we use milk chocolate so ours are very light in colour and texture, with gooey pieces of melted chocolate. Simply delicious.*

1. Preheat the oven to 180°C (160°C fan/350°F/Gas 4). Melt the butter and 225g (8oz) of the chocolate in a bowl set over a pan of hot water until the mixture is smooth and glossy.

2. Break the eggs into a mixing bowl, add the sugar, milk, and the melted chocolate mixture, and beat with a wooden spoon to combine. Sift in the flour and mix until smooth.

3. Stir in the remaining chocolate, then pour into the tin and bake for 45–50 minutes or until well risen and cooked in the middle. Leave to cool, then cut into 12 squares.

### IN THE AGA

Bake on the grid shelf on the floor of the roasting oven, with the cold sheet on the second set of runners, for 45 minutes or until well risen and cooked in the middle.

## PREPARE AHEAD AND FREEZE

*The brownies can be made up to 2 days ahead. Freeze for up to 3 months.*

# INDEX

**Editor** Megan Lea
**Senior art editor** Sara Robin
**Jacket designer** Saffron Stocker
**Jackets co-ordinator** Lucy Philpott
**Producer, pre-production** Heather Blagden
**Senior producer, pre-production** Tony Phipps
**Producer** Samantha Cross
**Creative technical support** Tom Morse
**Senior DTP designer** Tarun Sharma
**DTP designer** Umesh Singh Rawat
**Pre-production manager** Sunil Sharma
**Managing editor** Dawn Henderson
**Managing art editor** Marianne Markham
**Art director** Maxine Pedliham
**Publishing director** Mary-Clare Jerram

**Photographer** Georgia Glynn Smith
**Photography art direction** Sara Robin

NOTE: The author and publisher advocate sustainable food choices, and every effort has been made to include only sustainable foods in this book. Food sustainability is, however, a shifting landscape, and so we encourage readers to keep up to date with advice on this subject, so that they are equipped to make their own ethical choices.

This edition published in 2019
First published in Great Britain in 2010 by
Dorling Kindersley Limited
80 Strand, London WC2R 0RL

Text copyright © 2010, 2014, 2019 Mary Berry
Copyright © 2010, 2014, 2019 Dorling Kindersley
A Penguin Random House Company
10 9 8 7 6 5 4 3 2 1
001–315230–Oct/2019

A CIP catalogue record for this book is available from the British Library.

ISBN: 978-0-2413-9352-9
Printed and bound in Latvia

## AUTHORS' ACKNOWLEDGMENTS

Firstly, a huge thank you to the lovely Lucinda McCord, who was an essential part of the team that created the recipes with us for this book. Lucinda, thank you for your dedication, passion for your work, and friendship. We could not do what we do without you.

Thank you, too, to Mary-Clare Jerram at DK, who commissioned us to write this book and could see our vision for it. She has worked closely with us at every stage and always with a smile.

And a huge thank you to Dawn Henderson and Megan Lea, who edited the book with such dedication and commitment, and great understanding. It has been a joy to work with you.

Thank you to home economist lovely Lisa Harrison who made our recipes for the shoots, and to Georgia Glynn Smith for the stunning photography.

We would also like to thank our agents, Felicity Bryan and Michele Topham, who never seem to worry about our problems, but just sort them out fast!

Finally, thank you to you our readers for your amazing support.

## PUBLISHER'S ACKNOWLEDGMENTS

For the 2019 edition, DK would like to thank Alice Horne for project editing; Georgia Glynn Smith for photography; Lisa Harrison and Evie Harbury for the beautiful food styling; Hannah Wilkinson and Rob Merrett for prop styling; Sara Robin for photography art direction; Steve Crozier for image retouching; Tessa Wright for wardrobe styling; Jo Penford for hair and makeup; Vanessa Bird for providing the index; and Corinne Masciocchi for proofreading.

For the 2014 edition thanks are due to the following people: Project editors Michael Fullalove and Andrew Roff; photographer William Reavell; Managing editor Angela Wilkes; Managing art editor Christine Keilty; and in DK India: Head of publishing Arpana Sharma; Managing art editor Romi Chakraborty; Senior editor Saloni Talwar.

New photography © Georgia Glynn Smith
All other images © Dorling Kindersley
For further information see: www.dkimages.com

### A WORLD OF IDEAS:
### SEE ALL THERE IS TO KNOW

**www.dk.com**